THE
FREDS
AT BARNEYS NEW YORK
COOKBOOK

THE
FREDS
AT BARNEYS NEW YORK
COOKBOOK

MARK STRAUSMAN
WITH SUSAN LITTLEFIELD

GRAND CENTRAL
Life&Style
NEW YORK • BOSTON

Grand Central Life & Style
Hachette Book Group
1290 Avenue of the Americas, New York, NY 10104

grandcentrallifeandstyle.com
twitter.com/grandcentralpub

First Edition: April 2018

Grand Central Life & Style is an imprint of Grand Central Publishing. The Grand Central Life & Style name and logo are trademarks of Hachette Book Group, Inc.

The publisher is not responsible for websites (or their content) that are not owned by the publisher.

The Hachette Speakers Bureau provides a wide range of authors for speaking events. To find out more, go to www.hachettespeakersbureau.com or call (866) 376-6591.

Barney's, Inc. owns the BARNEYS, BARNEYS NEW YORK, FREDS, FREDS AT BARNEYS NEW YORK, GENES and GENES CAFÉ trademarks and related logos; and trademark rights in the menu item names from Freds, Freds at Barneys New York, Genes and Genes Café establishments. These trademarks are used with permission.

The photo of Fred Pressman on page xi is copyright Getty/Bettmann. The photo on page 6; the larger Freds Madison photo on page 8; and the photos on pages 11, 76–77, 94–95, 104, 179, 211, and 264–265 are by Mark Strausman. The smaller photo on page 8 of Freds Madison is courtesy of Barneys New York. All other photos by Sidney Bensimon.

Print book cover and interior design by Gary Tooth/Empire Design Studio

Library of Congress Cataloging-in-Publication Data

Names: Strausman, Mark, author. | Littlefield, Susan, author. | Freds at Barneys New York.

Title: The Freds at Barneys New York Cookbook / Mark Strausman; with Susan Littlefield.

Description: First edition. | New York, NY : Grand Central Life & Style, [2018] | Includes index.

Identifiers: LCCN 2017042674| ISBN 9781455537761 (hardcover) | ISBN 9781455537778 (ebook)

Subjects: LCSH: Cooking, American. | Cooking—New York (State) | Restaurants. | LCGFT: Cookbooks.

Classification: LCC TX715 .S8993 2018 | DDC 641.59747—dc23

LC record available at https://lccn.loc.gov/2017042674

ISBNs: 978-1-4555-3776-1 (hardcover); 978-1-4555-3777-8 (ebook)

Printed in the United States of America

LSC-W

10 9 8 7 6 5 4 3 2 1

M.S.
This book is dedicated to the American dream:
The dream my grandparents held on to when
they left their homeland and sailed to America;
The dream that gave Barney Pressman the
courage to hock his wife's engagement ring
so he could open a little store he named Barneys;
The dream that is alive and well in the
melting pot that is the kitchen of
Freds at Barneys New York.

S.L.
For Joseph and Daniel

CONTENTS

THE STORY OF FREDS AND ME   ix

Chapter 1. A Day in the Life of the Freds Kitchen   1

LUNCH   35

Chapter 2. The Freds Iconic Salads   37

Chapter 3. The Freds Lunch Classics   73

Chapter 4. A Year in Soup   109

DINNER   135

Chapter 5. Neighborhood Standards and Room Service   137

Chapter 6. Italian Classics   169

BRUNCH   205

Chapter 7. Brunch   207

DESSERTS   245

Chapter 8. Sweet Endings—Desserts and Fruits   247

Acknowledgments   274

Index   275

THE STORY OF FREDS AND ME

My life first intersected with Barneys when, at the age of thirteen, I was dragged there by my mother to purchase my bar mitzvah suit. Coming from a family of Jewish immigrant merchants, she wouldn't dream of purchasing that garment anywhere besides Barneys, *the* temple of menswear founded by Barney Pressman, patriarch of another Jewish immigrant merchant family. I didn't care where we bought the suit. I spent the subway ride from Flushing, Queens, to Manhattan sweating with dread at the prospect of standing exposed before some cranky tailor, who would invariably frown, tsk, and shake his head in dismay at my portly short frame, tugging roughly at too-tight trousers with a hand full of pins perilously close to my privates. Even more terrifying was the looming event for which I was being dressed. As a dyslexic reading Hebrew in front of a congregation full of school friends, I was in danger of my nerves destroying the pose of class clown I affected in order to cover up my learning disabilities. I survived both the fitting and the Torah portion, and my mother thought the suit looked terrific.

I couldn't have guessed that twenty-six years later my life would intersect with Barneys in an even more significant way, when I was asked to helm the restaurant in their new Madison Avenue flagship store—the restaurant that would become Freds. In those twenty-six years, Barneys had transformed, under the guidance of Barney Pressman's son Fred and his grandsons Gene and Bob, into a world-famous cutting-edge fashion destination, a true New York phenom. I had transformed, too, although not quite as spectacularly. I had become a chef and restaurateur— a perfect profession for someone with learning disabilities. I had spent four years training in classical European kitchens, eight years exploring Italy and Italian food, and had some visibility in the New York dining scene after opening several high-profile restaurants. I was mature enough to appreciate the parallels between Barney Pressman's Horatio Alger–type story and my own (again less spectacular) family's. And I was thin enough to fit into at least some of Barneys' clothing without needing the services of a tailor.

Now, more than twenty years after opening Freds in 1996, I see how well suited (pun intended) Barneys and I have been as collaborators. That, I think, has been the secret of Freds' success and the longevity of our partnership. From the beginning, I've tried to offer in food what Barneys offers in fashion: a luxury destination that provides a level of personal service second to none. My youthful dread of tailors notwithstanding, when we first opened Freds I developed a fast friendship with several of the Barneys tailors; we had a mutual respect and admiration. I saw that we were in a way doing the same thing. Like me, they were practicing an Old World craft, and our approaches were actually quite similar: classical techniques combined with a hospitality tailored to individual customer needs and requests.

My collaboration with Barneys New York is stronger than ever, and, as I look around the dining room with amazement, I'm proud to say that Freds has become an institution. It's not just that the restaurant is busier than it's ever been. It is, and that's no small accomplishment in New York, a town as tough on a business as Hollywood is on a marriage, where if you make it ten years you're an old-timer. What makes me happy, though, is that I know so many of the people *in* the restaurant: long-time staff, and customers who have been coming here regularly since we opened, whose families I have watched grow, people the staff and I count as friends.

At this writing, Freds Madison has satellite restaurants in Los Angeles, Chicago, and in Barneys' newest addition: Barneys Downtown, which re-opened in its original 7th Avenue location in Chelsea. Genes Café in the Madison Avenue store is also under the Freds umbrella. It was an honor to be offered the opportunity to create a restaurant for Barneys, and the collaboration has ultimately provided deep career satisfaction, beyond expectation. It constantly challenges me to flex my entrepreneurial muscles, is a canvas on which to express my creativity as a chef, gives me purpose and connection as a teacher and mentor to hundreds of employees, and affords me the pleasure of extending hospitality to the most interesting clientele in the world.

"No, I'm not Fred."

Much has been written about the history of Barneys, so there's no need for me to go over that subject. Suffice it to say that although it seems natural now that it should be located on the Upper East Side, Barneys' expansion there was a huge deal and propelled their reputation from downtown edgy to full-blown fashion-world force. The location, at the northwest corner of Madison Avenue and East 61st Street, could not be more perfect for a high-end retail business—and a restaurant. When you stand on that corner you almost literally have one foot in the offices of midtown while the other foot is grounded in one of the wealthiest residential corridors in the United States, the area within the boundaries of East 61st and 79th Streets, and Fifth Avenue and Lexington Avenue.

Any business venture needs a good name, and we were having trouble finding the right one. It's 1996 and I'm in a conference room at Barneys' downtown headquarters, sitting between brothers Gene and Bob Pressman, Barney Pressman's grandsons, the third generation of the Pressman family to run the store Barney created. I'm there because we're working out the details for the new uptown restaurant. The Pressmans know my Flatiron restaurant Campagna, with its rustic Italian food, and know me from my days at Coco Pazzo on East 74th Street, and at Sapore di Mare in the Hamptons, the part of Long Island where pretty much the entire Upper East Side decamps for the summer. The Pressmans are confident that I know the uptown neighborhood very, very well, and they're extremely positive about my plans for the restaurant so far. There's just one detail: We can't quite figure out a name. Gene and Bob are arguing about it; I wish I could remember the names we

Fred Pressman
in 1972

were considering, but each brother is adamant about his choice. As I recall there are heated words exchanged between them. I'm feeling uncomfortable because I don't particularly want to weigh in on the choices and be seen as preferring one brother over the other, especially so early in our partnership. There's a silent impasse between them, and suddenly an idea pops into my head that instantly and clearly seems the right thing.

"Freds!" I say. "The restaurant should be named after your father!"

They both turn to stare at me, and about one second later we have a deal.

Fred Pressman's legacy at Barneys was paramount. He was the man who brought Barneys into the modern era, who set it on the path from men's discount store to world-class fashion emporium, expanding its reach well beyond menswear to include women's, children's, and home sections. He (and his family) introduced Americans to cutting-edge European designers, including Giorgio Armani, Azzedine Alaïa, and Dries Van Noten, among many others. He insisted on the outstanding customer service Barneys is still famous for. The *New York Times* credits him as saying, "The best value you can offer a customer is personal attention to every detail, and they will return again and again."

I was also aware that naming a restaurant after a person usually implies a level of casualness and comfort, a feeling subconsciously that you're going to someone's house, and that was the vibe I was looking to create. I wanted the restaurant to be beautiful, but not so formal that you only visited on special occasions. Where you'd come dressed nicely, but didn't necessarily have to put on a jacket and tie. Where you'd feel cared for—whether you were simply stopping in for a bowl of Estelle's Chicken Soup on the way home from work, entertaining your best client at lunch, or celebrating with several generations of your family at Sunday brunch.

Fred Pressman passed away in 1996, just a few months before we opened his namesake restaurant.

At each Freds location I'm asked fairly regularly if I am Fred. No, I am not Fred. But I'm happy to say that I met him, and glad that his legacy lives on in Barneys.

The Move to the Ninth Floor

When I'm in Freds Madison, the sun-drenched space on the ninth floor, with its large windows and little balconies overlooking Madison Avenue, I have to strain to remember—and I'm willing to bet that even long-time regulars have forgotten this—that the restaurant was originally located in the basement, where the beauty and apothecary sections are now. It's not just any basement; much of the first floor above it was open so that you could peer down at the activity below. As a restaurant, the space was dark and intimate and at the same time built for the buzz of people-watching, whether you were looking down on the diners or up to the shoppers. Conveniently, you didn't necessarily have to enter the restaurant through the store; we had a designated entrance on 61st Street.

In 2001, Barneys decided to reorganize the store and move Freds from the basement to the ninth floor, where it is now. Change is usually disconcerting, and we were nervous about how this would be received. People liked the subterranean, clubby vibe downstairs and we anticipated a lot of complaints about moving. In addition, the restaurant would be losing its separate entrance, so we thought people might have a hard time figuring out how to actually get in when the store was closed (we were right about that, but it worked out eventually).

Over the summer of 2001, the new Freds was constructed, and by the end of August the kitchen was finished, new tables and chairs unpacked and arranged, silverware, plates, glassware set out, food ordered. Everything was ready for the City of New York Department of Health to come and inspect the new Freds on September 15, and then we could make a smooth, swift move. Of course, it didn't happen that way. On September 11, tragedy engulfed our city and our country. Like everyone else in those first overwhelming weeks afterwards, the staff and I were shell-shocked, unable to fathom the unfathomable, going through the motions of our lives and our work, knowing our understanding of the world had fundamentally changed. There was only energy for survival, certainly none for a major move, and even if there had been we couldn't move into the new space until it was inspected. The beleaguered, overwhelmed city agency had no time for anything like that.

It seemed like a lifetime, every day then seemed like a lifetime—looking back I wonder how they were able to manage it at all—but by late October the city was able to inspect the kitchen and we opened upstairs. The light that floods in from the huge windows there felt very healing, and seemed like a small gift after the terrible darkness and varying forms of loss we'd all experienced. As regular customers began to come in, one by one, there was the greeting, the spoken or unspoken understanding that we were all thankful to be alive, grateful to be a part of our community, one small, warm circle in the millions that make up life in New York City.

My Route from Queens to Madison Avenue

I was excited about the partnership with Barneys. It was a plum job—it still is. The opportunity to create a restaurant in a high-visibility destination that attracts visitors from all over the world was something that I, as a young, ambitious entrepreneur, was eager to take on. It was also a chance for me to break out of the role in which I had become typecast: that of Italian chef. I'm not Italian; I'm a Jewish boy from Queens who happened to fall in love with Italian food. I saw in Freds a way to expand my repertoire and resurrect some of the skills that I hadn't yet used in my professional career because they fell outside the scope of an Italian restaurant. But now I'm getting ahead of myself.

My route to becoming a chef was a little unusual, but I'd never been one to go by the book—and I mean that *literally*, because of my learning disabilities. After a dismal semester or three at several different colleges, I was struggling to finish a degree in

Hotel Management at New York Technical College, at the same time holding down a job I loved: cooking at the UN Plaza Hotel. I enjoyed cooking, and knew I had a talent for it. I'd taken over my mother's kitchen when I was in high school, shopping and cooking (but drawing a firm line at cleaning) when she went back to work after my father passed away. During my last semester at New York Tech, one of my professors, Dr. Thomas Ahrens, asked if I was interested in doing an internship in Germany. I jumped at the chance and went there expecting to stay three months. I ended up staying for four years.

The Grandhotel Hessischer Hof in Frankfurt, Germany, is where I was stationed for my internship. I'd never seen a kitchen so enormous and pristine. I knew within the first few days that I wanted to extend my stay, because it was clear that I couldn't possibly learn everything in three months. Working in Europe was going to be my college degree, my culinary Ivy League education. Despite its size, the Hessischer Hof was a farm-to-table restaurant long before that was a buzzword. Foragers and growers would show up at the back door hauling wicker baskets full of things like porcini mushrooms, chanterelles, or wild strawberries for the chef to look over.

Mark with Freds Madison executive chef Alfredo Escobar

Like any young apprentice I started with the lowliest of the low tasks as a *chef de commis* (junior cook), and I knew that hard work was the key to extending my stay. A high point was the day the head chef told me, "Ach, Herr Strausman, with that last name you might as well be German." I knew then that he approved of my work, and at the end of my internship he was happy for me to stay on as an employee. I spent the next year there, moving up the ranks, before deciding to branch out and see what I could learn from other places. I deliberately sought out jobs in large well-respected grand hotel kitchens, rather than smaller à la carte restaurants, because I wanted the experience of handling volume and variety. I spent about a year at what is now the Fairmont Le Montreux Palace, in Montreux, Switzerland, before returning to Frankfurt to work at the Kempinski Hotel. My last year was spent at the InterContinental Amstel in Amsterdam. At the Amstel I reached the coveted position of *chef de parti* (senior chef), unheard of for an American at that time. I even got a little local press when I revived their tradition of the grand Sunday brunch, complete with decorative ice sculptures.

After four years in Europe I reached a point where it seemed like I could either stay and make a life there permanently, with my network of friends and culinary connections, or I could leave it all before I got in any deeper, and come back home to New York City. Fate intervened with that decision when my grandmother Estelle (she of Estelle's Chicken Soup) died and I came back for the funeral. I was glad to be back home, and I realized I didn't really want to live the life of an expat in Europe and that I was in a fine position to conquer New York City. Or so I thought.

When I left for Europe, the big culinary hero in America was Paul Bocuse, one of the originators of *nouvelle cuisine*. By the time I came back to New York in 1986, Americans had stopped idolizing European cuisine and were embracing American regional cooking. As I pounded the pavement, clutching a resume that detailed my impressive roster of European experience, I was repeatedly asked, "Yes, but where have you worked in America?" That wasn't what I was expecting, and that disappointment was my first lesson as an entrepreneur: adapt or perish.

I was offered a job as a cook at Mortimer's, Glenn Bernbaum's Upper East Side society haunt *extraordinaire*, and I reluctantly took it. Mortimer's was an amazing place; on any given day, walking by the dining room from the kitchen to the bathroom, I would catch glimpses of some Kennedy family member, Nan Kempner, Nancy Reagan, or a famous CEO. Still, it wasn't the kind of job I wanted. I was disappointed in myself, and discouraged, and afraid my mother was disappointed in me, too. A Jewish mother sends her son to Europe to get what amounts to a doctorate in food and he comes home to take a job as a short-order cook. I lasted at Mortimer's for about nine months before the indignity of flipping Glenn's famous "twin burgers" (small patties that were easier to eat than regular size ones) got to me. Glenn understood why the job wasn't for me, but it wasn't the happiest parting when I left. Years later, Mario Buatta reintroduced us and we laughed about it. I was too naive at the time to truly appreciate Mortimer's, but looking back I see that I learned a great deal in my short time there. It was absolutely pivotal to my understanding of what hospitality is, at least on the Upper East Side of Manhattan. And subconsciously it created a template for what Freds would become. From Mortimer's I learned that, generally speaking, the richer a person is, the simpler their tastes. Plus, Glenn was a master at the complicated social equation of seating a dining room, which itself was an education, and I liked how pampered he made his regular customers feel.

After Mortimer's came a year spent cooking at Jacqueline's, a champagne bar on East 61st Street. The proprietor, Swiss French transplant Jacqueline Noss, was the only person I'd met in my job search who knew the reputation of the places I'd worked at in Europe. She got it, and I was relieved. My time there was significant because it's the place where I met my future- and eventually ex-wife, Susan, mother of my children and co-writer of this book. My culinary education wasn't over yet, however. One day in my search for a job that had more creative potential, I met with Italian restaurateur Pino Luongo. That meeting, arranged by the late, unofficial culinary matchmaker Marc Sarrazin, who was president of the whole-sale meat purveyor DeBragga and Spitler and who also understood my training, began a partnership that lasted seven years, sparked a friendship that has out-lasted the partnership, created several of New York's hottest restaurants in their time, and welcomed me into the world of Italian cooking, a place where I thrived for many years.

Pino, a Tuscan actor-turned-restaurateur known for bringing Tuscan food to New York at Il Cantinori, was seeking a chef for Sapore di Mare, a restaurant he was opening in East Hampton, New York. I wasn't trained in Italian cuisine, but Pino liked my enthusiasm and the fact that I'd worked in Europe. Plus, we're both talkers, so we hit it off right away. In the spring of 1988, we headed to Wainscott, the village in East Hampton where Sapore was located. Housed in an old mansion with a long porch overlooking tony Georgica Pond, Sapore was the first New York City restaurant to land in the Hamptons, and it's impossible to overstate the buzz that restaurant generated. *Everyone* came, a clientele out of a celebrity-obsessed dream, on a nightly basis. Calvin Klein, John Kennedy, Jr., and his sister, Caroline, Italy's Agnelli family, and a roster of artists and art dealers: Ross Bleckner, Mary Boone, Leo Castelli. The celebrity sighting reached its absolute zenith on the night Jackie Onassis joined her daughter for dinner and stunned the whole restaurant into silence. It was madness, and I absolutely thrived on it. I also thrived on establishing relationships with the local farmers who were there at that time (the old-timers are long gone, but happily there are still some wonderful farms out there), and I loved being able to live and cook according to the seasons. Susan and I got married after that first crazy summer, and spent a six-week honeymoon traveling around Italy, the first of many Italian trips over the next few years. The travel nourished my relationship with Italian food, and I began to develop my own style within the genre.

Pino and I opened Coco Pazzo on 74th and Madison Avenue in 1991. I was the *coco pazzo*, the "crazy chef," with my wild creations, the pickling, butchering, and curing, the enormous, groaning antipasto table, and my complete love of my craft. Coco Pazzo was a sensational success, and I was proud, as an American, to earn a three-star review for an Italian restaurant from the *New York Times*. I drew on that success to open my own restaurant, Campagna, in 1993.

Campagna was the ultimate expression of my love affair with Italian food. By the time it opened I had steeped myself in Italian food and culture and had refined my own approach to Italian cooking. *Campagna* means "country" in Italian, and Campagna's food was big, rustic, and flavorful. And popular. In the early years we would still be seating people for dinner at midnight. *New York* magazine dubbed Campagna "media central" because of all the music business people, artists and art dealers, and other creative types who hung out there. Campagna was not without its detractors, on the grounds of it not being a "real" Italian restaurant. It's not the kind of thing that factors into the conversation these days when someone opens an ethnic or regional restaurant, but I spent a lot of time back then justifying having an Italian restaurant as a non-Italian. At the same time I was beginning to feel constrained by the Italian label and found myself wanting to meander away from it at times. I started reviving some of the Jewish foods of my youth, offering up chicken soup and latkes at the Jewish holidays, for example. So when Barneys offered me the opportunity to run their restaurant I was eager to do so.

Credit where credit is due: I can't overstate the platform that Barneys, with its massive retail star power, provided for me to expand my career. My training in Europe was still relatively fresh in my mind, and I was ready for the challenge, but I'm not sure I could have stepped outside of the Italian box, and succeeded with such an eclectic menu, without their clout behind me.

I figured an eclectic menu wouldn't be out of place in Freds because the whole of Barneys is a curated mix of luxury brands from all over the world. Clothing from Belgian designer Dries Van Noten hangs across the sales floor from Dolce & Gabbana. So why can't Belgian fries share the menu with lasagna? Why on earth can't bouillabaisse coexist with spaghetti and meatballs? And since people from all over the world shop at Barneys, as well as the well-traveled locals in the neighborhood, there was bound to be appreciation of the classic European dishes I wanted to mix with the Italian ones. Barneys provided the legitimacy, the infrastructure, and the exposure for me to utilize all of my training and experience to realize one of my dreams: creating a restaurant with a cuisine that could encompass all my influences, and a kitchen on a par with the ones where I'd worked in Europe.

Freds' Influences

What kind of restaurant do you put in a temple of fashion? As I considered that question and planned the menu, there were many influences. My Italian food would be heavily represented, of course, because that's what people knew me for;

they'd be disappointed if that wasn't on the menu. The Pressmans and I thought about Harrods Food Hall and the restaurants in Harvey Nichols in London. Certainly I looked to society restaurants such as Mortimer's and the Brown Derby in L.A. Elements of all those places are in Freds.

But I also kept returning to a distinct restaurant moment I remember from my travels in Europe. Susan and I were driving through Normandy. It was lunchtime as we pulled into the center of a small town. There was absolutely no one around, the shops were closed; it was spookily quiet, like the day after the apocalypse. We were starving, so we headed to an inviting-looking restaurant on one corner of the town square. As soon as I opened the door I was hit with a blast of sound: It was the chatter of people talking, plates and silverware clanging, the glug of wine being poured. *Everyone* in the town was there, the owners of those closed shops, other local business people, probably lawyers, accountants, doctors. We had a delicious meal of brasserie-style food, but the food wasn't as memorable as the feeling we had when we opened the door and felt ourselves lucky to be in the midst of the bustle of life, to have stumbled into the warm, inviting center of that particular universe. That's exactly the feeling I wanted people to have when they came to Freds.

Someone recently referred to Freds Madison as "kind of a neighborhood coffee shop," and even though I'd never thought of it that way, I had to admit that's quite apt. I probably wouldn't have been pleased with the coffee shop label when I was first starting out in my career, when I longed, like most young chefs, to be an innovator, to blaze new culinary trails with my food. Of course I still want people to love my food; every time I pick up a pan to make something I'm looking to knock someone's socks off. But, really, I just like to make my customers happy. I'm like a Jewish grandmother that way, just with some classical culinary underpinning. If I had to describe my style of food, I'd say that it's Escoffier meets Grandma.

The reason the coffee shop name applies is because I've purposefully put together a menu of relatively uncomplicated food that you can eat every day. In fact, when we first opened I served the entrée salads in Buffalo china bowls, utilitarian china that's commonly used in diners. Freds' food isn't looking to outshine my guests; it's not unlike fashion in that way, where you want people to notice *you*, not the clothes you're wearing. At Freds you might notice that what you're eating tastes really good, but you probably won't interrupt the flow of your conversation to comment on it. I like simple classics, but as anyone who's ever watched *The Great British Bake Off* knows, simplicity is a hard thing to pull off because every element has to be absolutely perfect. So although it's important to me that my food has classical underpinning, nurturing my guests is where I get the most pleasure.

As I wrote this book, I realized how much the Freds menu is personal to me. I read it like a memoir, or a road map back to my past, because virtually every dish comes from a moment, a place, a time. It's the culmination of every place I've worked, of every trip I've taken, and of meals I've loved, mixed with memories of a Jewish food culture that's in danger of disappearing.

How to Use This Book

This book actually has a dual purpose. It's a cookbook; that's obvious. But it also serves as an archive of Freds menus. That's why the chapters are grouped by meal period, instead of the food type (meat, vegetables, etc.) as they are in most cookbooks. There's overlap with some items, of course; for example, soup is served at both lunch and dinner, but generally speaking that was the guideline. And because many people know me from my work in Italian cooking, the Italian-inspired recipes have their own chapter.

Although the vast majority of recipes here are simple and perfect for home cooks, there are a few—the Lobster Bisque springs to mind—that you might be less likely to make at home because they contain a daunting list of ingredients or require a big time commitment. I've included them in the book anyway, since they're dishes that are so popular and integral to the Freds menu that they simply must be included. But also because the teacher in me hopes they will inspire home chefs who welcome a culinary challenge.

Some of the recipes are not *just* recipes, they're processes. Things like stocks, or the Belgian Fries, or my Foolproof Pizza Dough have multiple steps and obviously lean toward the complicated side. For those, I've tried to give detailed instructions to make them a bit easier because I really do want them to be manageable, even if they take a little practice and experimentation. In many instances where a recipe calls for special equipment, and for most of the recipes in The Foundations of the Freds Kitchen...and Yours (page 5), I've also included an equipment list before the list of ingredients. The more ambitious recipes, particularly, give a window into the tasks that underpin a restaurant's menu, the kind of prep and technique that goes on behind the scenes in the kitchen, whether it's in the Freds kitchen... or yours.

CHAPTER 1

A DAY IN THE LIFE OF THE FREDS KITCHEN

Belgian Fries / 9

> *Garlic Mayonnaise / 10*

> *Sauce Calypso / 10*

Freds Herb Mixture / 12

Freds Pesto / 13

Clarified Butter / 14

Homemade Croutons / 15

Steamed Potatoes / 16

Blanched Vegetables / 17

Oven-Cooked Bacon / 18

Roasted Turkey Breast / 19

Estelle's Chicken Soup Trilogy / 22

> **Chicken Stock / 24**

> **Fortified Chicken Stock / 25**

> **Estelle's Chicken Soup / 27**

Vegetable Stock / 28

Demi-Glace / 30

> **Veal Stock / 30**

> **Demi-Glace / 31**

Court Bouillon / 32

To walk through the swinging doors from the dining room into the kitchen at Freds Madison is to enter another world. I thrive on the hushed buzz of a busy dining room, and I have to admit that there's a special frisson that comes from tending a roomful of fashionable people, a room that on any given day is sprinkled with movie stars, sports heroes, famous writers, well-known fashion designers, Broadway producers, and even former presidents and first ladies, in one of the world's most exclusive stores, in one of the world's wealthiest neighborhoods. That's the visible element, the public satisfaction of my job, and I love it. But I derive just as much satisfaction, possibly even more, and of a more personal nature, from the less visible world behind those swinging doors: the world of the kitchen.

The dining room is the proverbial tip of the iceberg in my business, although maybe an iceberg makes it sound ominous. Better is the analogy the *New York Times* used when it called Freds "A hidden nest atop Barneys to make deals." If the dining room is the "nest" in which we feed and coddle our customers, then the kitchen is the tree holding that nest, branching down its roots to the network of food systems that sustain it—farmers, growers, grain millers, cheese makers, delivery people, and the like. The growth and nurturing of that tree, the training, support, and employment of the scores of people who work at Freds, is actually the crux of my job, and there would be no hospitality without it. Maybe it sounds corny, but creating a place for people to work and support their families, being part of that life cycle, is quite moving to me, and a deep source of satisfaction. Many of the employees at Freds have been working there since we opened; some even worked with me at my previous restaurants. I've watched their children grow up, seen those kids graduate from college, and attended their weddings, as they've seen my kids grow (and evolve from toddlers who dreaded the smallest speck of parsley in their food to full-fledged vegan hipsters). One of the things I'm most proud of in my career is the stability of the kitchen staff at Freds, and I believe that the consistency that comes from having a stable staff is a major factor in Freds' longevity and success.

I had good role models for my training. The European kitchens where I trained were demanding, but at the same time quiet and industrious. When I look back now, I see that the head chefs who I considered to be the most exacting were actually careful teachers from whom I learned a great deal. That's the model I try to emulate, and the natural teacher in me enjoys passing on my knowledge to others.

A Peek Behind the Scenes

At Freds, the day starts many hours before we seat the first customer for lunch. We serve a large volume of food every day, and, since we're in New York City where storage space is so precious, each day is *literally* a fresh start: We cook pretty much everything from scratch each morning. The first cooks get to the restaurant by 6:30 a.m., many arriving on the #7 train from Queens, just as I did at the start of my career.

When they get here, huge paper bags of bread from Orwashers bakery, baked in the wee hours, are already waiting by the front door. We'll get another bread delivery, from Grandaisy Bakery and Hudson Bread, in the afternoon, which we'll use for dinner service. Some of our breads are made in house—the focaccia, pizza dough, and bagels and bialys, if it's the weekend—and those will start baking soon. The ovens will be turned on, ready to roast, tray after tray, the thirty or forty chickens and turkeys needed for a typical day of salads and sandwiches. Parts of other chickens will end up simmering for the next few hours in enormous stockpots, the first step in making Estelle's Chicken Soup. Peter, our purchasing agent, is checking in the delivery orders that are streaming in, hauled up the 60th Street service elevator to our 9th floor kitchen by truck drivers praying he'll check the order quickly so they can avoid getting a parking ticket, one of the constant irritations—and costs of doing business—of the food vendors who supply New York City kitchens. Fish and shellfish will be whisked into the walk-in fridge, and soon will be cleaned, scaled, fileted, shucked, or steamed, accordingly. A towering city of boxes filled with vegetables and salad greens makes the kitchen a temporary obstacle course, but within the space of a few minutes they're all unpacked and refrigerated. And a morning full of prep work begins.

COMMAND CENTRAL: THE PURCHASING OFFICE

The Freds purchasing office is where the magic actually begins. You can't make good food without *starting* with good food, so sourcing meats, vegetables and fruits, and other products is obviously a huge part of my job. Luckily, it also happens to be one of my greatest pleasures in life—anyone who travels with me has to drag me away from the food markets if they want to see anything else! I love New York City's Greenmarkets as much as any New Yorker, but the fantasy of the chef going to the market early in the morning to see what's good just isn't practical on a daily basis, at least not with the volume of business we do at Freds. That doesn't mean I don't spend hours searching for the best products and testing them, sourcing locally whenever possible. I have close relationships with many growers and producers, and I love to visit them whenever I get the chance. But this little office, with my purchasing agent, Peter, on the phone, is where the

deals get cinched. Peter knows what I want, the specifications of what I'm looking for, the quality I require, and how much I'm willing to spend, and he also keeps an inventory of what we're likely to need on any given day. Peter is kind of the wizard of the kitchen. Like a wizard, he somehow magically knows exactly where everything is all the time. The volume we do requires a great deal of coordination for delivery and storage, and Peter is the point person for that.

Once the food is delivered to Freds, we then start our own mini food chain. We begin processing the raw product to our specifications. Obviously, although I use the word *processing*, I don't mean it in the negative sense of corporate commercial food factories, or adding chemicals and additives. We *process* just the way you do at home, by cleaning, peeling, trimming, cutting, portioning, and the like.

A 60-SECOND PURCHASING LESSON

1. Purchase the best ingredients you can afford because quality ingredients make quality food.

2. Buy fruit and produce when they are in season, when they are at their best, most plentiful, and cheapest. When they're out of season the quality won't be as good.

3. Whenever possible, purchase food that's cultivated nearby.

4. Shop with all your senses. Don't just judge with your sight, but with smell and touch, too. Trust yourself. If it doesn't look good or smell good, it's not good. When I say looking good, I'm not talking about glamour specimens, but indications of freshness like crispness, unwilted leaves, and delicious aroma.

THE KITCHEN TOUR

The kitchen at Freds is actually three separate kitchens: the prep kitchen, where the bulk of the work is done; the à la carte kitchen, the line where the actual orders are cooked; and the pastry kitchen, which is separate so as not to mix the savory with the sweet.

The Prep Kitchen

In the European brigade system, the à la carte chefs—the ones who sauté, make pan sauces, and *cook à la minute*—are the superstars. But in my opinion, and in the Freds kitchen, the real superstars are the prep cooks. Where would we be without their support? Like a foundation holds up a building, the prep kitchen holds up a restaurant's menu and reputation. The prep kitchen is where I spend the most time, training and working with my staff. Perfection in the kitchen begins at the most minuscule level; every task, down to cutting the most finely minced shallot or whisper of chives, needs to be perfect. The prep area resembles a finely tooled watch. There are lots of moving parts in a small space, so the work needs to be precise and coordinated. In the space of a few hundred square feet, the prep cooks clean, peel, chop, trim, roast, par-cook, and so forth literally hundreds of pounds of vegetables per day. They prep the ingredients for our most popular items: the lunch entrée salads and our famous Belgian Fries. And that's not all. They roast the chickens and turkeys, make soups and sauces, pasta, and focaccia (and bagels and bialys, if it's the weekend). They prepare virtually all the *mis en place* that the line cooks will use later when cooking during service. I like to have designated point people doing certain tasks for the sake of consistency. The same two people, week in and week out, make all the salad dressings, for example. The same guys make the pizza dough and fresh pasta, as well as the bagels and bialys each weekend.

The à la Carte Kitchen (aka The Line)

Of course, all that prep work is in the service of the final goal: cooking the food and getting it out to the customers. The buck, as they say, stops here—with the à la carte kitchen. I didn't mean to imply earlier that my line chefs aren't superstars; they definitely are. On a busy day, they're like cooking machines, making constant split-second decisions to make sure things are not under- or overcooked. And of course there's all the drama of the open flame, the flourishes as they deftly flip stuff in pans. It's a show in itself, just like you see on reality TV. All the hard work of the prep kitchen enables the line cooks to focus on the task at hand; with the right prep, or *mis en place*, as it's known in the kitchen, they've got everything they need at their fingertips, and they never stop moving. Virtually everything is prepped and laid out for them, so they don't even need knives on the line.

THE BUTCHER BLOCK

My favorite part of the prep kitchen, in fact my favorite part of the entire kitchen, is the butcher block. It's the heart of the kitchen, the epicenter, and at Freds it's *literally* in the center, the first thing you see when you come in from the delivery entrance. A massive expanse of solid wood in a sea of stainless steel, it's the Ellis Island of the kitchen: Every piece of protein that is cooked at Freds stops at the butcher block—to be weighed, portioned, shaped, or manicured—on the way to its eventual destination. To me, that chunk of wood is an icon. It's huge, unmoving as a rock (which is important in a production kitchen because the shiny stainless-steel tables in the rest of the workspace won't stand up to all the pounding the butcher does), and an earthy symbol that we do everything from scratch. Being a butcher in a restaurant the size of Freds is a huge responsibility. The butcher is the de facto head of the prep kitchen, and he's handling thousands of dollars of expensive food every day. It's kind of a colorful job, because anytime blood, guts, bones, and sharp knives are involved it's a bit theatrical. But, most importantly, from my point of view, the butcher is pivotal to creating the consistency that Freds, like any good restaurant, is known for. That's why there's only one butcher at Freds. If we had a rotating crew of butchers, each one would do things slightly differently, and we'd lose consistency.

The butcher needs to be skilled in butchering and carefully manicuring the meats and poultry, the steaks, chops (when we have them), and paillards. He also portions the tuna, the branzino, and other fishes. The butcher has to have a good eye, because everything needs to be beautiful, trimmed and ready for the line cooks to pop in the pan. How food looks raw is how it's going to look cooked, and so it's up to the butcher to make sure it looks nice. He also delicately seasons and shapes every one of our crab cakes—and hamburger patties, too. The work that the butcher does is equivalent to the butchering you'll find in a top meat market.

The Pastry Kitchen

Tucked around the corner from the main kitchen is the pastry kitchen, which is its own separate entity. In European kitchens, the pastry kitchen would be even more set apart, probably in a separate room with a door, and with its own ovens and stoves. Here in New York City prime real estate, we're fortunate to at least have a pastry alcove, even if we don't have a whole room. It's right next to the prep kitchen, but the pastry kitchen is as tranquil as the prep kitchen is bustling. The art of making pastry requires precision, and that requires focus and concentration. Amid the hubbub that is a working kitchen, it's like trying to perform a sterile operation in a jungle. The pastry department has its own designated equipment—knives, strainers, mixers, cutting boards, pans, etc.—and no one from the prep kitchen is allowed to touch them. It's the closest we can get to hermetically sealing the pastry department. The goal is to avoid cross-contamination with anything savory. Who wants to get a whiff of garlic as you bite into your dessert? That's definitely not a sweet way to end the meal!

The Foundations of the Freds Kitchen...and Yours

I think a lot about the word *foundation* in regard to my business. Like the foundation of a house, the work that goes into supporting a restaurant menu is unseen, except by those who do it. And as concrete and steel form the foundation of a house, the techniques, methods, and, of course, the recipes in the hands of skilled employees are what supports a restaurant's menu and builds the consistency that is important to any successful endeavor.

Foundations matter just as much in the home kitchen as they do in a restaurant. The rest of this chapter contains a sampling of useful kitchen methods and techniques, plus recipes for several of Freds' most iconic dishes, tailored for the home cook.

HOW TO CHECK FOR DONENESS IN MEAT

When you're cooking an individual portion of protein, whether poultry, fish, or meat, it can be challenging to figure out when it's cooked to the degree you like it. Of course you could slice it through the middle and look, but it isn't going to look as pretty after that, especially if you need to do so more than once. A good sauté cook is a master at determining a food's degree of doneness. And my Tire Test can help you learn that skill, too. This method is for individual portions; if you're cooking a larger item, such as a roasted turkey or chicken, you need to use a meat thermometer.

Imagine the protein you're cooking is a tire, and use the chart and your sense of touch (using a spatula, of course) to help you determine its degree of doneness.

THE TIRE TEST

Well done: the tire needs no air

Medium well: the tire needs a touch of air

Medium rare: the tire definitely needs air

Rare: you can't ride on it

Temperatures for Doneness

Red Meat (beef, lamb, and game)

Rare: 110°F to 115°F

Medium rare: 120°F

Medium: 130°F to 145°F

Medium well: 155°F

Well done: 165°F or over

Poultry

Safe: 165°F

MIS EN PLACE

If I had to pick just one concept from a restaurant kitchen that's most useful for home cooks, *mis en place* would be it. It's crucial to a smooth running professional kitchen, but just as useful for home cooking. *Mis en place* means "everything in place," and the *mis en place* for any given dish is all the little things—the chopped garlic, minced herbs, butter or oil, stocks, etc.—that you'll need to cook the final dish. If you're organized and take the time to gather your *mis en place* beforehand, you can focus on cooking, rather than jumping back and forth to the cutting board or fridge for something you've forgotten.

BOUQUET GARNI/SACHET

Traditionally, the fresh herbs used in a sauce or stock are tied together with kitchen twine to form a bouquet garni so it's easy to remove them before serving or straining. Another alternative is to place the herbs, along with whole spices and aromatics, such as peppercorns, cinnamon sticks, cloves, etc., into a small square of cheesecloth and tie it together with kitchen twine to make a sachet.

ESCOFFIER FOLD

I'm a destroyer of oven mitts, I admit it. I get pretty involved when I cook; things get messy. Anyone who turns me loose in their home kitchen has to be resigned to the fact that if they have decorative mitts they're going to be unrecognizable by the end of the night. It's the price they pay for a good meal. Mitts look beautiful hanging in the kitchen, but they're not up to the task of serious cooking. Either they're too thick, too thin, too large, too small, too unwieldy, or

CLASSIC CUTS

Escoffier said it first, in fact he's the one who invented it, but it's helpful to have a baseline kitchen vocabulary. The following is a guideline of terms professional chefs use for different knife cuts.

¾"

½"

¼"

⅛"

Large dice (mirepoix): ¾-inch cubes
Medium dice: ½-inch cubes
Small dice: ¼-inch cubes
Brunoise: ⅛-inch cubes
Fine Brunoise: 1/16-inch cubes
Batonnet: ½-inch strips
Allumette: ¼-inch strips
Julienne: ⅛-inch strips
Fine julienne: 1/16-inch strips
Chiffonade: 1/16-inch (think coleslaw-thick) shreds
Whisper: finely minced (as herbs, chives)

too pretty for the job. You'll never find them in a professional kitchen.

A professional kitchen is stocked instead with an endless supply of good-quality, cotton kitchen towels, which chefs use for any number of tasks, among them moving hot pots and pans. The Escoffier fold, as it was known earlier in my career (that term seems to have fallen into disuse, but deserves to resurface), is a way of folding a kitchen towel so that it's thick enough to protect one's hands. It's pretty simple and straightforward: Fold a good cotton kitchen towel in half three or four times (depending on the size of the towel), so that you end up with a square several layers thick—thin enough to hold flexibly, but thick enough to protect your hands during the hottest tasks, such as removing pans from the oven.

The kitchen towels we used in Europe were a sturdy cotton/linen blend, but any good-quality 100-percent-cotton kitchen towel will serve the purpose. Invest in ten good ones that you use and wash over and over again, and you'll never have to rely on another flimsy oven mitt.

Sachet of aromatics

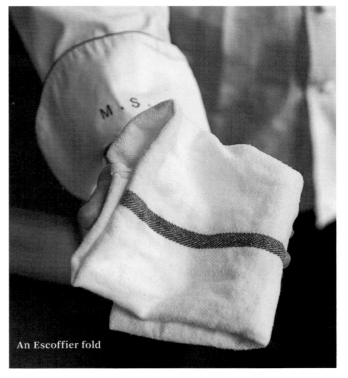

An Escoffier fold

Freds at Barneys New York, Madison Avenue (above and at right)

BELGIAN FRIES

I had to put our Belgian Fries at the beginning of the book because they're our most-loved menu item by far. Any tour of the kitchen will include the sight of the mountains of potatoes that—every single day—we clean, peel, slice, and parboil before frying golden brown and sending out to the dining room in Freds' distinctive cone glassware, along with our signature trio of sauces: Garlic Mayonnaise, Sauce Calypso, and, of course, ketchup.

I learned how to make fries properly in Amsterdam, which was my last working gig in Europe. I chose to work in Amsterdam because I knew the competition for restaurant jobs was less there than in places like Paris, and if I landed in a Michelin-starred place the training would be just as rigorous. However, if I'd known about the Dutch love of *frietkjes*—due to their proximity to the potato-loving Belgians—that alone might have been enough to lure me there. The city is dotted with Flemish *frituur* stands, and I ate them every weekend of my yearlong stint. Money was tight, *frietkjes* were cheap, and I needed to work my way through the two dozen sauces on offer, everything from simple mayonnaise, to peanut and curry sauce. At my favorite stand I eventually settled on a regular order of "special sauce," which was more or less like my childhood favorite, Russian dressing. You can take the boy out of Queens, but you can't keep him away from Russian dressing. Standing in line, far from home, I used to dream of having a restaurant someday where I would serve *frietkjes* like those, and Freds presented the perfect opportunity. Barneys threw a party a few years ago for the fabulous Belgian designer Dries Van Noten. I cooked him an order of our fries and brought them to him at his table. I rolled out one of the few phrases I knew in Dutch, which I must have heard a million times standing in line at the *frituur* in Amsterdam: *Frietjes zijn erg lekker*. ("Fries are delicious.") He looked up and rattled back an answer in Dutch, which of course I didn't understand, so I was forced to confess that I had just used up all the Dutch I knew. Fortunately, he laughed, and then said, "Well, you make fries like a Belgian." That's a great compliment coming from a Belgian, and one I'll never forget.

Makes 4 to 6 servings

EQUIPMENT	INGREDIENTS
Large stainless-steel bowl	Ice
2 large baking sheets (or platters)	6 Idaho potatoes* (about 4 pounds)
Paper towels	6 cups peanut oil
8-quart stockpot	Kosher salt
Deep fry/candy thermometer	Garlic Mayonnaise and Sauce Calypso (page 10), or your favorite sauce, for serving
Stainless-steel spider skimmer (available in stores that sell Asian cooking utensils or online)	
Long-handled wooden spoon	*Idahos are the potato of choice for making fries because they're drier than other types of potato—in a good way.*

CONTINUES

Fill the bowl with ice water and set it by your cutting board. Peel the potatoes and cut into ¼-inch-thick fries. Drop the fries into the ice water as you cut them to keep them from becoming discolored.

Line each baking sheet with several layers of paper towels. Place the peanut oil in the stockpot and heat over medium-high heat to 300°F, gauging the temperature of the oil using the candy thermometer. With paper towels, pat very dry as many fries as will fit comfortably in the pot—10 to 15.

Being careful not to overcrowd the pot, add the batch of fries and cook until they just begin to brown, about 5 minutes. Using the spider, transfer them to the paper towels to drain. Repeat with the remaining potatoes. Let stand for 30 minutes. Set the oil aside but do not discard it. (At this point you can store the potatoes in the refrigerator for up to 4 hours to fry later, but be sure to pat them well before cooking, since there will likely be condensation that might make the oil splutter.)

Reheat the oil to 350°F over medium-high heat. Add the fries, again in batches, and cook until golden brown. If needed, gently separate them with a long-handled spoon so they don't stick together. Transfer the cooked potatoes to a paper towel–lined baking sheet, sprinkle with salt, and serve immediately with your choice of sauces—although I recommend Garlic Mayonnaise and Sauce Calypso.

GARLIC MAYONNAISE

Makes 1 cup

EQUIPMENT

Whisk

INGREDIENTS

1 tablespoon minced garlic

¼ teaspoon kosher salt

1 cup good commercial mayonnaise

Sprinkle the minced garlic with the salt and use the side of your knife to mash the salt into the garlic to make a smooth paste. Whisk the paste into the mayo until it's well mixed. Set aside in the refrigerator for at least 2 hours (or overnight, ideally) in an airtight container before serving. Use within 3 days.

SAUCE CALYPSO

Makes 1½ cups

EQUIPMENT

Citrus juicer

Food processor (or bowl and a whisk)

INGREDIENTS

½ cup good commercial mayonnaise

¼ cup ketchup

1 teaspoon Dijon mustard

Juice of 1 Florida orange

Juice of 1 lemon

1 tablespoon juice from bottle of horseradish

1 tablespoon cider vinegar

1 teaspoon kosher salt

Freshly ground black pepper

1 tablespoon cognac

4 shakes Worcestershire sauce

Place the mayo, ketchup, and mustard in a food processor and blend on medium speed until well blended. With the processor on low, drizzle in the citrus juices and then the horseradish juice, vinegar, salt, and pepper. Blend well and switch the setting to low. Slowly drip in the cognac. Even though the cognac is a small amount, do not dump it in at once, but add it slowly or it may not blend in. When the dressing is emulsified, add the Worcestershire sauce and mix well. Taste and adjust the seasoning, if desired. Chill well before using. This sauce will keep in the refrigerator for 2 weeks.

And the Oscar goes to...Belgian Fries at Freds Beverly Hills

FREDS HERB MIXTURE

A container of our own finely chopped fresh herb blend sits on most of the stations around the kitchen because we use it in so many dishes—in salad dressings, in pastas, a pinch as a garnish for soup or on top of a chicken paillard, and more. It's an aromatic, similar to the famous herbes de Provence, except that ours is always made with fresh herbs and is our own blend.

This mixture is a great trick for home cooks, too. I don't know about you, but whenever I buy a bunch of herbs for home use, I end up using about half, and then the rest goes bad. Chopped finely and blended this way, and then stored in a sealed container in the fridge, the mixture should stay good for about one week. It also freezes well, although I would freeze it in individual portions. Spend a little time making this mixture and you will reap the reward of having fresh herbs on hand to toss into salads, mix into salad dressings, sprinkle over fish, omelets, or steamed vegetables, or use in a million other ways. Tailor-make your own blend just the way you like it—you might like tarragon more than I do, for example, or you might want to include dill, which we don't at Freds.

The key is to remove all the leaves from the stems (except for chives, obviously) and chop them very finely. On the illustration of Classic Cuts (see page 6), the cut for this mixture would be *whisper*. It's easiest to finely chop the herbs with a mezzaluna, but you can also use a large chef's knife. Since you are chopping so finely, use a large stable cutting board, and make sure to give yourself lots of elbow room for leverage. It's tempting to use a food processor, but that's not the best option in this case because it will tend to grind the juicier herbs (the basil and parsley) too much and turn the whole thing into a paste. What you're looking for here is a slightly dry mixture resembling sawdust.

When talking about bunches of herbs, I'm aware that the size of a *bunch* can vary wildly, depending on the store and the time of year (summer bunches of basil are usually enormous!). As a point of reference, consider each *bunch* used in this recipe to be the standard, medium-size bunch you find in the supermarket. Depending on your need, you can obviously adjust it to the smaller single-size packages that are so widely available.

Yield varies according to the size of the bunches

EQUIPMENT

Mezzaluna (can substitute knife)

INGREDIENTS

1 bunch fresh Italian parsley

1 bunch fresh chives

1 bunch fresh thyme

1 bunch fresh rosemary

1 bunch fresh basil

1 bunch fresh chervil

1 bunch fresh oregano

½ bunch fresh tarragon

Pick the leaves off the stems of all herbs, with the exception of chives, and discard the stems. Pile the leaves on a large cutting board, and, ideally using a mezzaluna, chop them all together very finely, until the mixture almost resembles sawdust. Store in an airtight container in the refrigerator for up to 10 days.

FREDS PESTO

This is not a traditional pesto because it does not contain pine nuts or cheese—but that actually makes it more flavorful and more versatile. I omitted the nuts because of the spike in nut allergies among my customers. There's no cheese, either, because I like to drizzle the pesto over fish and, in Italian food cooking, mixing cheese and fish (or seafood) is a big no-no. If you miss the flavor of cheese, feel free to throw in a handful of Parmesan cheese at the last minute of the grinding process.

While I've given the recipe amounts as a guideline, the size of bunches of basil varies widely. You may need more or less oil, or salt, depending on the quality and amount of basil. You're looking to use just enough oil to emulsify the basil into a creamy sauce, and that might take a little less or a little more than I've indicated. Make this with the beautiful, abundant basil of summer and then freeze it in small containers to use during the long winter.

Makes 1½ to 2 cups

EQUIPMENT

Food processor

INGREDIENTS

2 very tightly packed cups fresh basil leaves (roughly 2 large summer bunches fresh basil, or 4 smaller hydro bunches)

2 cloves garlic, peeled

Juice of ½ large lemon (or 1 whole small lemon)

½ cup extra-virgin olive oil

½ teaspoon kosher salt (or to taste)

Pick the leaves from the basil and discard the stems. Using a food processor, blend the basil, garlic, and lemon juice until they become a fine sauce. With the setting on low, drizzle in the olive oil until the pesto is thick and creamy. Add salt, taste, and adjust the salt, if needed.

Pour immediately into an airtight storage container, cover, and freeze; or refrigerate and use within a day or two.

CLARIFIED BUTTER

Clarified butter is great to have on hand for several reasons. It keeps longer in the fridge than butter. Plus, you can use it to cook things at a higher heat and for longer, which is especially handy for sautéing. Browned butter—which is what happens when the milk solids in butter turn color when sautéed—has its place, but for most things clarified butter works better. I especially like to use it to cook eggs and potatoes. It's a magical combination with those things.

Clarified butter is the pure fat that is separated from the water and milk solids that are contained in cream. (Butter itself is actually just cream that's been over-whipped.) It is the fat of choice for haute cuisine (also known as *ghee*, it's a staple in Indian cooking, too), in the way that olive oil is for Italians.

In the restaurants where I worked in Europe, we would churn our own butter on Sunday nights if we ran low at the end of an unusually busy day, in case the delivery was late the following morning. Running out of butter simply was unthinkable. We've never had to do that yet at Freds, maybe because our calorie-conscious guests often leave butter untouched on the table, or prefer the olive oil we also serve with our bread.

Makes approximately 1½ cups

EQUIPMENT

Strainer

Cheesecloth for straining

Ladle

2-quart stainless-steel mixing bowl

2-quart saucepot or soup pot

1 sterile glass jar, with lid

INGREDIENTS

4 sticks (1 pound) unsalted butter

Get the equipment ready before you start melting the butter: Line the inside of the strainer with a layer of cheesecloth and set it aside with the ladle and mixing bowl.

Place the butter in the pot over a low to medium heat. As the butter melts, adjust the heat to keep the butter from sizzling and so that the milk solids don't brown. However, if the heat is *too* low, the water will not evaporate and release the milk solids to allow them to sink to the bottom of the pan. (The fat and the milk solids have different weights, so they naturally separate when heated. You'll see that the milk solids are a lighter color than the fat.)

Once the fat and solids have melted and separated, remove the pot from the heat and work fairly quickly to strain the fat. (Do not stir the butter once it's separated and even take care moving the pan so they don't merge again.) Use a ladle to skim the fat off the top, and pass it through the strainer. Don't dip the ladle down to catch any of the milk solids. The cheesecloth will catch any stray drops of the solids.

Let the strained fat sit for 10 minutes to cool slightly, and then pour it into the glass jar. Alternately, you can pour it into small containers to freeze for individual use. Clarified butter will keep in the refrigerator for a week and the freezer for much longer.

HOMEMADE CROUTONS

Crunchy, slightly buttery croutons are the perfect garnish for any soup or salad. This recipe calls for fresh mint, but feel free to substitute Freds Herb Mixture (page 12), or any herbs or seasonings that appeal to you—or leave out the herbs entirely. White bread is the easiest to use for croutons as it dries out quickly and thoroughly in the oven. It's possible to substitute whole grain bread, but it may need to toast a bit longer.

If you're making larger croutons to use for Lobster Bisque (page 124), follow these instructions, but use ½-inch-thick slightly diagonal slices of baguette, instead of the diced pullman loaf.

Makes approximately 2 cups

EQUIPMENT

Large mixing bowl

Baking sheet

INGREDIENTS

4 slices pullman-style white or brioche bread, crusts removed, cut into dice

4 fresh mint leaves, finely chopped (can substitute other fresh herbs)

2 tablespoons clarified butter (see page 14; can substitute olive oil)

Kosher salt

Preheat the oven to 350°F. Place the diced bread and mint in a mixing bowl and gently mix together. Warm the butter just until it's melted and drizzle over the bread. Sprinkle with salt and mix gently to coat all the pieces. Spread the bread onto the baking sheet and toast in the oven for 4 to 6 minutes, until the croutons are golden brown. Remove from the oven and set aside to cool. Store the croutons in a covered container at room temperature for up to 2 days.

STEAMED POTATOES

When I worked at the Hessischer Hof in Frankfurt, a whole new world of potato cookery opened up to me. Germans take potatoes seriously, and there was an entire room of the kitchen devoted to potato preparation. Each main course came with a different potato dish, whether it was a gratin, new potatoes turned in butter, potato salad, pommes frites, and on and on. That's where I learned to steam potatoes instead of boiling them. It was kind of a revelation, because potatoes are so much more flavorful when they're not waterlogged. This method is especially good for more waxy types of potatoes, such as fingerlings, Yukon Golds, red bliss, or russets, but not really suited for dry, fluffy potatoes like Idahos. Steamed potatoes are good chilled in salads, but steaming is also a good way to cook them ahead to serve later, perhaps sautéed with a little butter.

The best tool for steaming potatoes is a bamboo steamer basket, which should fit on top of a 5-quart pot. Alternatively, you can use a vegetable steamer basket.

Makes 1 cup

EQUIPMENT

5-quart stockpot

Bamboo steamer basket with lid

INGREDIENTS

1 tablespoon salt

¾ pound fingerling potatoes (or larger potatoes cut into your desired size)

Fill the pot about halfway full of water, and add the salt. Peel (if desired) and cut the potatoes and place them in the steamer. Place the steamer on the pot, cover with the lid, turn the burner to high, and steam until the potatoes are tender. Once the water comes to a boil, check the potatoes every 3 minutes or so for doneness by inserting a paring knife into the center of a piece. The potatoes are done when there is no resistance, or, as the saying goes, when it's "like a hot knife through butter." Do not use an ice bath to cool the potatoes. Simply turn off the heat and remove the steamer basket from the pot. Let the potatoes cool at room temperature and use within 1 hour. Refrigeration will change the texture, so it's best to make only the amount you need.

BLANCHED VEGETABLES

Blanching is a great method for cooking vegetables because it gives you the maximum amount of control over the cooking process. You can use the same technique for any vegetable—string beans, asparagus, broccoli, cauliflower, etc.—that will not be ruined by immersing in cold water. The key to the control is making an ice water bath to immerse the vegetables in immediately after they're cooked. The cold "shocks" the vegetables and arrests the cooking at the perfect moment so they stay just the right amount of crisp and green. The shock of the cold water eliminates any carry-over cooking time, which is cooking that goes on in food even after it's removed from the heat.

Makes 1 cup

EQUIPMENT

5-quart stockpot

Large stainless-steel bowl

Colander

Kitchen towel

INGREDIENTS

¾ pound vegetables

Kosher salt

Ice

Clean the vegetables, trim, and cut as desired. Fill the stockpot with water that measures approximately two to three times the volume of vegetables. Add salt and bring the water to a boil.

While you're waiting for the water to boil, prepare the ice water bath: Place a generous amount of ice in a large stainless-steel bowl and add some cold water, but not enough that it will completely melt the ice. Set the bowl to the side in your sink and set a colander next to it for draining the vegetables.

When the water comes to a boil, add the vegetables and let them boil with the lid off so you can keep track of their color. When they're cooked to your liking, quickly drain them in the colander and then immediately place them into the ice water bath. If they melt all the ice, add more ice to keep the ice bath extremely cold. When the vegetables are cold, or at least at room temperature, remove them from the ice water, and pat dry with a kitchen towel. Use immediately or store in the refrigerator for later use.

———

OVEN-COOKED BACON

We cook mountains of bacon every day, and not just for brunch: Both our Club Salad (page 61) and Madison Classic Club Sandwich (page 97), lunchtime staples, contain bacon. The oven makes it easy to make perfect bacon, and there's nothing better than perfect bacon. Even if you're not cooking the vast amount we are, it makes sense to bake it in the oven, rather than stand in front of a spluttering frying pan. Since all the bacon cooks at the same time, you can actually sit down and eat at the same time as your family, although I can't help you with that if you're also making pancakes!

We tend to cook the bacon crispy because that's the way most Americans like it. Europeans prefer it on the slightly chewy side, with the meat cooked but the fat portion still a bit soft and pale, like it is on a cooked steak. However you like it, keep a close eye on it, especially toward the end of the cooking time when it can turn from crispy to burnt in a matter of seconds. If you're making it to use for sandwiches later in the day, like we do, you'll also need to keep an eye out to make sure your family members don't make strips "mysteriously" disappear before you can use them!

We use it at room temperature for salads and sandwiches, but if you want to warm it before serving, place in a 250°F oven for just a few minutes.

Makes 12 strips

EQUIPMENT

Parchment paper

Heavy-duty restaurant-quality
half sheet pan with at least 1-inch sides

Paper towels

Baking sheet

INGREDIENTS

1 (1-pound) package good-quality bacon
(we use Nueske's applewood-smoked)

Preheat the oven to 350°F. Spread parchment paper to cover the sheet pan. Arrange the bacon on the paper evenly and in rows, with pieces not touching. Place in the oven and bake for about 5 minutes, then lower the heat to 300°F. Continue baking until the bacon is to your liking (crispy or not), 8 to 10 minutes; check every 2 minutes to make sure it's baking slowly and not burning.

While it's baking, spread a layer of paper towels on the baking sheet. When the bacon is done to your liking, remove it from the oven and set the pan aside to sit for 2 to 4 minutes. Then, using a spatula, transfer the bacon to drain on the paper towels. Serve immediately or set aside to cool, covered loosely with a paper towel, to use later for sandwiches and salads.

Allow the fat that's in the pan to cool for 30 minutes before you discard it.

ROASTED TURKEY BREAST

At Freds, we roast whole bone-in turkey breasts instead of whole turkeys. We cook six to eight whole large breasts each and every day at Freds Madison to use in our Madison Classic Club Sandwich (page 97) and our Club Salad (page 61). At Freds New York City Downtown location, we roast them for our Jewish Boy from Queens Sandwich (page 101). You can usually find whole bone-in turkey breasts at better supermarkets and butcher shops; if they don't have them in stock they can order one for you. Like whole turkeys, you'll find them in different sizes—the smaller ones weigh 6 to 8 pounds, so choose the size that makes sense for your household. Certainly for a home cook it's simpler—and quicker—to roast a breast than a whole bird because you don't have to worry about the breast drying out while the legs are finishing cooking. The advantage of roasting your own turkey is not just better flavor; it's a great "leftover" to have on hand in the fridge for holidays, weekends, for the Little League team, or for the teenagers in your life who tend to travel through in packs.

Makes 6 to 8 servings

ROASTING A TURKEY BREAST

Check the weight of the breast so you can gauge approximately how long it will take to cook. The rule of thumb for roasting turkey, whether you're roasting a whole bird or just the breast, is to roast it at 325°F for 18 to 20 minutes per pound. The breast is not done until the internal temperature has reached 165°F. Gauge this by using a meat thermometer, which you stick into the center of the breast, right next to the bone.

A layer of carrots, onions, celery, and garlic in the roasting pan adds a layer of flavor to the turkey. Even if they char, which they likely will, that adds a nice, very subtle smokiness to the meat.

EQUIPMENT

Large poultry roasting pan

Flat rack to fit in the roasting pan

Baster

Aluminum foil
(to make a tent over the turkey)

Meat thermometer

INGREDIENTS

2 carrots, cut into 2-inch chunks

2 onions, cut into 2-inch chunks

4 stalks celery, cut into 2-inch chunks

1 head garlic, cloves separated and peeled

1 (6- to 8-pound) whole, bone-in turkey breast

3 tablespoons salt

2 teaspoons coarsely ground black pepper

¼ cup olive oil

2 cups dry white wine
(can substitute water)

CONTINUES

Preheat the oven to 325°F.

Place the rack in the roasting pan and lay the vegetables and garlic on the rack. It's fine if some fall through to the pan; they're going to end up there anyway as they cook. Rub the bottom of the turkey breast with 2 tablespoons of the salt and 1 teaspoon of the pepper. Turn it over and rub the skin with the olive oil and sprinkle with the remainder of the salt and pepper. Place on the rack, and carefully pour the wine into the pan, but do not pour it over the turkey. Roast according to the weight of the breast (18 to 20 minutes per pound). Check every 30 minutes to make sure the skin is not burning, and baste each time using liquid from the pan. If the skin does start to get too brown, use a large piece of aluminum foil to carefully cover the top for the remainder of the roasting time.

Near the end of the roasting time, check the internal temperature of the breast by inserting the meat thermometer deep into the meat on the bottom side, close to the bone. Once you get a reading of 120 or 130°F, you need to keep an eye on the time and check the temperature every 10 minutes. (If you have a digital thermometer you can't leave it in while the breast is cooking, but if you have a standard, oven-proof one you can.)

When the breast is cooked to an internal temperature of 165°F, remove it from the oven and set aside to cool for at least 30 minutes, or ideally 1 hour. Once it's cool enough to touch, remove the meat from the bone. Alternatively, you can leave it on the bone, although it's easier to slice neatly if the bone is removed.

If desired, freeze the bone to use next time you make stock.

———

ESTELLE'S CHICKEN SOUP TRILOGY

"Grandma's recipe to cure colds and stay thin"

Some things never go out of style: a crisp white shirt, a little black dress, a cashmere sweater. In the food world, chicken soup is one of those things. And it's tailor-made for the fashionable: It packs a lot of flavor and nutrition into something satisfying, plus it's low calorie, a combination that's basically the Holy Grail for my customers. With the current popularity of bone broth, this soup is on point. Some of my regulars eat it nearly every day for lunch; it's that satisfying. I probably get more compliments about this soup than any other menu item, because people can't believe how flavorful it is and how good they feel after eating it.

On a personal level, Estelle's Chicken Soup, named for my maternal grandmother, is a touchstone for me. It's the merging and distillation of everything in my career and my past. I've described my food style as "Escoffier meets Grandma." Well, this is Escoffier meets Bubbe. I was a Jewish kid growing up in Queens in the '60s and '70s. Do you have any idea how much chicken soup—errr, Jewish penicillin, as the cliché goes—I ate in my childhood? My mother, daughter of the eponymous Estelle and as fashionable as any of my customers, even if she couldn't afford high fashion, lived on the stuff because "it's not fattening." So for most of my youth it was the last thing I wanted to eat, except maybe once a year at Passover. And certainly it was the last thing I wanted to cook as a starry-eyed aspiring chef fresh from a four-year stint in Europe. Europeans don't have the same obsession with chicken that we have here in America. It did not factor at all in my classical training and was a more humble dish than I was interested in cooking. I explored Italian peasant food in my career, but the peasant food of my own roots? Not interested.

But thankfully time mellowed me, as it has a way of doing, and one year, in a nostalgic mood, I decided to put a couple of Passover foods on the menu during the first two nights of the holiday (we now do a very popular full Passover menu). Chicken soup was one of them. I saw how deeply it resonated with my customers, many of whom have similar backgrounds to mine. I decided to use my knowledge as a chef to make the best chicken soup possible, the Socratic ideal of chicken soup. This is not the somewhat weak (sorry, Mom) broth my mother dashed together in between working full-time and taking care of us kids. This is a fortified broth—fortified using a three-day process that packs in more marrow and nutrition than you can believe. For me, Estelle's Chicken Soup is more than soup: It's a poem of my life and a big, warming bowl of love.

I call this a *trilogy* because it takes three days to make properly. If you stop after the first day you'll have a perfectly sound chicken broth to use as a base for cooking, to use in soups and other dishes. It's the second day—the fortifying of the stock—that takes the soup over the top and makes it truly special. It's well worth the time, in my opinion, especially if you're serving it for a special occasion.

STOCK-MAKING BASICS

Escoffier, who was thinking about the foundations of cooking long before I was born, elegantly called stock "the humble foundation for all that follows." There are gigantic stockpots simmering all the time in our kitchen, in various stages of making the three main types of stock we use: chicken, vegetable, and veal. In addition we also make lobster stock for our lobster bisque.

You don't need me to tell you that stock making at home is quite an undertaking. In fact, I think of it as being a little bit like mountain climbing. It's a big project that requires a lot of preparation, but the similarity doesn't stop there. In climbing, everyone assumes the danger is when you're ascending the slope, but actually there's as much danger, if not more, when you're coming down off the mountain. You're basking in your accomplishment, but you really can't give in to the temptation to relax because you still need to stay on your guard. In stock making, that point is when the cooking time is finished and you are faced with a large pot of extremely hot liquid and bones that you need to carefully drain and strain.

If you are brave enough to tackle it, it's a great weekend project. Make it two or three times a year, divide it into small containers for individual use, and freeze it so you always have some on hand. However, don't feel badly if you aren't up to making your own. There are now many first-rate commercial stocks available: canned, in soft packaging, and in the freezer sections of supermarkets and gourmet stores. Good-quality convenience items like this make home cooking increasingly easy, delicious, and pleasurable.

GENERAL TIPS FOR GOOD STOCK

- Count on about a 30-percent reduction in liquid. For example, if you want a 2-quart yield, start with 3 quarts of water.
- Put everything—bones, vegetables, herbs, and water—in the pot before you turn on the burner. Then slowly let it come to a simmer. Don't let the liquid boil rapidly at any point during the process or the stock will become cloudy.
- Do not salt the stock. Save it for when you're seasoning the final dish you're using the stock in.

- Leave the pot uncovered. Slowly simmer chicken stock for 4 to 6 hours, vegetable stock for 2 hours, veal for 6 to 8 hours.
- As the stock cooks, a frothy residue (I hesitate to use the unappetizing term *scum*, but that's really what it is) will periodically rise to the top. Use a ladle to skim it off and discard it. As it simmers, the stock will gradually produce less and less of it.
- When the stock is cooked, turn off the heat and let it sit 20 to 30 minutes to cool slightly. **Use great care** when removing the bones and straining the liquid, because the stock will still be **very** hot.
- Give yourself plenty of elbow room to work as you move the stockpot. Place it on a stable space on the counter, ideally next to the sink, where you have placed a container to ladle the stock into. Place a large garbage bag or container near you for discarding the bones and vegetables. **Remember:** The bones will also be **very** hot!
- Place a China cap or mesh strainer over the container in the sink. Use a large measuring cup or small pitcher to scoop out the stock and pour it through the strainer which will catch any small bits of meat, bone, and vegetable.
- When you can't scoop out any more liquid, discard the bones. For safety reasons, do not tilt the stockpot until you reach the very last bit of liquid, and only after you have removed all the bones from the pot.
- Place the strained stock in storage containers with lids. Do not completely fill the containers; fill two-thirds full so that there is enough air for the stock to breathe as it cools or you risk it turning sour. Place in the fridge to cool.
- When chicken or veal stock is chilled, fat will congeal on the top. Scoop it off to discard it. It's not possible to get rid of 100 percent, there will always be a little left. But remove as much as possible, or the stock may go sour more quickly.
- Freeze any stock you won't be using within 2 days. I recommend freezing in 1- or 2-pint containers so you can thaw them as needed. Stock will keep for 3 months in the freezer.

I strongly recommend using chicken necks and backs as a base for the first two steps because it's more economical and less wasteful than using whole chickens. I also recommend freezing leftover bones and carcasses when you have roasted chicken so that you can use them for stock making. On the third day you should use a whole chicken because you will want to include the shredded meat in the final dish. On the regular menu, we serve Estelle's Chicken Soup with shredded chicken meat and just a sprinkling of fresh herbs. At Passover we add matzoh balls and slivers of carrot and celery. We also sometimes offer a Passover version that contains thinly sliced baby artichokes, spring peas, and a little bit of rice. If you want something heartier and autumnal, cubes of parsnips, carrots, and potatoes are a nice addition, too.

CHICKEN STOCK
(DAY ONE)

Makes about 6 quarts

EQUIPMENT

10- to 12-quart stockpot

Heavy-duty potholders for lifting stockpot
(or kitchen towels in the Escoffier fold, see page 6)

Tongs

Long-handled ladle

Mesh or China cap strainer

Smaller stockpot

INGREDIENTS

5 pounds chicken necks and backs
(can substitute 5 pounds chicken pieces)

4 medium red onions, cut into 2-inch cubes

3 carrots, cut into 2-inch cubes

1 head celery, cut into 2-inch cubes

3 leeks, white and light green parts, trimmed,
well-washed, and roughly chopped

2 parsnips, cut into 2-inch cubes

½ bunch fresh Italian parsley

½ bunch fresh thyme

¼ bunch fresh marjoram

6 fresh sage leaves

8 black peppercorns, smashed

2 bay leaves

3 whole cloves

Cold water to cover

Ice

Place all ingredients (through cloves) in the stockpot and cover with cold water. Bring to a gentle simmer over high heat, watching so that it does not at any point go into a full boil, which will cause the stock to become cloudy. Reduce the heat to medium low and simmer, uncovered, for 4 to 6 hours. Check on it intermittently and if, during the first 2 hours, the liquid reduces so that it is no longer covering the vegetables and chicken, add more water to cover them.

Make an ice water bath in the kitchen sink by placing enough ice and cold water so that half the pot will be submerged when added. Carefully place the pot in the ice water bath to quickly bring down the temperature. If a large quantity of ice is not available, let the stock cool slightly on its own. Then use tongs to remove the solids and carefully ladle the stock, which will still be quite hot, through the strainer into the smaller stockpot, so any small bits are filtered out. Place the strained stock in the refrigerator to finish cooling overnight. Use as a base for the next step (Fortified Chicken Stock, page 25), or freeze in individual containers to use as chicken stock.

FORTIFIED CHICKEN STOCK

(DAY TWO)

Makes about 6 quarts

EQUIPMENT

Large slotted spoon

10- to 12-quart stockpot

Heavy-duty potholders for lifting stockpot
(or kitchen towels in the Escoffier fold,
see page 6)

Tongs

Long-handled ladle

Mesh or China cap strainer

Smaller stockpot

INGREDIENTS

About 6 quarts cold Chicken Stock
(from Day One)

3 pounds chicken necks and backs
(can substitute other chicken pieces)

2 medium red onions, cut into 2-inch cubes

2 carrots, cut into 2-inch cubes

¼ head celery, cut into 2-inch cubes

1 leek, white and light green parts, trimmed,
well-washed, and roughly chopped

½ bunch fresh Italian parsley

½ bunch fresh thyme

6 fresh sage leaves

8 black peppercorns, crushed

2 bay leaves

3 whole cloves

Cold water to cover

Ice

Use the slotted spoon to skim off the layer of solid fat that has risen to the top of the cold stock.

Place the stock and the remaining ingredients (through cloves) in the stockpot and add water to cover as needed. Bring to a gentle simmer over high heat, watching so that it does not at any point go into a full boil, which will cause the stock to become cloudy. Reduce the heat to medium low and simmer, uncovered, for 4 to 6 hours.

Make an ice water bath in the kitchen sink by placing enough ice and cold water so that half the pot is submerged when added. Carefully place the pot in the ice water bath to quickly bring down the temperature. If a large quantity of ice is not available, let the stock cool slightly on its own. Then use tongs to remove the solids and carefully ladle the stock, which will still be quite hot, through the strainer into a smaller stockpot, so any small bits are filtered out. Place the strained stock in the refrigerator to finish cooling overnight. Use as a base for the next step (Estelle's Chicken Soup, page 27), or freeze in individual containers to use as chicken stock.

CONTINUES

ESTELLE'S CHICKEN SOUP
(DAY THREE)

Makes about 6 quarts, serving 8 to 10

EQUIPMENT

Large slotted spoon

10- to 12-quart stockpot

Tongs

INGREDIENTS

6 quarts Fortified Chicken Stock
(from Day Two)

1 (4-pound) chicken, preferably
all-natural or organic, cut into 8 pieces

1 carrot, trimmed, peeled, and cut
into ¼-inch cubes

1 small onion, cut into ¼-inch cubes

1 leek, white part only, trimmed,
well-washed, and sliced very thinly

1 celery stalk, cut into ¼-inch slices

Kosher salt

Freshly ground black pepper

Optional garnish: 12 sprigs fresh
parsley, chopped; 1 bunch fresh chives,
cut into whisper-thin pieces

Use the slotted spoon to skim off the layer of solid fat that has risen to the top of the cold stock.

Combine the stock and the remaining ingredients (through celery) in the stockpot. Bring to a gentle simmer over high heat, watching so that it does not at any point go into a full boil, which will cause the stock to become cloudy. Reduce the heat to medium low and simmer, uncovered, for 1½ hours, or until the chicken is tender and cooked through.

Using a pair of tongs, carefully remove the chicken pieces from the soup. Set them aside until cool enough to pick the meat from the bones. Discard any gristle and the bones. Shred the meat, and return to the soup. Season the soup with salt and pepper to taste. If you're serving the soup immediately, heat it through. Ladle into serving bowls, making sure everyone gets some chicken meat in their bowl, and garnish with the chopped herbs. If you're serving it later, refrigerate or freeze immediately.

VEGETABLE STOCK

An actor or musician plays to their audience, and as a chef that's also how I approach the dishes I offer my guests. Sensing trends and the way people want to eat is fundamental to the way I approach my craft and my business. I might have been trained in classical European cooking, with its reliance on the foundation of veal-based demi-glace, but my use of vegetable stock at Freds is pure American. It's light, and more in line with the way most of my customers want to eat right now. We use it as a foundation for many of our soups, for risotto, and as a flavorful stand-in for water (perhaps with a touch of saffron) when cooking couscous and other grains. Sometimes we use it for poaching fish, too.

Even if you're not a vegetarian, there are several reasons you might want to use vegetable stock. It's quicker to make than animal-based stocks, cooking in 2 hours as opposed to 4 to 6. And it's made with ingredients you're likely to have on hand.

Makes 5 quarts

EQUIPMENT

Cheesecloth sack

10- to 12-quart stockpot

Heavy-duty potholders for lifting stockpot (or kitchen towels in the Escoffier fold, see page 6)

Ladle

Mesh or China cap strainer

Large measuring cup or small pitcher (for scooping stock)

Smaller stockpot for cooling

INGREDIENTS

2 bay leaves

12 whole black peppercorns

8 fresh sage leaves

8 fresh rosemary sprigs

8 quarts water

1 head celery (about 12 stalks), stalks separated and trimmed

4 medium onions, peeled

1 pound button mushrooms, thickly sliced

2 bulbs fennel, trimmed

4 large carrots, trimmed

2 turnips, trimmed

2 parsnips, trimmed

3 leeks, white and green parts, cut in half and well-washed

2 large handfuls fresh parsley sprigs

1 head garlic, cloves separated and peeled

Ice

Make a bouquet garni by tying the bay leaves, peppercorns, sage, and rosemary in the cheesecloth sack. Chop all the vegetables into ¾-inch pieces (mirepoix).

Place the bouquet garni in the large stockpot and add the water. Add the mirepoix, parsley, and garlic. Place the pot over medium-high heat and heat, uncovered, just until the liquid starts to simmer. Reduce the heat to medium low and simmer gently for about 2 hours, until the vegetables are very soft. If scum surfaces at any point, simply skim it off.

Make an ice water bath in the kitchen sink by adding enough ice and cold water so that half the pot is submerged. Carefully place the pot in the ice water bath to quickly bring down the temperature. If a large quantity of ice is not available, let the stock cool slightly on its own. Remove the bouquet garni, then ladle the stock through the strainer into the smaller stockpot. If you like, push down on the vegetables to squeeze all the liquid and some of the vegetable pulp into the stock, which will give it more body (this will make the stock a bit cloudy).

Use immediately, or refrigerate (keeps about 2 days) or freeze (keeps for 3 to 4 months) to use later. Vegetable stock does not "jell" the way bone stock does because it contains no animal protein, nor will it have a layer of congealed fat on top when it's cold, as meat stocks do.

VEGETABLES TO USE FOR MAKING VEGETABLE STOCK

Experiment using different vegetables for stock, especially if you're looking to accentuate a particular flavor, such as asparagus or mushroom. In that case, use more of that particular vegetable, and make sure to use all of it, including the woody stems that you normally would discard.

	Vegetables NOT to Use
Carrots	
Celery	Potatoes (including sweet potatoes)
Onions	Beets
Leeks, ramps, and other alliums	Broccoli, cauliflower, or other "flowering" vegetables
Mushrooms	Cabbage
Asparagus	Leafy greens
Fennel	Tomatoes
Parsnips	Eggplant
Turnips	Peas
	String beans
	Squash

DEMI-GLACE

Demi-glace is a reduction of veal stock that's made from roasted veal bones. It's a two-step process of making the stock and then reducing it, which creates the glossy sheen and rich flavor French sauces are known for. Demi-glace is a wonderful base for a wide variety of sauces, which can incorporate herbs, mushrooms, leeks, red wine, bone marrow, and other flavorings as desired.

When roasting the bones for the stock, keep an eye on them so they brown, but do not burn, since burned bones will result in bitter demi-glace.

VEAL STOCK

Makes 5 quarts

EQUIPMENT

Large roasting pan with 2- to 4-inch sides

Tongs

12-quart stockpot

Heavy-duty potholders for lifting stockpot (or kitchen towels in the Escoffier fold, see page 6)

Long-handled slotted spoon

Smaller stockpot for cooling

Mesh or China cap strainer

Ladle

INGREDIENTS

5 pounds small (or cut-up) veal bones, cracked if possible (your butcher can do this for you)

2 carrots

3 onions, peeled

3 celery stalks

2 leeks, split lengthwise, well-washed

1 large handful fresh parsley sprigs

4 sprigs fresh rosemary

4 sprigs fresh thyme

12 black peppercorns

3 cloves

2 bay leaves

1 head garlic, cut vertically in half (do not peel)

2 cups dry red wine

2 cups milled or crushed canned Italian plum tomatoes

2 tablespoons tomato paste

Water to cover

Ice

Preheat the oven to 425°F. Place the bones in the roasting pan and roast for 1 to 1½ hours, until the bones are browned and nicely caramelized. Check now and then while they are roasting to make sure they don't burn.

While the bones are roasting, cut the vegetables into ¾-inch dice (mirepoix).

Once the bones are brown, carefully transfer to the stockpot. Add the mirepoix, remaining ingredients (through tomato paste) and enough water to cover it all. Place over medium-high heat and cook until the liquid is almost—but not quite—boiling. Reduce the heat to medium low and simmer gently, uncovered, for 6 to 8 hours. Don't let the stock boil or it will become cloudy. During the first 4 hours, add water as needed to keep the ingredients covered, but don't add water during the last 2 to 3 hours or the flavor will become watery.

Make an ice water bath in the kitchen sink by adding enough ice and cold water so that half the pot is submerged. Carefully place the pot in the ice water bath to quickly bring down the temperature. If a large quantity of ice is not available, let the stock cool slightly on its own. Then use tongs to carefully remove the large pieces of bone from the stock and discard. Place a smaller stockpot next to you and place the strainer on top of it. Using a ladle, strain the stock through the strainer into the smaller stockpot. As you do so, press down on the solids to squeeze out all the juices. Refrigerate the stock for up to 4 days.

——

DEMI-GLACE

Makes 2½ quarts

EQUIPMENT

8-quart stockpot

Long-handled spoon

INGREDIENTS

5 quarts Veal Stock (opposite)

2 cups red wine

Place the veal stock and red wine in the stockpot over medium heat until it just starts to boil. Immediately reduce the heat to low or medium low so that it's barely simmering. Simmer this way, uncovered, for about 2 hours, until the stock reduces by half, checking and stirring frequently to make sure it's not burning. The color will darken and the liquid will thicken as it reduces. Check for the proper viscosity by placing a teaspoon of the sauce on a small plate, and then tilting the plate. When the demi-glace is reduced to the proper thickness it will not run when the plate is tilted.

Freeze demi-glace in half pint airtight containers to use as needed. Stored this way it will keep for six months.

——

COURT BOUILLON

Instead of poaching delicate seafood and fish in plain water, I prefer the classical method of using the flavored broth called court bouillon. Court bouillon is simple to make, and the added flavorings give the end product an extra dimension of flavor. Besides containing an assortment of aromatics (such as garlic and peppercorns) and water, court bouillon always contains some kind of acidic liquid, most commonly white wine vinegar, which lends brightness to the poached seafood or fish.

In this book I use court bouillon for cooking whole lobsters (see page 49), but it also works beautifully for poaching seafood and fish: anything from individual filets to a whole side of salmon.

Makes 8 cups

EQUIPMENT

Large (10- to 12-quart) stockpot with lid

INGREDIENTS

1 large red onion

8 cloves garlic, peeled

8 cups water

1 cup white wine vinegar

2 bay leaves

4 juniper berries

16 whole black peppercorns

½ bunch fresh Italian parsley

Stud the onion with the cloves by sticking the stick end of each into the flesh of the onion. Place the onions and remaining ingredients in the stockpot and bring to a boil over high heat. Once the liquid is boiling, lower the heat to medium. Carefully add the seafood (or fish) and cook according to the instructions.

That old real estate adage that the three most important factors for determining value are location, location, location applies to Freds' success, too. Being in Barneys' Madison Avenue flagship store, at the intersection of 61st Street and Madison Avenue, means that we stand with one foot in the well-heeled Upper East Side, and the other foot in the office towers of midtown. It's the perfect position for a busy lunch business, attracting both the captains of industry and the ladies who lunch, although these days the ladies are actually more likely to be executives, foundation heads, and Broadway producers. Being in Barneys also means that, well, we're in *Barneys*, a shopping mecca for people from all over the world. When we opened Freds, I had a hunch that lunch was going to be big, but I couldn't have imagined *how* big. It's packed, every day, and has been for over twenty years. In fashion terms, lunch is the event we get dressed up for. Sometimes the room feels like one big party, because everyone knows each other, either from business, the charity circuit, the neighborhood, or all of the above. The table-hopping is out of control. I love it, and as much as I'd like to take credit, I have to admit that a lot of our success has to do with our location.

CHAPTER 2
THE FREDS ICONIC SALADS

Mark's Madison Avenue Salad / 43

Freds Chopped Chicken Salad with Balsamic Dressing / 45

The Palace Warm Lobster Salad with Freds Bistro Dressing / 48

The Palm Salads / 53

    Palm Beach Shrimp Salad with Green Goddess Dressing / 53

    Palm Springs Shrimp Salad with Green Goddess Dressing / 55

      Baked Fresh Baby Artichoke Hearts / 56

Freds Niçoise Salad / 57

The Club Salad / 61

Autumn Salad / 63

Vegan Salad with Salsa Verde Vinaigrette / 65

Beverly Hills Asian Chicken Salad / 68

There's one dish that's far-and-away the customer favorite at lunch: salad. We offer a large range of entrée salads, and serve them in iconic large white bowls. When I look around the dining room at lunch, those bowls are everywhere. Sure, a cone of Belgian fries is sprouting up from the center of almost every table, because who can resist them? But that's a guilty pleasure made for sharing. My customers will pick at a fry or two, but what most of them are *really* eating for lunch is salad. It makes sense; Freds is housed in the world's most fashionable store, in the world's most fashionable neighborhood, and while my customers are extremely health conscious, they also want to enjoy something delicious.

I think it's always been that way in society restaurants. It's no accident that many of the world's famous, classic salads were invented to amuse and feed the crème of society. The Cobb salad was invented at the Brown Derby restaurant in Los Angeles, for example. And, of course, there's Waldorf salad, invented right here in New York City at the Waldorf Astoria Hotel.

My good customer John Gutfreund used to quote the stock market adage, "Let trend be your friend," and I've found that's useful wisdom for the restaurant business, too. If my customers want to eat salad, why fight it? That just means I need to try and create the most delicious, satisfying salads I can. On the original menu for Freds, I included a number of entrée salads. All the originals—Mark's Madison Avenue Salad, the Club Salad, the Palace Warm Lobster Salad (which I named in honor of my time working at the Montreux Palace in Switzerland), to name a few—are still on the menu to this day, even though we keep adding new ones to keep up with current trends. In Freds' regional locations, I like to include salads that reflect the culinary culture of the area. For example, on the Beverly Hills menu I've included an Asian Chicken Salad, which has turned out to be our biggest seller there, although I doubt it would be as popular on Madison Avenue.

The traditional entrée plate is like a rock band, with the meat, starch, and veg standing in for the guitarist, bass, and drummer. It's solid, makes a statement, even if it's somewhat basic. A great salad, by contrast, is more like a symphony, with a wider range of ingredients, textures, and tastes to give it complexity and subtlety. The salads we make at Freds are even, in the culinary world, called *composed* salads, so the analogy actually kind of works.

Besides the fact that serving salads made business sense, I had my own personal reasons for creating them. My favorite part of working in Europe was learning about the classical cold kitchen. In American restaurants, there's really no counterpart to the lavish buffets that are popular with weekend diners in the grand European hotels where I worked. I worked in three different grand hotels at various points: the Amstel Hotel in Amsterdam, the Montreux Palace on Lake Geneva, and the Hessischer Hof in Frankfurt, but there's at least one in every major European city. Sure, we have beautiful hotels here in New York City—some of them are Freds' neighbors—with wonderful restaurants, but for the most part hotels in America are geared for travelers, not for locals. And even the best ones offer no counterpart to the grand hotel buffets in Europe. It's just not part of our culture, but there, it's a tradition to dine graciously on Sunday afternoons, dressed in your very best, in the grand, flower-filled turn-of-the-century dining room of the local grand hotel. Impeccably set buffet tables are piled high with lavish and decorative platters of the very best seasonal produce—perhaps poached white asparagus, or spring artichokes, or fresh chanterelles and porcini, and other salads—as well as cured meats, aspic, gelée, and pâté, every single thing made in house. The cold kitchens in the places where I worked produced a staggering variety of foods and the presentations were stunning.

I was dazzled and intrigued by the artistry of it. Most aspiring chefs long for the glory of the sauté station, but I much preferred the cold station. In fact, I became obsessed. I did my stint sautéing, and obviously I'm glad for what I learned, but at a certain point, I found flipping hunks of protein and making pan sauces a bit boring compared to the artistry of those buffets. I wanted to know how to make everything on them. My final time in Europe was spent working at the Amstel Hotel (now the InterContinental Amstel), and the head chef there, seeing my love of the cold kitchen and my willingness to work hard and learn, was happy to station me there. By the time I left, I was master garde manger in charge of the whole department, unheard of for an American at that time. When I came home I had notebooks full of scrawled recipes for the dressings, cold vegetable preparations, pâté, and cured meats I had learned to make.

When I got back to New York City, the culinary scene had changed. French and continental food, the epitome of fine dining when I left, was no longer in demand. Regional Italian food was all the rage, and I, along with everyone else, fell in love with it. I tucked away the notebooks from my training and pursued a mad love affair with Italy for the next ten years. My cold kitchen skills weren't entirely unused, however. My penchant for curing or pickling every meat and vegetable I could get my hands on earned me the title *Coco Pazzo* (crazy chef), hence the restaurant of the same name. But other than that, my notebooks remained tucked away. Creating the

original menu at Freds, knowing that I'd be cooking for a well-traveled audience who would appreciate classic continental cuisine, gave me a reason to dig them out. I'd forgotten some of the fantastic things I made back then. Some—meats in aspic, for example—don't really translate to the American palate. But the salad dressings definitely do, and they became my secret culinary weapon.

Honestly, they're really the secret to the success of Freds salads. *It's the dressings.* Everyone loves the ease of a simple vinaigrette whisked together *à la minute*, and there's a time and place for that. But most of the salad dressings at Freds are a bit more complex than that, and I think that's part of their appeal. Their flavors elevate a salad to something a bit special, which is what you want when dining out—or when you're entertaining. Even though some of the dressings in this chapter might look a bit daunting, with more ingredients than you might use on an average day, I encourage you to try making them, especially for special occasions when you want to dazzle your guests. I love all the dressings in this chapter, but my personal favorite is Freds Bistro Dressing; if I had to choose one dressing to eat for the rest of my life that would be it, so if you're going to try making one, that's a good place to start.

When dressing salads, I subscribe to the haircut theory, which means to start small and change in increments. It's an inverse haircut theory, really, because you're adding, rather than taking away, but, in any case, start by adding less dressing than you think you need, toss the salad, and then add more, a little at a time, if needed. It's always possible to add more, but once you've added too much it's almost impossible to fix it. Sure, you can add more greens, but the balance of other ingredients will be completely thrown off.

Like a lot of Freds dishes, these salads are processes, not just recipes. At Freds we have a full staff to do the prep work to pull everything together to compose the final dish. Remember, these dishes are designed specifically to be a bit more special than what one would make at home. A salad like Mark's Madison Avenue Salad has a million ingredients and requires a daunting amount of prep for a home cook. Because this book is about Freds, I'm documenting the recipes as we make them there, but please feel free to vary or simplify them to make them more practical for your life.

Tips for Good Dressings

OILS

I'm a huge fan of the wonderful bitterness of freshly pressed Italian extra-virgin olive oil, and for simple vinaigrette there's nothing better. It's one of the reasons Italians are known for the perfect simplicity of their cuisine. Our olive oil of choice at Freds is Monini Originale Extra Virgin Olive Oil. Monini is a three-generation-old company that cold presses their oil from 100 percent Italian olives. It's what we pour at the table with bread, and what we use in the kitchen. It's the real deal, fairly priced for its high quality, and pretty easy to find in better supermarkets. Monini has different olive oil blends—their Fruttato may be the easiest to find—and they all are of the highest quality.

As much as I love olive oil, sometimes, especially in salad dressings, you need an oil that has a milder flavor that doesn't overpower the other ingredients. A number of our dressings call for using peanut, grapeseed, or soybean oil because they allow the other flavors in the recipe to shine through.

VINEGARS

Most of the vinaigrette recipes call for red wine vinegar, and I recommend using a high-quality one that has 6 to 7 percent acidity (it will be listed somewhere on the bottle). Other vinegars that are good for vinaigrettes and are acceptable substitutes for red wine vinegar are white wine, champagne, and cider vinegar. Purchase the highest quality you can afford for the best taste. Balsamic vinegar, of course, is much loved, and is great for making a balsamic vinaigrette. But it's so singular in flavor (and color) that it doesn't really play well with other more subtle ingredients, so unless it's specified as an ingredient I wouldn't use it.

SAFE RAW EGG SUBSTITUTES

In their original, classical form, many of the dressing recipes in this chapter called for raw egg yolks, but the USDA does not, nor do I, recommend consuming raw eggs due to the risk of salmonella poisoning, especially for the very young, very old, and those with compromised immune systems. Fortu-

nately there are good alternatives available. At Freds, we use frozen pasteurized egg yolks, but unfortunately those seem to be available only for professional kitchens at this time.

At home, one possibility is to use pasteurized boxed eggs, which are available in some markets. A better alternative, however, is to substitute a small amount of good commercial mayonnaise, which provides similar emulsification properties without the risks posed by raw eggs. For this book I've already modified the dressings that originally called for raw egg, and here's the ratio I used: 1 tablespoon mayo equals 1 egg yolk. If a recipe calls for more than 1 egg, use 1 tablespoon mayo for the first egg and ½ tablespoon for each subsequent egg.

EMULSIFICATION AND STORAGE

Most of the dressings in this chapter are better if they're made in a food processor, rather than by hand. When I was in Europe, we made all the dressings by hand, since a food processor wasn't yet a household item, but why would you do that now?

For one thing, a food processor is needed to break up larger items, such as olives or herbs. Some of the recipes contain mayonnaise, for which a food processor provides brisker emulsification. Also, the recipes each make enough dressing for four or more salads, and a food processor is better at handling the volume.

All dressings should be stored in the refrigerator after they're made. They will be good for about a week, although they reach their peak of flavor the day after they're made. Refrigerated dressings should be brought out to sit at room temperature for 30 to 45 minutes before serving because that will bring out the best flavor. If the dressing has separated, simply give it a good shake (or whisk) to re-emulsify it.

Freds Beds—Salad Blends

A good foundation is just as important when it comes to salad as it is for any other dish. At Freds, we give a great deal of thought to the greens we use, both where we purchase them and how we use them. A substantial part of our morning prep is trimming, cleaning, and mixing mountains of salad, every single day. Each type and variety contributes different qualities to a salad. The loose-leaf lettuces—Bibb, Boston, Little Gem, and the like—are mostly mild, soft, and sweet. Some others, like romaine, give a refreshing crispness. Bitter chicories, such as endive and radicchio, can stand up to stronger flavors and more assertive dressings. And there's arugula, which contributes its own wonderful and distinctive flavor.

Part of my job in making salads interesting for my customers is putting together the right lettuce blends, something a little more special than they might make for themselves. Obviously, you won't be replicating our salad blends exactly at home. For one thing, the salad you use will depend on what's freshest in your market. At better supermarkets, it's easy to find an array of ready-made, packaged organic blends. But for the record, the following are the most common salad blends we mix at Freds.

SOFT BED SALAD BLEND

(Used in Palace Warm Lobster Salad, page 48; Freds Chopped Chicken Salad, page 45; Palm Salads (page 53).)

The mild flavors and soft texture of this blend make it a perfect base to augment the delicate flavor of crustaceans: lobster, shrimp, crab. Dress the leaves lightly, however, and serve immediately after dressing as they can quickly become soggy and mushy. Often I don't dress the greens when I use this blend, but rather dress the other things in the salad— seafood or vegetables—place them over the lettuces, and drizzle a little more dressing over it all.

Boston	*Butter*
Bibb	*Baby red romaine*
Little Gem	

MADISON SALAD BLEND

(Used in Mark's Madison Avenue Salad, page 43; Club Salad, page 61.)

This blend offers a little sample of everything: a little mild, a little bitter, a little crisp.

Red oak	*Radicchio*
Green oak	*Organic mesclun mix*
Boston	*Lola Rosa*
Hearts of romaine	*Frisée*

TRICOLORE SALAD BLEND

(Used in Vegan Salad, page 65.)

Italians love their bitter greens, and this is *the* classic Italian salad. The Vegan Salad contains lots of different kinds of heirloom beans, and the strong flavors of these lettuces give dimension to a salad that would otherwise be quite mild.

Arugula

Endive

Radicchio

MARK'S MADISON AVENUE SALAD

This is the original chopped salad at Freds, the one that started them all. It was on the opening menu at Madison, and it's still going strong, more than twenty years later. A little caveat: You'll probably look at the recipe, note the million ingredients, and immediately begin to envision all the blood, sweat, and tears required to make it. But I think it's worth it, and chances are you already have some of the ingredients on hand, or can get them already prepared. Plus, I won't tell anyone if you leave out an item or three.

I started chopping salads years before I opened Freds, when I was the chef at Coco Pazzo a few blocks north on Madison Avenue. I simply wanted to make it easier for my customers to eat salad without dropping pieces on their expensive Chanel suits. This salad got its start there, and it turned out to be a career epiphany for me, thanks to my friend Ronnie Lane.

I first met Ronnie and her husband, Bill, when I was the chef at Sapore di Mare in East Hampton. At the time it was *the* place to eat and be seen in the Hamptons, and it was crazy in the summertime. Ronnie and Bill ate there every weekend, and eventually she started asking me to make her something different, off-menu. I could never indulge her because the kitchen was always too busy. I promised to make her something if I came back to Manhattan, which I figured would never happen. She called in that promise when we opened Coco Pazzo. On one of our first nights open, always a crazed time in any new restaurant, Ronnie beckoned me over to her table to remind me what I'd said. I didn't have the heart to renege, but I also didn't want to confuse my newly hired kitchen crew with something off-menu when they were just getting used to cooking there. Out of desperation I grabbed a large serving bowl, put in some greens, and then went down the line of vegetable *mis en place* and put a little bit of every single thing that was on the line into the bowl. I tossed everything with our homemade vinaigrette, and topped it with some chunky Italian tuna. Ronnie loved it. I did, too, because it's light and a delicious mix of flavors. The vegetables we use now are the same ones that were on hand the first night I made the salad for Ronnie.

The epiphany that came with this salad became a guiding force in my career and in my philosophy as a restaurateur. I started to understand the importance, as a host, of listening to and honoring customer requests. True hospitality sometimes means being able to improvise a little, and it's extremely satisfying to offer someone something they're really craving.

Make the dressing first, so the flavors can blend while you chop and mix the salad ingredients. When you chop the vegetables, make an effort to chop them all roughly the same size.

Serves 4 as a main course, 6 as an appetizer

CONTINUES

½ cup finely chopped tomatoes

½ cup finely minced onion

½ cup blanched green peas

½ cup chopped blanched asparagus

2 white button mushrooms, finely chopped

¼ cup minced raw zucchini

¼ cup minced red bell pepper

¼ cup minced yellow bell pepper

¼ cup cooked beets, cut into small cubes

¼ cup finely minced blanched green beans

½ cup boiled potatoes, cut into small cubes

¼ cup chopped scallions

4 large handfuls Madison Salad Blend (see page 41), or preferred salad blend

¼ cup cooked lentils

¼ cup cooked white beans

1 (12-ounce) can Italian tuna, drained of oil or water

Madison Avenue Dressing (below), to taste

Combine all the vegetables in a large mixing bowl. Finely chop the salad greens and mix lightly into the vegetables. Add the lentils and beans, then crumble in the tuna. Drizzle with dressing to taste, and toss well until everything is mixed together. Divide among four or six plates and serve immediately.

MADISON AVENUE DRESSING

Makes 1 cup

1 clove garlic

¼ cup red wine vinegar

¾ cup extra-virgin olive oil

Dash of kosher salt

Freshly ground black pepper

Peel the garlic clove, smash it with a chef's knife, and place in a stainless-steel bowl. Add the vinegar and set aside for 1 hour to let the flavors meld, then remove the garlic.

Add the olive oil and whisk together. Add the salt and pepper, mix again, and then taste and adjust seasoning if needed.

FREDS CHOPPED CHICKEN SALAD
WITH BALSAMIC DRESSING

This salad is an addictive combination of flavors and textures that ensures it's a perennial Freds favorite: savory, freshly roasted chicken combined with the sweetness of pears and balsamic, the creaminess of avocado, the freshness of greens. We roast twenty-four to forty-eight chickens per day, every single day, at Freds—specifically for this salad. We start roasting them early in the morning, so they can be cooked and pulled apart by lunchtime. As you can imagine, this process takes several hours of work by my dedicated prep crew, assembled around the kitchen worktable. Since this is an everyday ritual, and the kitchen a relatively small space, their deftness in working together rivals any dance company, except that the performance is punctuated with passionate opinions on soccer leagues and the World Cup.

Whole roasted chicken isn't something we serve at the restaurant, but the technique here is my basic method for roasting a whole bird, whether you plan to use the meat in a salad or are carving it for dinner. For salad, make sure to cook it at least 3 hours ahead so it has time to cool. Whatever you do with the meat, be sure to freeze the carcass to use to make stock (page 24)!

When prepping the vegetables and pear, make sure the pieces are more or less the same size. The uniformity makes for a more attractive final product. Sprinkle the pear with lemon juice to keep it from discoloring, and cut the avocado just before assembling the salad.

Serves 4 as a main course, 6 as an appetizer

EQUIPMENT

Flat rack to fit inside the roasting pan

Roasting pan

Cooking twine

Meat thermometer

Food handler gloves (optional)

CHICKEN

1 (4-pound) chicken, preferably all natural or organic

1½ tablespoons salt

½ bunch fresh thyme

1 lemon

2 cloves garlic, peeled

1 tablespoon extra-virgin olive oil

1 teaspoon freshly ground black pepper

SALAD

4 large handfuls Soft Bed Salad Blend (see page 41), or preferred salad blend

1 cup 1-inch diced fresh pears, sprinkled with 1 tablespoon lemon juice

1 cup string beans, blanched (see page 17) and cut into 1-inch pieces

1 cup cherry tomatoes, halved

½ cup minced onion

2 ripe avocados, pitted, peeled, and cut into 1-inch cubes

Balsamic Dressing (page 46), to taste

CONTINUES

To roast the chicken: Preheat the oven to 350°F. While the oven is heating, prepare the chicken. Quarter the lemon and squeeze 1 tablespoon of juice to set aside for the pears. Place the rack in the roasting pan. Rinse the chicken, rub 1 tablespoon of the salt around the inside of the cavity, and then stuff it with the thyme, lemon, and garlic. Tie the legs closed with cooking twine. Rub the olive oil over the entire bird, and sprinkle with the remaining ½ tablespoon salt and the black pepper. Place on the rack and roast for 72 to 80 minutes. Test for doneness by inserting a meat thermometer into the leg, close to the bone. The chicken is done when the thermometer reads 165°F. Remove the thermometer if the chicken is not done, and test again in a few minutes. Remove from the oven and set the chicken aside to cool.

When cool enough to handle (remember, it will be hotter internally), remove the meat from the bones: We use food-handling gloves when pulling apart the chicken. Make sure you have a large container nearby to put the meat in. First, remove the skin from the chicken. Then pull off the wings, legs, and thighs and remove the meat from them. To remove the breasts, place your thumbs on either side of the breastbone and slide your finger underneath the breast, between the breast and the bone, moving up and down to loosen the meat. Use your hands to shred the breasts into 2-inch strips. At the bottom of the breast is the wishbone. Find it to make sure the thin pieces are not stuck to the breast meat so they won't find their way to the plate. If the wishbone is intact, make a wish and break it. There is meat on the back of the carcass, so make sure to pull that off, as well as any meat that's remaining on the bone. If you're not going to make the salad for a few hours, place the chicken meat in the fridge, but be sure to remove it and let come to room temperature for 30 to 45 minutes before you serve it, to bring out the best flavor.

To compose the salad: In a large stainless-steel mixing bowl, combine the greens, pear, beans, tomatoes, onion, avocado, and half of the chicken meat. Add some of the dressing and toss to make sure everything is lightly coated, adding more dressing if needed. Divide the mixture among four or six plates, distributing it equally. Lay the rest of the chicken on top and serve immediately, passing the remaining dressing in case people want to add more.

BALSAMIC DRESSING

Makes 1 ½ cups

¼ cup balsamic vinegar

¼ cup Dijon mustard

¼ cup soy sauce

2 tablespoons sugar (optional)

1 teaspoon kosher salt

½ teaspoon freshly ground black pepper

1 cup extra-virgin olive oil

Place all the ingredients except the oil in a food processor and pulse for about 30 seconds, until everything is mixed together. With the machine on low, slowly drizzle in the olive oil until the dressing is emulsified.

THE PALACE WARM LOBSTER SALAD
WITH FREDS BISTRO DRESSING

Barneys is a luxury destination; it's part of the company brand, so of course our menu at Freds reflects that. And what's more luxurious than lobster? Naturally, since we like to pamper our customers, we do all the work and remove the meat from the shell. Maine lobster is pure Americana, one of the foods our country does best. The Montreux Palace hotel in Switzerland, where I worked and for which this salad is named, would import Maine lobsters at great expense, because even though there are wonderful crustaceans in the Mediterranean, there's nothing like an Atlantic lobster. I didn't learn about lobsters in Europe, though; my mother, like any self-respecting Jewish matriarch, taught me at a young age how to pick out every morsel of flesh from a lobster, at Sunday dinners at Paddy's Clam House on 34th Street in Manhattan. What *did* come from Montreux, however, is the dressing, and it's my all-time favorite.

Like all Freds salads, this is a process. We have a team to do it at the restaurant, which you don't have at home. Don't let that stop you, though. Everything that needs to be done for this salad can be done ahead of time—making the dressing, cooking the potatoes, blanching the beans, and, of course, cooking and shelling the lobster.

The lobsters we use at Freds are from the Atlantic, mostly Maine, but sometimes Canada, depending on the season. Since we're going to remove the meat anyway, and they're not for show, we buy culls, which are missing a claw. We look for culls that are 1 to 1¾ pounds; they're less expensive than the two-clawed glamour models.

If you're on the Eastern seaboard, especially during the summer, you're probably able to find a fishmonger who sells freshly cooked lobster meat; you'll need about 1 pound. But whether you cook it yourself or buy it from the fishmonger, be sure to use fresh lobster. Canned or frozen lobster meat will not be good in this salad.

We serve this with the lobster, potatoes, and string beans slightly warmed, which really brings out their flavors. If you don't want to take the step to warm them, make sure they're room temperature before you dress and serve them. Perhaps with a nice chilled bottle of champagne to toast to the fruits of your labor!

Serves 4 as a main course, 6 as an appetizer

Large (10- to 12-quart) stockpot with lid

Large stainless-steel bowl (for ice bath)

Large metal tongs

Lobster cracker (or nut cracker)

Lobster fork

LOBSTER

Double recipe Court Bouillon (page 32), or 4 quarts water

4 (1- to 1¼-pound) lobster culls

Ice

SALAD

2 endive, leaves separated

6 large handfuls Soft Bed Salad Blend (see page 41) or preferred salad blend, coarsely chopped

Freds Bistro Dressing (page 50), to taste

3 scallions, trimmed and finely sliced

½ pound fingerling potatoes, steamed (see page 16), chilled, peeled, and cut into ½-inch cubes

½ pound string beans, blanched and shocked (see page 17), and cut into ½-inch pieces

1½ pints cherry tomatoes, halved

To cook and clean the lobsters:

Prepare the court bouillon in the stockpot, and when it's boiling add the lobsters. The water may not cover them completely, but that's fine. Cover the pot and turn the heat on high until the liquid comes back to a boil, then turn the heat down so the liquid is simmering, not boiling vigorously. Simmer for 5 minutes and then turn off the heat. Keeping the pot covered, let the lobsters sit in the pot for 3 minutes. Prepare an ice water bath by placing ice in a large stainless-steel bowl in the sink and adding water.

Using great care because of the steam, remove the lobsters from the pot with the tongs and place them in the ice water bath. They should cool in the bath for about 30 minutes. You will need to add more ice to the bath as it melts in order to quickly bring down the temperature of the lobsters so the meat won't be overcooked and tough.

Extracting the meat from the lobsters is a messy job, so make sure you pick a spot that has plenty of space and a countertop that won't be damaged by the water and lobster juices that are inevitably going to flow. Remove each lobster from the bath one at a time and pat dry. Holding the lobster tail in one hand and the body in the other, twist until the tail and body come apart. You may be able to easily pull the meat from the tail, but if not, cut through the soft underbelly of the tail shell just enough to open it. Try to keep the tail meat intact if you can. If you're lucky, the cavity of the body might contain coral (the firm red stuff, which is actually lobster roe), and it will definitely contain tomalley (the green gooey stuff, which is the lobster's liver).

Don't throw these away! You won't use them in the salad, so if you're like me just eat them right then and there. But you can also refrigerate or freeze them, along with the shells, to use in making lobster bisque.

To open the claws, tear off the small pincer and use the lobster cracker to crack the big pincer so you can pull the meat out in one piece. Twist the knuckles of the claws to open them and use the lobster fork to pull out the meat. Chop the meat, including the claws, into approximately 1-inch pieces. Unless you're composing the salad immediately, store the lobster meat in the refrigerator, but use it within 24 hours.

To compose the salad: Arrange 4 or 5 endive leaves in a star pattern on each serving plate. Chop up any remaining endive and add it to the salad blend. Mix together, *without* dressing, and divide among the plates.

Place ½ cup Freds Bistro Dressing in a large mixing bowl.

Place 2 tablespoons of water in a nonstick skillet, and then add the scallions, lobster, potatoes, and string beans. Warm over low heat, stirring gently, until the water evaporates and everything is just barely warmed, NOT hot. Place in the mixing bowl with the dressing, and mix gently, then add the tomatoes. Add more dressing, if desired, a little at a time, according to your taste, and mix together one more time so that everything is well coated. Divide among the serving plates, making sure each plate has an equal portion of lobster, and serve immediately.

FREDS BISTRO DRESSING

This is my all-time favorite salad dressing. I could eat it every single day. There's just something magical about it. It's creamy without cream; substantial but light. The grated onion really amps up the flavor, and the pickle juice adds a little zing. It's great with the Palace Warm Lobster Salad, but then again it's great with *any* salad, honestly. Three words, borrowing from Nike: Just do it.

Makes about 2 cups

1 red onion

½ cup red wine vinegar

¼ cup German mustard
(or Dijon mustard for a little extra spice)

¼ cup kosher pickle juice

2 tablespoons good commercial mayonnaise

1½ cups peanut or soy oil

1 tablespoon kosher salt

1 teaspoon freshly ground black pepper

Peel the onion and grate it, using the finest setting on the grater. Make sure you retain the juices that emerge. Combine the grated onion and juices, the vinegar, mustard, pickle juice, and mayo in the processor and pulse until they form a smooth paste. On a low speed, slowly drizzle in the oil until the dressing emulsifies. Add the salt and pepper and churn for 30 seconds more. Store in the fridge until you're ready to use it. This dressing actually tastes best the day after you make it because the flavors have a chance to meld, but will keep for 3 or 4 days.

Palm Springs Shrimp
Salad (page 55)

PALM BEACH SHRIMP SALAD
WITH GREEN GODDESS DRESSING

I dreamed up this recipe during a week I spent in Palm Beach, Florida. Many of Freds' customers spend the winter down there, and at one point I was invited to gig as a guest chef at a private club. The avenues lined with palm trees inspired the use of hearts of palm, and the soft lettuces and avocado seem to match the town's unruffled ease. Something about the vibe on Worth Avenue, though, put me in mind of a long-lost American classic: Green Goddess dressing. Jumbo shrimp seemed the obvious pairing for a salad with a tropical vibe. When I got back to New York, we ran it as a special as a tribute to the snowbirds. It was an instant hit and was added to the permanent menu. I'm pleased that this salad is the go-to favorite lunch of Barneys' CEO Daniella Vitale, who once told me, "I don't know what you put in the Green Goddess dressing, but I can't get enough." I guess with the publication of this book, my secret will be out.

Serves 4 as a main course, 6 as an appetizer

4 large handfuls Soft Bed Salad Blend (see page 41), or preferred salad blend

2 avocados, pitted, peeled, and cut into 1-inch cubes

1 cup cherry tomatoes (we use a mixture of red and yellow), halved

8 stalks hearts of palm, blanched* and cut into 1-inch pieces

1 clove garlic, sliced

2 tablespoons extra-virgin olive oil

16 jumbo shrimp (ask your fishmonger for Mexican or Ecuadorian white shrimp, U-12 size), peeled and deveined

¼ cup white wine

Kosher salt

Freshly ground black pepper

½ cup Green Goddess Dressing (page 54), or to taste

4 hard-boiled eggs (see page 217), peeled and cut into halves or quarters

At Freds, we use fresh hearts of palm, blanched in salted water for about 30 to 40 minutes, and then chilled (see Blanching Vegetables, page 17). Since you may have difficulty finding fresh hearts of palm, canned ones are perfectly acceptable.

Trim and rinse all the lettuces and dry in a salad spinner. Gently tear them into bite-size pieces and place in a large mixing bowl. Add the avocado, tomatoes, and hearts of palm and gently mix together. Set aside while you cook the shrimp.

Cook the garlic in the olive oil in a sauté pan over medium heat until it starts to brown. Add the shrimp, then the wine, and sprinkle with salt and pepper. Simmer gently for 4 to 6 minutes, until the shrimp are just cooked. Turn off heat and set aside while you dress the salad.

Drizzle dressing to your taste (start slowly—you don't want to overdress, and you can always add more) into the bowl of salad and mix together well. Divide the salad equally among four or six plates. Place the shrimp, divided equally, on top of the salads and arrange the eggs on top. Serve immediately. Refrigerate any leftover dressing.

CONTINUES

GREEN GODDESS DRESSING

Legend has it that Green Goddess dressing was invented in San Francisco in the 1920s as an homage to an actor in a play of the same name, but it really hit its apex during the '70s; it was on menus everywhere. Maybe it got overplayed because it kind of disappeared as time went on, at least on restaurant menus. It's too bad, though, because it's a terrific dressing, full of flavor. Also, it raises one of life's biggest questions: Why has it never achieved the same status of Caesar dressing (who conquered even the salad world, I guess)?

You can use any combination of herbs, but chervil and tarragon are core flavors in the original dressing, so don't omit those. I throw in a little spinach because I want to make sure the dressing has a nice green hue.

Like many salad dressings, it's optimal to make this a day before serving, to let the flavors meld and reach their peak. If you can't manage a full day, at least make it 2 hours before you use it. It's best to make it in a food processor so it will come out very smooth and emulsified. However, it is possible to make by hand or with an immersion blender; if you do, be sure to chop all the herbs, the shallot, and the anchovies very, very finely, with a mezzaluna or sharp chef's knife, before blending together.

Makes about 3 cups

¼ cup chopped fresh chervil leaves

2 tablespoons chopped fresh tarragon leaves

¼ cup chopped fresh basil leaves

¼ cup chopped fresh chives

¼ cup chopped fresh curly parsley

6 fresh mint leaves, chopped

½ cup raw spinach, finely chopped

1 shallot, minced

2 anchovy filets, mashed

2 teaspoons kosher salt

½ teaspoon white pepper

¼ cup warm water

6 tablespoons cider vinegar

3 tablespoons plain yogurt

2 tablespoons good commercial mayonnaise

1 tablespoon Dijon mustard

1 cup extra-virgin olive oil

2 tablespoons fresh lemon juice

2 shakes Worcestershire sauce

2 shakes Tabasco sauce
(optional, if you like it a little spicy)

Place all the herbs, the spinach, shallot, anchovies, salt, white pepper, and water in the bowl of a food processor. Blend together until the mixture forms a paste. Add the vinegar, yogurt, mayonnaise, and mustard and slowly blend together well. With the processor on a low speed, slowly drizzle in the oil in a slow stream until the dressing is emulsified. Add the lemon juice, Worcestershire, and Tabasco (if using), and blend together well. Store in a tightly covered container in the refrigerator for at least 2 hours before using. Will keep for up to 1 week.

PALM SPRINGS SHRIMP SALAD
WITH GREEN GODDESS DRESSING

When we opened Freds in Beverly Hills, I adapted the Palm Beach Shrimp Salad to include two of California's most famous crops: artichokes and asparagus, and named this new version for another snowbird destination, Palm Springs (although these days it's more famous for its proximity to Coachella).

This spinoff is identical to the Palm Beach salad, but with the addition of blanched, chilled asparagus and baked baby artichokes. If you can't find fresh baby artichokes, you can substitute canned ones, which you would use as is, without needing to bake them.

Serves 4 as a main course, 6 as an appetizer

1 bunch asparagus, blanched and chilled (see page 17), and cut into 1-inch pieces

Baked Fresh Baby Artichoke Hearts (page 56), cooled to room temperature and quartered

Palm Beach Shrimp Salad (page 53)

Add the asparagus and artichokes to the salad in the first step when you add the avocado, tomato, and hearts of palm, and continue with the recipe for Palm Beach Shrimp Salad.

———

CONTINUES

BAKED FRESH BABY ARTICHOKE HEARTS

Besides using them in the Palm Springs salad, these are wonderful on their own, especially as part of an antipasto platter with other vegetables and/or meats and cheeses. If you make them in advance and store them in the refrigerator, make sure to let them sit out for 30 minutes or so to bring them to room temperature for fullest flavor.

Serves 4 to 6

2 tablespoons fresh lemon juice

12 fresh baby artichokes

3 tablespoons extra-virgin olive oil

Kosher salt

Freshly ground black pepper

2 cloves garlic, thickly sliced

¼ cup chopped fresh mint

Preheat the oven to 325°F.

Fill a large mixing bowl with cold water and add the lemon juice. Pull off the outer leaves of each artichoke until you get down to the pale yellow leaves at the center. (Discard the leaves you tear off, since baby artichoke leaves don't have any edible flesh as large artichokes do.) Use a paring knife to trim the stem at the base to make the bottom flat. As you finish each artichoke, place it into the lemon water so it won't discolor while you trim the rest.

When all the artichokes are trimmed, drain them and pat dry. Arrange in a large baking dish with a cover. Drizzle the olive oil over the artichokes, sprinkle with salt and pepper, and dot with the garlic and mint. Cover the baking dish and bake for 30 to 45 minutes, until the artichoke bottoms are tender when pierced with a sharp knife. Remove from the oven and set aside to cool to room temperature.

FREDS NIÇOISE SALAD

Master perfumer Frédéric Malle gave me one of my favorite compliments: He said that Freds Niçoise salad is the best he's had this side of the Atlantic. Certainly I made enough Niçoise salads during the time I worked in Europe, so I hope I learned something.

I made one New World change to this Old World classic, which is to use fresh, sushi-grade yellowfin or bigeye tuna, the kind of fresh tuna you can find in any good fish market, instead of the canned tuna in the traditional French version. We don't serve our Niçoise in the iconic bowls, but rather on a plate, because it is the most composed of our composed salads. Everything is laid out on the bed of greens and the dressing is drizzled on top, rather than tossed.

As with all our classic salads, the Niçoise starts with a process, or several processes, really. A number of items—string beans, potatoes, eggs, and, of course, the dressing—need to be prepared and chilled beforehand. Only the assembly of the plates and the searing of the tuna are done at the last minute. Be sure to remove chilled items from the fridge about 30 minutes before serving, as room temperature brings out the fullest flavor. I prefer to steam, rather than boil, the potatoes for this recipe, and instructions for doing so can be found on page 16.

Serves 2 as a main course, 4 as an appetizer

12 small red bliss potatoes, steamed (see page 16) and cut into 1-inch cubes

1 cup green beans, blanched (see page 17)

12 black olives, pitted*

Niçoise Dressing (page 58), to taste

4 large handfuls Madison Salad Blend (see page 41), or your preferred blend

2 endive, leaves separated

1 small head radicchio

1 pint mixed cherry tomatoes, halved

4 hard-boiled eggs (see page 217), peeled and halved

4 (6-ounce) pieces sushi-grade fresh tuna, preferably 1-inch thick

Kosher salt

Freshly ground black pepper

2 tablespoons soybean or peanut oil

8 anchovy filets

We use Gaeta and Niçoise olives, which are both black. We never buy olives that are pitted; we pit our own fresh every day. It's imperative to take serious care and make sure every olive is pitted, because we never want a customer to crack a tooth on one! I know it might sound like overkill, but after pitting, we count every olive and every pit to make sure we have the same number of each.

CONTINUES

If you like tuna well done, preheat the oven to 450°F. If you like it rare, you can cook it entirely on the stovetop.

Assemble the salad plates before you cook the tuna: Place the potatoes, green beans, and olives in a large mixing bowl, add 2 tablespoons dressing, and toss together to coat.

To lay out the serving plates, begin by separating the 2 endive into individual leaves, and lay 5 leaves, arranged with the tips facing out, to form a star on each of four plates. Trim the base from the heads of radicchio and separate the whole leaves. Lay 3 leaves together in the center of each plate, so it looks a bit like an open flower. Place a scoop of the potato mixture, dividing equally among the plates, in the center of the radicchio bed. Artistically arrange the tomatoes and halved eggs in a border around the potato mixture.

Sprinkle the tuna steaks on both sides with salt and black pepper. Heat the oil in a sauté pan (oven-proof if going into the oven) over medium heat until very hot. Carefully place the tuna pieces in the pan, laying them away from you so you don't get splattered with hot oil.

Cook on one side until browned slightly, about 2 minutes, then turn over to sear on the other side. If you like the tuna rare, at this point it will be perfect for you, especially if it's a cut that's thinner than 1 inch. If you'd like it cooked through, place it in the oven for a few minutes.

When the tuna is done to your liking, remove it from the pan, and place it on a clean cutting board. Slice each piece into four or five slices, and lay slices decoratively on top of each salad. Lay 2 anchovies in an "X" pattern on top of the salad, and drizzle each portion with a tablespoon or so of dressing. Serve immediately, placing the extra dressing in a container to pass at the table in case anyone wants more.

NIÇOISE DRESSING

The amounts of mustard and lemon in this dressing balance each other well, so that one doesn't overpower the other. If you prefer a stronger flavor of either one, add a bit more of whichever one you desire.

Makes 1 cup

¼ cup Dijon mustard

¼ cup fresh lemon juice

2 teaspoons each chopped fresh parsley and chives

1 small clove garlic, mashed

Kosher salt

¾ cup extra-virgin olive oil

Using the food processor, blend all the ingredients except the oil until a smooth paste is formed. With the machine on low, slowly drizzle in the olive oil until the dressing thickens and is emulsified. Taste and add more salt if desired. Store in the fridge for up to 1 week.

THE CLUB SALAD

This salad, one of the original classic salads on the menu since day one, is basically a deconstructed club sandwich, without the bread. The indulgence vs. virtue ratio is pretty balanced, I think. I threw in a little bleu cheese for good measure, simply because bleu cheese and bacon taste so great together. It's a flavor combo that is near and dear to my heart because as a child I remember watching my father enjoy it.

The Club Dressing is a pared down version of my all-time favorite: Freds Bistro Dressing (page 50). The mustard and shallots are a dead giveaway of its French pedigree. We use a lightly flavored oil in this dressing. You can substitute olive oil; just know that it might overpower the other flavors more than a mild oil.

Serves 4 as a main course, 6 as an appetizer

4 large handfuls Madison Salad Blend (see page 41), or your preferred salad blend

2 cups ¼-inch cubed roasted turkey breast (see page 19)

1 endive, roughly chopped

½ small red onion, thinly sliced

4 plum tomatoes, cut into ¼-inch pieces

1 scallion, finely minced

Club Dressing (page 62), to taste

8 strips smoked bacon, cooked until crisp and crumbled

½ cup crumbled Danish or domestic cow's milk bleu cheese

Place the salad mix in a large salad bowl. Add the turkey, endive, onion, tomatoes, and scallion. Add the dressing and toss gently until everything is evenly coated. Divide the salad among four or six serving plates and top evenly with the crumbled bacon and bleu cheese. Serve immediately.

CONTINUES

CLUB DRESSING

Makes 1½ cups

¼ cup Dijon mustard

¼ cup red wine vinegar

2 tablespoons good commercial mayonnaise

2 shallots, minced

1 teaspoon kosher salt

Freshly ground black pepper

¾ cup neutral-tasting oil, such as peanut, soybean, or grapeseed

Place the mustard, vinegar, mayonnaise, shallots, salt, and pepper in a food processor and whiz together. With the machine on low, slowly drizzle in the oil. Taste for salt and pepper. Store in the fridge for up to 1 week and shake before using.

―――

AUTUMN SALAD

As compensation for the chill in the air and the diminishing bounty of summer, autumn gives us brilliantly colored leaves, pumpkins and gourds, and the addictive little Brussels sprout. I think it's a fair trade. To me, butternut squash and Brussels sprouts are the quintessential autumn vegetables. And they go so well together, with the sweetness of the squash and the nutty flavor of the sprouts made more intense by the caramelization of the roasting process. This salad is a distillation of fall for me and, with the addition of goat cheese, it's my take on simple French bistro cooking.

An added bonus: I'm honored that it's a favorite dish of prior Barneys' CEO Mark Lee.

Serves 2 as a main course, 4 as an appetizer

1 pound Brussels sprouts, trimmed and quartered

½ large butternut squash, peeled, seeded, and cut into 1-inch cubes (or 1 pound pre-cut butternut squash)

5 tablespoons extra-virgin olive oil

1 teaspoon kosher salt

2 tablespoons red wine vinegar

½ teaspoon freshly ground black pepper

1 head radicchio, trimmed and chopped into 1-inch pieces

2 endive, trimmed and sliced into 1-inch pieces

1 (5-ounce) clamshell box arugula, roughly cut

6 ounces fresh goat cheese, cut into 4 slices

Preheat the oven to 375°F. Place the Brussels sprouts and squash in a mixing bowl and sprinkle with 1 tablespoon of the olive oil. Toss to coat, spread the vegetables on a large baking sheet, and sprinkle with ½ teaspoon of the salt. Roast for 12 to 15 minutes, until the vegetables are lightly caramelized and tender when pierced with the tip of a knife. Set aside to cool for at least 10 minutes.

Make the vinaigrette by placing the vinegar in a small container. Drizzle in the remaining 4 tablespoons olive oil and whisk until the vinegar and oil are mixed. Add the remaining ½ teaspoon salt and the pepper and mix together again.

Mix together the radicchio, endive, and arugula and divide among two or four plates. Divide the roasted vegetables among the salads and drizzle with vinaigrette.

Just before serving, place the slices of goat cheese on a baking sheet under the broiler (either in your oven or a toaster oven) for a few minutes, until they are golden brown on the top but not so melted that they lose their shape. Quickly divide among the salads and serve immediately.

——

VEGAN SALAD
WITH SALSA VERDE VINAIGRETTE

I'm a bit of a Jewish grandma, always fretting that everyone's not getting enough to eat. So when my guests started requesting vegan dishes, I wanted to make sure they didn't go hungry. I started packing salads with beans, grains, legumes, and good fats like avocado, foods that are really satiating. I prefer to eat this way myself now. This salad contains five types of beans, in addition to quinoa. See what I mean about being a worried grandmother?

If you make this at home you are unlikely to make it exactly the way we do at Freds. We have a huge staff who prepares all the different types of beans every day, in addition to making two different types of quinoa. You at home likely do not. So while this recipe documents the way we serve this at the restaurant, there are ways to modify it to make it more practical for home use, without losing any of the flavor and contrast. For one thing, you may want to use only one kind of quinoa, and only one or two types of beans. We use heirloom beans cooked from scratch in our kitchen, but at home feel free to use readily available canned beans such as cannellini, kidney, black, or pinto beans. That said, I encourage you to at some point shop for some heirloom beans in your local gourmet market or online and cook them yourself. They're plumper, firmer, juicier, and more flavorful than most canned beans.

If you opt for cooking your own beans, you need to start preparing them 24 to 30 hours before serving, to account for soaking, cooking, and chilling. In that case, prepare more than you need for this salad so you'll have leftovers for a couple of days. Directions for cooking beans and quinoa are given on the next page.

Besides the beans, the other item in this recipe that benefits from advance preparation is the pungent, herb-infused dressing. The flavors meld and reach their peak the day after it's made. With a little planning you can make it at the same time you set your beans to soak. Store the dressing in the fridge after it's made, of course, but take it out about 45 minutes before serving for fullest flavor.

Serves 4 as a main course, 6 as an appetizer

CONTINUES

¼ cup cooked and chilled Anasazi beans

¼ cup cooked and chilled bayo beans

¼ cup cooked and chilled calypso beans

¼ cup cooked and chilled garbanzo beans (chickpeas)

¼ cup cooked and chilled pinto beans

¼ cup cooked and chilled red quinoa

¼ cup cooked and chilled white quinoa

¼ cup minced carrot

¼ cup minced celery

¼ cup minced onion

4 handfuls Tricolore Salad Blend (see page 41)

Salsa Verde Vinaigrette (opposite), to taste

2 ripe avocados, pitted, peeled, and cut into ½-inch cubes

Place all the ingredients except the dressing and avocado in a large mixing bowl. Toss to mix and then slowly add dressing, tossing to coat, until the salad is dressed to your liking. Divide the salad among four or six serving plates. Arrange cubed avocado on top of each salad and serve immediately.

─────

SALSA VERDE VINAIGRETTE

Like Green Goddess (page 54), this dressing leaves plenty of room for improvisation when it comes to herb selection. Chervil and tarragon should be the predominant herbal flavor, so feel free to add those with a heavy hand. The other herbs are suggested guidelines, but if you have more or less of one of them, use what you have. And if you're missing one—except for the chervil and tarragon—substitute more parsley.

Makes about 3 cups

½ cup chopped fresh chervil leaves

¼ cup fresh basil leaves
(8 large or 12 small leaves), torn

¼ cup chopped fresh curly
parsley leaves

2 tablespoons chopped fresh
marjoram leaves

1 tablespoon chopped fresh
tarragon leaves

1 tablespoon chopped fresh
thyme leaves

1 tablespoon chopped fresh
sage leaves

4 black olives, pitted and chopped

6 capers, rinsed of salt or brine
and chopped

½ cup red onion, minced

2 cloves garlic, minced

½ cup red wine vinegar

2 tablespoons olive juice

2 tablespoons fresh lemon juice

½ teaspoon kosher salt

¼ teaspoon freshly ground
black pepper

1½ cups extra-virgin olive oil

Place all the herbs, the olives, capers, onion, and garlic in the bowl of a food processor and pulse until a paste forms. Add the vinegar, olive juice, lemon juice, salt, and pepper and pulse again to combine. With the processor on low, pour in the oil in a very slow stream, mixing until the dressing is emulsified. Taste to check seasoning and add more salt and pepper, if desired. Refrigerate for at least 2 hours, but preferably 24 hours, before using.

BEVERLY HILLS
ASIAN CHICKEN SALAD

Don't roll your eyes and pass up this West Coast classic because of all the low-brow Asian chicken salads out there. There's not a canned Mandarin orange in sight in our version, just a whole lot of fresh shredded vegetables, two types of crunchies—fried wonton wrappers and rice noodles—to keep it interesting, and a craveable homemade dressing. The creation of the executive chef in Beverly Hills, Chef Emanuel Pradet, this salad is our biggest seller in L.A.

You should make the dressing the day before you serve because, as with all dressings, the flavors mature with a little time. You can also shred the vegetables beforehand, and fry the wontons and rice noodles—as long as you store the veggies in the fridge and the wontons and noodles in a sealed container in your cupboard to keep them crunchy. The chicken, however, should be cooked shortly before serving; it doesn't need to be hot, but ideally it should still be tender from being freshly cooked. Wonton wrappers and rice noodles should be easy to find in the Asian section of your local supermarket.

Serves 4 as a main course, 6 as an appetizer

EQUIPMENT

Kitchen knife

Baking sheet

Paper towels

Deep fryer (or large stockpot)

Candy thermometer

Spider skimmer

Large mixing bowl

12-inch ovenproof skillet

CHICKEN SALAD

6 wonton wrappers

1 (approximately 8-ounce) package thin rice noodles

2 cups peanut oil for frying (can substitute soybean oil, or pure olive oil—but not extra-virgin)

18 snow peas, blanched (see page 17) and julienned

1 head Napa cabbage, shredded

2 heads romaine hearts, shredded

1 cup shredded carrots

1 cup julienned daikon radishes

1 cup sunflower sprouts

4 (6- to 8-ounce) chicken breasts

Kosher salt

Freshly ground black pepper

1 tablespoon soybean oil

2 teaspoons soy sauce

Asian Dressing (opposite), to taste

½ cup lightly salted roasted cashews

Fry the wontons and rice noodles:
Cut the wonton wrappers into ½-inch-thick strips. Break up the rice noodles, splitting each noodle into three pieces. Spread a couple of layers of paper towels on a baking sheet and place it within easy reach of the stove.

Heat the peanut oil (with candy thermometer, if you have one) in a deep fryer or large stockpot until it's very hot (350°F on the thermometer). Once it's hot, turn down the heat slightly to maintain a steady temperature and not overheat. Fry the wonton strips a few at a time, making sure they don't stick together. When they are golden brown, remove them with a spider skimmer and place them on the paper towels to drain. Then fry the rice noodles a handful at a time. You don't want them to brown, you simply want them to puff up, which they will do quite quickly, within 1 to 2 minutes. Transfer to the paper towels to drain as well. When the wontons and noodles have cooled, set them aside or place them in an airtight container to use when you make the salad.

Combine the snow peas, cabbage, romaine, carrots, radishes, and sprouts in a large mixing bowl (or a storage container if you are serving the salad later). Set them aside while you cook the chicken.

Preheat the oven to 350°F. Sprinkle the chicken breasts with salt and pepper. Heat the soybean oil in a 12-inch ovenproof skillet over medium heat. When the pan is hot, add the whole chicken breasts and cook for about 4 minutes, turning at the 2-minute mark to lightly brown both sides. Transfer the pan to the oven and bake for 8 to 10 minutes, until the internal temperature of the chicken is 165°F. Remove the pan from the oven and place on the stovetop. While the chicken is still very hot, drizzle the soy sauce over it. Turn the pieces so the chicken is lightly but evenly coated and slightly caramelized. Set aside for a few minutes, until the chicken is cool enough to touch. Cut or shred the meat into strips.

Assemble the salad: Place half of the chicken, along with half of the wontons and rice noodles, into the bowl with the vegetables. Add dressing, a bit at a time so as not to overdress, and mix well until it's dressed to your taste (you will have leftover dressing). Divide the salad among four or six plates and top with the remaining chicken, wontons, and rice noodles, and the cashews. Serve immediately with extra dressing on the side for those who want it.

ASIAN DRESSING

Makes 6 cups

1 cup plum sauce

¾ cup rice vinegar

½ cup hoisin sauce

½ cup peanut butter

¼ cup soy sauce

½ cup Dijon mustard

2 tablespoons sesame oil

½ cup chopped fresh cilantro

½ cup chopped fresh ginger

¼ cup chopped garlic

1½ cups olive oil

Place all ingredients except the olive oil in the food processor and blend until well mixed and smooth. With the machine on low, slowly drizzle in the oil until the dressing is well blended and emulsified. Place in the fridge for at least 2 hours, or until ready to use.

CONTINUES

Beverly Hills Asian Chicken Salad (page 68)
with *mis en place* in background

The Jewish Boy from Queens
with Russian Dressing

CHAPTER 3
THE FREDS LUNCH CLASSICS

Avocado Toast / 75

    Pico de Gallo / 76

Tuna Tartare with Cucumber Carpaccio, Ginger, and Crostini / 79

Roasted Shrimp with Lime and Ginger with Warm White Cannellini Beans / 81

Grilled Hen of the Woods Mushrooms in a Balsamic Glaze with Arugula and Shaved Parmesan / 84

Sautéed Chicken Livers on Crostini with Shallots and Port Wine Sauce / 86

Pan-Seared Salmon with Sautéed Spinach, Tomato and Scallion Salad, Salsa Verde Vinaigrette, and Roasted Fingerling Potatoes / 87

Baltimore Crab Cakes with Rémoulade and Classic Coleslaw / 91

Join the Club: The Freds Club Sandwiches / 94

    Beverly Hills Club / 94

    Lobster Club / 96

    Madison Classic Club / 97

        Freds Potato Chips / 98

The Jewish Boy from Queens with Russian Dressing / 101

Chicken Paillards with Tomato, Arugula, and Red Onion Salad / 103

Upper East Side Filet of Sole with Sautéed Carrots and Snow Peas / 106

Lunch might be mostly about salad, but it's not *all* about salad. That would make for a pretty unbalanced menu. Salad drives lunch, but lunch drives Freds, so it's important to make sure there's something for everyone. In fact, Freds is famous for having an extensive menu, and it's one of the reasons business people can entertain clients there several times a week without getting menu fatigue.

I'm a traditionalist, and I love what I think of as classic hotel dishes: club sandwiches, crab cakes, pan-seared salmon, chicken paillards. The art for me as a chef is to take a classic dish and make the best version I can possibly imagine, with the highest quality ingredients. Our Club Sandwich, for example, is made with thick slices of turkey, freshly roasted that morning, perfectly crispy Nueske's applewood-smoked bacon, and the juiciest vine-ripened tomatoes, all on toasted bread from a buttery pullman loaf baked during the night. It's served with our own homemade potato chips. It's simple, and the challenge with a simple dish is that every element has to be done perfectly for it to be outstanding. And at Freds we always aim for outstanding.

I think the simplicity of these classic dishes helps facilitate Freds' reputation as a popular place to socialize or cut a business deal. The food has to be delicious, but it's not demanding to be adored. It stands back, because it's always the guest that's the star of the show.

AVOCADO TOAST

Avocado toast has taken over the world. In the Freds sphere, it first conquered Freds Beverly Hills, because of course it's California. It didn't stop there, though, and rapidly made its way to our New York locations, because there's just no stopping the craving people have for it. I really love our version, which is loaded with contrasting flavors and textures, and is shamelessly indulgent and delicious. It starts with the bread: We use a dense, slightly sweet pullman loaf from Orwashers bakery that's rich with spelt, raisins, sunflower seeds, and honey. We toast it, and then we spike the flavor, in a trick borrowed from the Italians, by rubbing on raw garlic. We soften the sharpness of the garlic with a little spread of cumin butter (there's the indulgence) before we mound on the avocado, then top the whole thing off with some piquant pico de gallo and sunflower sprouts for added crunch and to echo the sunflower seeds in the bread. It's anytime food: bar snack, appetizer, or even an entrée when topped with one of our blue Araucona eggs. Credit for the pico de gallo goes to Freds Madison executive chef Alfredo Escobar. He and the team at Freds Madison have brought a new energy to my career, and vibrancy to the Freds menu, by encouraging me to explore Latin American ingredients and seasonings.

Serves 1 or 2 as an appetizer

½ tablespoon unsalted butter, softened

Pinch of cumin

2 slices dense whole grain bread, preferably with raisins, nuts, and seeds

1 clove garlic, peeled and halved

1 small ripe avocado

Pinch of Maldon sea salt (or any sea salt that has crystal-like shards)

2 tablespoons Pico de Gallo (page 76)

Sunflower sprouts for garnish

Drizzle of extra-virgin olive oil

Mix the softened butter and cumin together. Toast the bread until it's well toasted. Rub each piece of toast on both sides with the cut side of the garlic. Press down a little on the garlic so that the oils and flavor permeate the bread as you rub it, but not hard enough to tear the bread. Spread each slice lightly with the cumin butter. Cut the avocado in half and remove the pit. Use a spoon to scoop out the flesh, and chop it roughly. Spread each slice of bread with half the avocado and mash and spread it to cover the entire surface of the slice. There should be enough avocado on each slice that you can mound it a bit in the center. Sprinkle with the sea salt, place a generous spoonful of pico de gallo on each slice, and garnish with the sunflower sprouts and a tiny drizzle of olive oil. Serve immediately before the avocado begins to discolor.

CONTINUES

PICO DE GALLO

Makes approximately ¾ cup

1 small plum tomato, finely minced

¼ to ½ fresh jalapeño pepper (depending on how spicy you like it), finely minced

2 tablespoons finely minced red onion

1 tablespoon finely minced scallion

1 teaspoon finely minced cilantro

Juice of ½ lime

½ teaspoon kosher salt

Place all ingredients in a mixing bowl and mix well together. Let sit at room temperature for 30 minutes so the flavors meld. Store any leftover pico de gallo in the refrigerator and use it within 24 hours.

TUNA TARTARE
WITH CUCUMBER CARPACCIO, GINGER, AND CROSTINI

The raw fish trend of the moment may be poke, but when we opened Freds, the hot (not *literally* hot, of course) raw fish of the moment was tartare. Japanese fashion and taste was especially in vogue in the '90s, and Barneys was out front with the trend. Comme des Garçons suits and shirts were all the rage, and sushi was becoming commonplace. Fish tartare was a way of addressing the trend, even if your restaurant wasn't Japanese. This dish is light, flavorful, and satisfying, with the cool, crisp sensation of the cucumber counterbalancing the tangy umami flavors that season the tuna. It's stood the test of time, and is still one of Freds' most popular appetizers.

Obviously, this dish requires the very best and freshest sushi-quality tuna. The best tuna is a deep burgundy; the rich depth of color, as in Japanese indigo-dyed denim, is how you can tell a premium-quality piece. It's also important to feel it, as the high fat content of a premium cut will give it a slightly soft feel.

While beef tartare is traditionally put through a meat grinder, that's a bit rough for delicate fish: Better to use a sharp knife to mince the tuna. The cucumbers we use for this are the long hydroponic ones, and they should ideally be sliced paper-thin, so use a mandoline or Japanese vegetable slicer if you have one, or a very sharp knife. Prepare the cucumbers and crostini first so you can plate everything and serve it immediately. To achieve the prettiest presentation, use a round metal mold to shape the tuna on the plate. If you don't have a mold, simply mound it in the center of the cucumber ring. It will taste just as good! Of course, people with compromised immune systems, as well as the very young and very old, should not consume raw fish.

Serves 4 as an appetizer

CONTINUES

CUCUMBER CARPACCIO

1 Japanese cucumber

2 teaspoons sesame oil

2 teaspoons soy sauce

1 teaspoon rice wine vinegar

Pinch of kosher salt

CROSTINI

12 (½-inch-thick) slightly diagonal slices of baguette

2 cloves garlic, peeled

TUNA TARTARE

12 ounces sushi-grade tuna

¼ cup minced fresh chives

4 teaspoons minced fresh ginger

4 teaspoons sesame oil

4 teaspoons soy sauce

2 teaspoons extra-virgin olive oil

2 teaspoons rice wine vinegar

Pinch of kosher salt

Pickled ginger for garnish

Make the cucumber carpaccio: Slice the cucumber paper-thin and arrange decoratively on each serving plate, overlapping them to create a kind of flower circling the center, leaving a 2- to 3-inch circle in the middle for the tuna. Mix together the sesame oil, soy sauce, rice vinegar, and salt in a small bowl and set aside.

Make the crostini: Toast the baguette slices. Cut the tips off the garlic cloves and, while the toasted bread is still warm, rub the cut end around the edges of each slice to release the garlic aroma into the bread.

Make the tuna tartare: With a very sharp knife, cut the tuna into ¼-inch strips. Lay the strips flat and cut them lengthwise again to make even thinner strips. Chop the strips into tiny cubes, as small as possible. Place them in a small bowl and add the remaining tartare ingredients. Mix together very gently and let it sit for 1 or 2 minutes to let the flavors meld.

To plate each service: Place a 2- by 3-inch round metal mold in the center of the cucumber, pushing the slices so they are just touching the outside of the mold. Stuff tuna tartare into the mold so that it forms an even ¼-inch-thick patty. Turn it over gently and remove the mold. Drizzle the cucumber dressing over the cucumber, garnish with a small pile of pickled ginger, and place the crostini at intervals around each plate. Serve immediately.

ROASTED SHRIMP WITH LIME AND GINGER

WITH WARM WHITE CANNELLINI BEANS

The early part of my career was spent immersed in Italian cooking, and happily that meant traveling to Italy on a regular basis. One of my favorite places is the town of Forte dei Marmi on the Tuscan coast. Tuscans are famous for their love of beans, and the combination of seafood—usually octopus or shrimp—with white beans is a classic Tuscan beach dish. Although the beans in this recipe are wonderful with shrimp, they can stand on their own, too, sopped up with a nice, crusty piece of bread. Either way, cook them the day before you want to serve them, and remember you'll need to soak the dried beans for 24 to 48 hours before cooking. So while this recipe doesn't require a lot of hands-on work, it does require advance planning.

At Freds we use U-12 size white shrimp from Mexico or Ecuador. If you specify U-12, your fishmonger will know what you mean. They're meaty and the perfect size for skewering with the rosemary. We peel off most of the shell, leaving the tip of the tail for presentation, and marinate them, covered in the fridge, for about 24 hours, although you can cut that to 6 hours, if necessary.

Serves 4 as an appetizer

16 jumbo shrimp (ask your fishmonger for Mexican or Ecuadorian white shrimp, U-12 size)

4 thick sprigs fresh rosemary, large enough for skewering

Juice of 2 limes

1½ tablespoons extra-virgin olive oil, plus more for drizzling

2 tablespoons minced fresh ginger

1 scallion, minced

Kosher salt

2 cups Warm White Cannellini Beans (page 83)

1 bunch fresh watercress for garnish

Rinse the shrimp and peel off the shells, leaving the tail bits on. To devein the shrimp, use a paring knife to remove the vein going up the center back of each. Skewer 4 shrimp onto each rosemary sprig and place the skewers in a dish large enough for them to lay flat.

Combine the lime juice, olive oil, ginger, and scallion in a small bowl. Pour the marinade over the shrimp skewers, making sure each shrimp is well coated. Cover and marinate in the refrigerator for 6 to 24 hours.

CONTINUES

Preheat the oven to 450°F. Lightly coat a large nonstick roasting pan with olive oil. Place the skewers in the pan and lightly drizzle the shrimp with olive oil and sprinkle with salt. Roast for 5 to 7 minutes, until the shrimp are firm to the touch.

While the shrimp are in the oven, gently warm the beans in a small pot, adjusting the seasoning if needed.

Ladle ½ cup beans onto each serving plate. Lay a shrimp skewer across each plate and garnish with watercress by placing it beside and slightly under the shrimp skewer. Drizzle with a small amount of olive oil and serve immediately.

WARM WHITE CANNELLINI BEANS
(Fagioli in Fiasco)

These creamy, tender white beans are a Tuscan peasant recipe that dates from long before the invention of modern home conveniences. As the wood embers in the home hearth were dying down for the day, the resourceful Italian mama would put beans, extra-virgin olive oil, water (so the oil wouldn't fry the beans), black pepper, and some whole rosemary sprigs inside a *fiasco*, a wine flask. Then she'd place the flask in the embers. When morning came, the beans were cooked, soft, and plump. We don't have any embers in which to cook our white beans at Freds, so I had to figure a modern way to reproduce this ancient technique. We make these beans every two days or so.

Do not add the salt until the beans are cooked, as it causes the bean skins to break down during cooking.

Makes about 6 cups

1 pound dried cannellini beans

3 cups extra-virgin olive oil

1 cup water

2 cloves garlic, thinly sliced

2 large sprigs fresh rosemary

1 tablespoon coarsely ground black pepper

1 bay leaf

Kosher salt

Place the beans in a container large enough to hold twice the amount of water as the volume of beans. Cover the beans with water and soak for 24 to 48 hours.

Drain the beans, place in a large stockpot, and add the oil, water, garlic, rosemary, pepper, and bay leaf. Cover and cook over very low heat until the beans are extremely tender and creamy, 2½ to 3½ hours. Make sure they are on a very low simmer to prevent the water from evaporating. When they are tender, remove the pot from the heat and cool the beans slightly. Remove and discard the bay leaf. Add salt to taste, mixing thoroughly.

Store in the refrigerator for up to 3 days.

GRILLED HEN OF THE WOODS MUSHROOMS
IN A BALSAMIC GLAZE WITH ARUGULA AND SHAVED PARMESAN

This dish is one I've been serving almost my entire career, and I haven't grown tired of it yet, and neither have Freds' customers. The combination of warm, sweetly savory mushrooms, spicy arugula, and pungent cheese is irresistible. People still stop me in the dining room to tell me how much they love it. When I first created it, hen of the woods mushrooms—which are also known as maitake mushrooms—were not as widely available as they are now. Our hen of the woods are from Pennsylvania, where some of the best mushrooms in the world are cultivated. These mushrooms, like the ubiquitous portobello, but more delicious, are a good stand-in for meat for vegetarians. The balsamic is used in a classically Italian way, not to make vinaigrette, but to deglaze the mushrooms. This adds an umami flavor and, combined with a drizzle of olive oil, serves as an *à la minute* dressing for the salad.

Serves 4 as an appetizer

1 pound hen of the woods mushrooms (large clusters, if possible)

Kosher salt

Freshly ground black pepper

3 cups baby or wild arugula

¼ cup extra-virgin olive oil

2 cloves garlic, sliced

6 tablespoons 12-year-old balsamic vinegar

12 shaved slices Parmigiano Reggiano cheese

Drizzle of extra-virgin olive oil

1 tablespoon minced fresh chives

Preheat the oven to 325°F. While the oven is heating, trim the bases of the mushrooms, but make sure each cluster stays in one piece. Place in an ovenproof nonstick pan with a lid and sprinkle with salt and pepper. Cover, place in the oven, and bake for 20 minutes. Slide the mushrooms onto a plate and set the pan aside to cool, since you'll be using it to sauté the mushrooms.

While the mushrooms are baking, divide the arugula among four serving plates.

When the mushrooms have cooled enough to handle, place the pan over medium-high heat and add the olive oil and garlic. Sauté until the garlic starts to brown. Tear the mushrooms into evenly sized chunks, add to the pan, and sauté until they are a little crispy on each side. Lower the heat to medium and pour the balsamic over the mushrooms. Mix to coat the mushrooms and cook 3 to 5 minutes, until the balsamic is thickened and the sharpness of the vinegar is cooked out, similar to when you're cooking with wine or other alcohol.

Place the hot mushrooms on the arugula, forming kind of a teepee shape. Lay the Parmesan over the mushrooms. Drizzle with olive oil, sprinkle with chives, and serve immediately.

SAUTÉED CHICKEN LIVERS
ON CROSTINI WITH SHALLOTS AND PORT WINE SAUCE

This dish flies in the face of every modern food trend. You could say that it's so *out* that it's *in*. And it's been a customer favorite at Freds since the day we opened. Part of its appeal is the fact that it contains brown butter, one of the world's most irresistible foodstuffs. And part of it is that for a lot of my customers, and for me, chicken livers are a part of our cultural heritage and yet they are something we tend to not make at home. If you cook a lot of chicken, as we did in my childhood home, you're going to end up with a lot of chicken livers, so I grew up watching my dad savor them. This classical preparation treats the humble liver, a peasant dish, with the same respect as a rich man's filet mignon.

At the restaurant, we serve three livers per person, but if you serve this at home, you may find that one or two per person is enough. This dish works very well for family-style serving; just make sure everyone gets some of the sauce. Most people like chicken livers cooked "pink," the way my father preferred them, which means medium to medium rare. If they overcook and become too firm, their texture becomes grainy. Be sure to use ruby port, not tawny port, because it adds a nice touch of sweetness to the sauce. While you can make your own demi-glace, there are good-quality ready-made ones available in the freezer section of most good supermarkets.

Serves 4 to 6 as an appetizer

¼ cup (½ stick) unsalted butter

1 tablespoon extra-virgin olive oil

¼ cup minced shallots

2 small cloves garlic, minced

12 plump chicken livers, trimmed of fat and connective tissue

Kosher salt

Freshly ground black pepper

½ cup ruby port wine

½ cup demi-glace (page 31 or store-bought) or Fortified Chicken Stock (page 25)

4 to 6 slices peasant bread

2 small cloves garlic, cut in half

Heat the butter and olive oil in a large skillet over medium-high heat, swirling the pan as needed, until the butter foams and browns. Add the shallots and garlic and cook, stirring, until translucent, 2 to 3 minutes. Season the livers with salt and pepper and add to the pan. Brown them for a moment, turning once, then add the port. Simmer for 1 minute, then add the demi-glace, and reduce the heat to medium low. Swirl the pan and continue cooking the livers until done to your liking, 4 to 6 minutes total cooking time for medium rare. Nick the bottom with a paring knife to check for the degree of pink you like. Taste the sauce and adjust the seasoning.

Toast or grill the bread and, while it's still warm, rub the slices all over with the cut garlic. Place a toast in the center of each plate and pile on 2 to 3 livers per serving. Drizzle the sauce over the livers and serve.

PAN-SEARED SALMON
WITH SAUTÉED SPINACH, TOMATO AND SCALLION SALAD, SALSA VERDE VINAIGRETTE, AND ROASTED FINGERLING POTATOES

I've always joked that salmon is the only fish that migrates up Madison Avenue, because I'm sure that on any given day on the Upper East Side, entire schools of salmon are consumed. Freds contributes greatly to that number, largely because of this dish. It's the kind of light, healthy, and flavorful dish you can eat every day and still feel good, and lots of my customers do.

I like to sear the salmon on both sides, so both the skin side and the fish side are crispy. It adds a nice umami flavor, but I'm always careful to watch so that the fish doesn't overcook. I think salmon is best cooked medium rare, with a bit of pink inside, but we get a lot of requests for it to be well done; that's fine, too, as long as it's not dried out. I love to eat crispy fish skin, but if you don't, simply use a spatula to remove it after it's cooked.

The Salsa Verde Vinaigrette is best made the day before, and the Tomato and Scallion Salad gathers a fuller flavor if you make it an hour before serving it. Also, use fully grown spinach, not baby spinach for this dish, because baby spinach becomes slimy when cooked.

Serves 2

TOMATO AND SCALLION SALAD

4 plum tomatoes, seeded and cut into ¼-inch cubes

2 tablespoons minced scallions

1 tablespoon chopped fresh basil

Pinch of salt

SALMON

2 teaspoons extra-virgin olive oil

2 (7-ounce) skin-on salmon filets

Pinch kosher salt

Pinch freshly ground black pepper

2 lemon slices

2 sprigs fresh rosemary

SPINACH

2 tablespoons extra-virgin olive oil

2 cloves garlic, thickly sliced

1 pound triple-washed curly spinach (*not* baby spinach)

Pinch of salt

Roasted Fingerling Potatoes (page 88)

2 generous tablespoons Salsa Verde Vinaigrette (page 67)

CONTINUES

Make the tomato salad: An hour before serving, combine all the salad ingredients and set aside in the fridge for the flavors to meld.

Make the potatoes: About 40 minutes before serving, make the Roasted Fingerling Potatoes (at right).

Make the salmon: Heat the olive oil in an ovenproof skillet over medium-high heat. Place the salmon in the pan, skin side up, and cook for a few minutes without moving so that the fish develops a golden brown crust; adjust the heat, if necessary, so the salmon doesn't burn. Use a spatula to turn the salmon over. (If it sticks it might mean that it needs more time cooking.) Sprinkle with salt and pepper and top with lemon slices and rosemary. Cook for a minute or two, then place in the 425°F oven. Roast for 12 to 15 minutes, depending on the level of doneness you desire. Thinner cuts of salmon that come from near the tail will cook more quickly; thicker cuts from the body will take longer.

Sauté the spinach: While the fish is cooking, heat the olive oil in a large skillet over medium heat. Add the garlic slices and cook until golden brown. Add the spinach, sprinkle with salt, and sauté, mixing around as needed, until the spinach is wilted.

To serve: Place spinach in the center of each plate. Place a salmon filet, skin side down, on top of the spinach, and spoon the tomato salad over the fish. Place the roasted potatoes around the spinach and drizzle everything with vinaigrette. Serve immediately.

ROASTED FINGERLING POTATOES

Serves 2

12 fingerling potatoes (or 2 to 3 large regular potatoes, cut into 1-inch cubes)

Kosher salt

Freshly ground black pepper

2 cloves garlic, thinly sliced

Leaves from 2 sprigs fresh rosemary

¼ cup extra-virgin olive oil

Preheat the oven to 425°F. Arrange the potatoes in a single layer in a nonstick baking dish or roasting pan. Sprinkle with salt and pepper, dot with garlic and rosemary, and drizzle with the oil. Roast, stirring occasionally, for about 30 minutes, or until tender all the way through when pierced with a knife. Serve immediately.

BALTIMORE CRAB CAKES
WITH RÉMOULADE AND CLASSIC COLESLAW

There's an art to making a good crab cake, and I learned that art from the best: Obrycki's Crab House, which was then located in the Fells Point neighborhood of Baltimore, Maryland. In a state famous for blue crabs, Obrycki's is a standout. In the early '90s, a new generation of American chefs was exploring regional American cuisine, and there was already a lot of good food happening in Baltimore. In 1993, I was lucky enough to spend time in the kitchen at Obrycki's for a week while hosting the Taste of Baltimore during the baseball All-Star Game week, and they showed me how to make a perfect crab cake.

They explained to me that the art comes from putting in just the right amount of binder. Too much and it loses its delicacy and you mainly taste the binding agents; too little, the cake falls apart and you just end up frying pieces of crab. It *is* supposed to be a cake, after all. Since we were talking baseball all week, it made sense when they used a baseball analogy: Hitting a 90-mile-an-hour fastball takes the same kind of nerve as it does to make crab cakes with as little binder as they do.

Their binder, too, was a revelation. I came in with a Yankee point of view, thinking they'd use some combination of flour, breadcrumbs, and eggs, but I was wrong. Their main binding agents were simply mayonnaise and saltine crackers (with some Old Bay seasoning thrown in, naturally), and their crab cakes were spectacular. I brought their advice (although not their actual recipe—I ended up sneaking in an egg, anyway, since I think it works better) back to New York, and have been making crab cakes their way ever since.

The other secret to making great crab cakes is to mix the crab and binder as little and as gently as possible. You don't want to break up the meat; you want to keep the nice, large hunks intact.

At Freds, we serve our crab cakes with Rémoulade Sauce and Classic Coleslaw, in addition to Belgian Fries. If you want to do the same, prepare the coleslaw and rémoulade ahead of time, and prep the potatoes for the fries so that they're blanched, chilled, and ready for the final fry, before you cook the crab cakes.

Serves 3 as a main course (2 cakes each), 6 as an appetizer (1 cake each)

THE 311 ON CRABMEAT

Not all crab is created equal. Crabmeat is sold in different grades, ranging from colossal (the best) to small claw meat. Crab is served in restaurants at many different price points, and a low price generally indicates that the crabmeat is of a lower grade. That doesn't mean it's bad; it just means that it comes in smaller pieces or flakes, and you'll probably need more binder to form a cake. The most succulent meat, with the choicest pieces, is packaged as jumbo lump crabmeat. At Freds, we use fresh jumbo lump crabmeat exclusively.

Jumbo lump crabmeat should be handled as delicately and as little as possible. The more it's handled, the more likely it is that the large lumps will break up, which will defeat the purpose of buying a premium grade.

CONTINUES

RÉMOULADE SAUCE

1 cup good commercial mayonnaise

2 tablespoons minced cornichons

1 tablespoon minced capers

1 tablespoon Dijon mustard

1 tablespoon minced fresh chervil

1 tablespoon minced fresh chives

1 tablespoon minced fresh parsley

1 teaspoon minced fresh tarragon

1 tablespoon minced shallot

1 teaspoon minced garlic

1 anchovy filet, mashed, plus
1 teaspoon olive oil from the jar or can

¼ teaspoon paprika

Kosher salt

Freshly ground black pepper

CRAB CAKES

1 pound jumbo lump crabmeat

½ cup good commercial mayonnaise

½ egg, whisked (optional*)

5 tablespoons roughly crumbled
saltine cracker pieces (crumbled well,
but not too)

1 tablespoon good commercial
mayonnaise mixed with ¼ teaspoon
cayenne pepper (or more cayenne
to taste)

1 tablespoon onion pulp (puree onion
in blender, grate very finely, or chop until
it's a mash)

1 tablespoon minced red bell pepper

1 tablespoon minced yellow bell pepper

*Purists (like Obrycki's) don't use egg, so feel
free to omit it. I add it because I find it helps
keep the cakes together without affecting
the taste.*

1 tablespoon chopped fresh parsley

1 tablespoon minced fresh chives

½ tablespoon Old Bay seasoning

½ teaspoon paprika

½ teaspoon celery salt

¼ cup finely pulverized saltine cracker
crumbs (about 10 crackers)

3 tablespoons soybean oil for frying

TO GARNISH

3 or 6 cups Classic Coleslaw (page 93),
1 cup per serving

Belgian Fries (page 9)

Make the rémoulade: Place all the
rémoulade ingredients in a food
processor and whiz together on
medium speed until everything is
well blended. Store in the refrigerator
in a sealed container. It will last for
a week in the fridge and the flavors
will become deeper.

Make the cakes: Line a sheet pan
with parchment paper and spread
out the crabmeat. Carefully and
gently, so as to keep intact the large
lumps, feel through it and remove
any pieces of shell and cartilage.
We usually pick through the meat
twice to make sure we get all the
shell out.

Place the cleaned meat into a large
mixing bowl and add the remaining
crab cake ingredients, except for
the fine saltine crumbs and the
soybean oil. Very gently, using a
rubber spatula or your hands, mix
everything together. Shape the
mixture into 6 equal patties, 1 to

1½ inches thick (about ⅓ cup each).
Roll the cakes in the fine saltine
crumbs to coat them thoroughly,
and place in the fridge to chill until
firm, 30 minutes to an hour.

Cook the cakes: Preheat the oven
to 350°F. In a large ovenproof skillet,
heat the oil over medium heat.
Carefully place the crab cakes in the
pan and cook until browned, about
2 minutes. Gently turn them over
and continue cooking for another
2 minutes, until browned on the
other side. Transfer the pan to the
oven and bake until the crab cakes
are heated through, about 10
minutes.

Garnish each serving with 1 cup
coleslaw, 2 tablespoons rémoulade,
and a handful of fries.

———

CLASSIC COLESLAW

Even if you didn't grow up eating in New York delicatessens like I did, it's impossible to imagine certain dishes without coleslaw, and our Baltimore Crab Cakes, on the menu since day one, is one of those dishes. We're not a deli, so we don't serve a side of this as a standard thing, although regular customers who know our slaw special order sides of it all the time. Besides the crab cakes, we also pile it on The Jewish Boy from Queens turkey sandwich (page 101), a relatively new menu item created for the downtown store. There are a lot of inventive slaw recipes out there these days, which I love, but this one is as classic as it gets.

Coleslaw is one of the first dishes I learned to make, long before I had any idea that I was going to become a chef. I still remember my mother's advice that the perfect amount of onion and caraway seed is what makes a good slaw shine, and this recipe definitely follows her template.

Cabbages vary in size, so you may need to adjust the amount of milk and mayo so that everything is coated. The amounts I've listed are for medium-size cabbages and carrots, neither puny nor colossal. I recommend using a mandoline to slice the cabbages. The Japanese and Swiss make good ones and they are easy to find in stores. Like its family member kale, cabbage softens up with a good massage, so make sure you wash your hands well before making this so you can give it a good working over. Then let it rest in the fridge for at least 2 hours—ideally overnight—before serving.

Makes 12 cups, serving 6 to 8

½ medium head red cabbage

½ medium head savoy cabbage

½ medium head white cabbage

2 medium carrots

1 red onion

1 cup good commercial mayonnaise

½ cup milk

2 tablespoons apple cider vinegar

½ tablespoon Worcestershire sauce

1½ teaspoons caraway seeds

1 teaspoon sugar

2 teaspoons kosher salt

½ teaspoon finely ground black pepper

Peel any rough outer leaves from the cabbage halves and cut out the large cores. Shred the cabbages with a mandoline on a setting that makes them about the thickness of a strand of regular spaghetti. Trim away the tops of the carrots and peel them. Grate the carrots using the larger shred of box grater (or in a food processor) and then toss the cabbage and carrots together in a large bowl.

Finely mince the onion by hand or by pulsing in a small blender, being sure to retain any liquid that emerges. Place the onion and its juices in a separate large mixing bowl and add the rest of the dressing ingredients. Use a whisk to mix it until it's well blended.

Add the cabbage and carrot mixture, a handful or two at a time, to the dressing, mixing as you go, until the vegetables are well coated. If the mixture seems dry, add a small amount of milk, a little at a time. Using your hands, massage the slaw rather strongly for several minutes, until the cabbage starts to soften and the orange color from the carrots is bleeding into the dressing. Taste and adjust the seasoning if necessary. Cover and store in the fridge for at least 2 hours or overnight before serving.

———

JOIN THE CLUB: THE FREDS CLUB SANDWICHES

The classic club sandwich is synonymous with the American power lunch. Every great hotel in the world has one on their room service menu, every bar or café has a version. To Europeans, they're as iconically American as blue jeans and cheeseburgers. A classic is a classic for a reason, and so I knew a lunch spot like Freds had to have at least one, done perfectly, served with our homemade potato chips or Belgian Fries. As it turns out, we have three.

BEVERLY HILLS CLUB

Makes 1 sandwich

2 ounces fresh Dungeness crabmeat

2 ounces cooked jumbo shrimp, cut into pieces

2 tablespoons Garlic Mayonnaise (page 10)

3 leaves romaine lettuce, cut into chiffonade

3 slices whole wheat health bread

3 slices cooked Nueske's applewood-smoked bacon (or any thick-cut brand)

3 (¼-inch-thick) slices beefsteak tomato

½ ripe avocado, pitted, peeled, and sliced

Belgian Fries (page 9), optional

In a small bowl, gently mix the crab and shrimp together with 1 tablespoon of the Garlic Mayonnaise. In a different bowl, mix together the lettuce and the remaining Garlic Mayonnaise so that it's the consistency of coleslaw. Set both bowls aside.

Toast the bread slices and lay them out in a row. Spread the shrimp and crabmeat mixture in an even layer on one slice and top with the bacon. Place the second slice of bread on top, then layer first with the tomato and then with the avocado slices. Spread the lettuce mixture on top of that. Cover with the final bread slice and press down gently. Cut the sandwich in half diagonally, making two triangles. We do not cut this sandwich in four pieces like a traditional club sandwich as it falls apart quite easily.

Serve with Belgian Fries, if desired.

THE FREDS LUNCH CLASSICS

LOBSTER CLUB

Makes 1 sandwich

3 leaves romaine lettuce, cut into chiffonade

2 tablespoons Garlic Mayonnaise (page 10)

3 slices seven-grain bread

4 ounces cooked lobster meat (see Palace Warm Lobster Salad, page 48)

3 slices cooked Nueske's applewood-smoked bacon (or any thick-cut brand)

3 (¼-inch-thick) slices beefsteak tomato

Belgian Fries (page 9), optional

In a small bowl, mix together the lettuce and 1 tablespoon Garlic Mayonnaise so that it's the consistency of coleslaw. Toast the bread slices and lay them out in a row. Spread the remaining Garlic Mayo on one slice of bread, making sure the surface is completely covered. Place lobster in an even layer on that slice and top with the bacon, then place the second slice of bread on top. Lay on the sliced tomato and spread the lettuce mixture on top of that. Cover with the final slice of bread and press down gently. Cut the sandwich in half diagonally, making two triangles. We do not cut this sandwich in four pieces like a traditional club sandwich as it falls apart quite easily.

Serve with Belgian Fries, if desired.

———

MADISON CLASSIC CLUB

Makes 1 sandwich

3 leaves romaine lettuce, cut into chiffonade

2 tablespoons good commercial mayonnaise

3 thick slices brioche pullman bread, toasted

4 ounces hand-sliced, freshly roasted turkey breast (see page 19)

3 slices cooked Nueske's applewood-smoked bacon (or any thick-cut brand)

3 (¼-inch-thick) slices beefsteak tomato

Handful of Freds Potato Chips (page 98), optional

½ sour pickle, optional

In a small bowl, mix together the lettuce and 1 tablespoon mayonnaise so that it's the consistency of coleslaw.

Toast the bread slices and lay them out in a row. Spread the remaining mayo on one slice of bread, making sure the surface is completely covered. Place the turkey on that slice, and lay the second bread slice on top. Then, lay the bacon and tomato, and spread with the lettuce/mayo combo. Top with the third and final slice of bread. To serve in the traditional way, poke four toothpicks into the sandwich equidistant in a square and cut the sandwich into four perfect triangles. Place each triangle on the plate so each tip touches another. Pile the potato chips in the middle of the plate, and garnish with the pickle.

CONTINUES

FREDS POTATO CHIPS

Serves 4

EQUIPMENT

2 large stainless-steel mixing bowls

Mandoline with ruffle blade

Baking sheet (or large platter)

Paper towels

8-quart stockpot

Deep-fry/candy thermometer

1 stainless-steel spider skimmer (these are easy to find online or in stores that carry Asian cooking utensils)

INGREDIENTS

4 large Idaho potatoes

7 cups peanut oil for frying

Kosher salt

Fill one stainless-steel mixing bowl with cold water. Peel the potatoes, and slice them with a mandoline using the ruffle blade. As they come off the mandoline, place the slices into the ice water.

Line the baking sheet or large platter with several layers of paper towels ready to drain the cooked chips. Have a handful of extra paper set aside by the bowl of potatoes to blot off excess water before frying.

Place the peanut oil in the stockpot, place the thermometer in the oil, and heat to 375°F over high heat. When the oil reaches the desired tempera-ture, lower the heat to medium high so that the temperature doesn't climb higher. In batches of 8 to 10, remove slices from the water and pat dry. Place in the hot oil and fry until golden brown, about 3 minutes. Do not crowd in the pot, and gently separate the slices with the spider as they cook so they don't stick together. Remove chips to drain on the paper towel–covered baking sheet, then transfer them to the second mixing bowl. Repeat to fry the remaining potatoes. Sprinkle with salt. Serve the chips immediately.

THE JEWISH BOY FROM QUEENS

WITH RUSSIAN DRESSING

Where I grew up in Queens, in a neighborhood where freshly roasted turkey was a staple foodstuff, the word for foodie was *fresser*. And, boy, was I a *fresser*. The day my father showed me how to combine ketchup and mayo is still a vivid memory. It was a formative *fresser* rite of passage. As an adult I realized that it's basically Russian dressing, but at the time it blew my young *fresser* mind. My mind was blown again the day I discovered that it was possible to order coleslaw *inside* my turkey sandwich, which then became my standing order at the local deli throughout my teenage years.

This sandwich, which I created for the opening of Freds in the new downtown store, is homage to Barneys' return to its original New York neighborhood and a nod back to the turkey sandwiches of my youth. Then, I would have had this sandwich on rye, but the grown-up *fresser* in me thought that it might taste even better on an onion roll. Orwashers bakery makes large, delicious, savory onion pockets—with minced onions swirled through the dough and sprinkled on top—that are as traditionally New York as bagels, and they're perfect for this sandwich. If you can't find them, it's fine to substitute a simple kaiser roll, or, of course, the traditional rye bread.

Originally only on the lunch menu, the Jewish Boy from Queens was so requested that it's now on the dinner menu as well. The other day a couple of twenty-something guys were sharing one (in another New York sandwich tradition, it's big enough for two) and called me over to say, "Thanks for putting it on at dinner. We love this thing!" It's gratifying for this Jewish boy from Queens to see a new generation of *fressers* enjoying my old neighborhood treat.

Makes 1 sandwich

1 large onion pocket roll

2 tablespoons Russian Dressing (page 102)

5 ounces sliced freshly roasted turkey (see page 19)

½ cup Classic Coleslaw (page 93)

1 leaf Bibb lettuce

1 thick slice vine-ripened red tomato

½ sour pickle, optional

Freds Potato Chips (page 98), optional

Cut the roll in half horizontally and toast it on a light setting so the onions don't burn. Spread Russian dressing on both halves, and then arrange the sliced turkey on the bottom half. Using a fork so that excess liquid drains off, place the coleslaw on top of the turkey. Top with the other half of the bun, press down slightly, and cut in half.

Arrange on a plate with the lettuce, tomato, pickle, and potato chips if desired.

CONTINUES

RUSSIAN DRESSING

Makes 1 ½ cups

1 cup good commercial mayonnaise

½ cup ketchup

4 shakes Worcestershire sauce

1 teaspoon kosher salt

Freshly ground black pepper

Place all ingredients into a mixing bowl and blend well together using a whisk or an immersion blender. Store in a covered container in the fridge for up to 1 week.

HOW TO POUND A PAILLARD
(OR SCALOPPINE, MILANESE, OR CARPACCIO)

This technique for pounding meat works whether you're making a paillard, a Milanese (breaded paillard), or carpaccio (raw pounded steak—not a suitable way to serve chicken, obviously!). The goal is to end up with a piece of meat that is evenly thin all over.

Use a countertop where you have enough elbow room for leverage and that's sturdy enough to stand up to pounding—we use a butcher block instead of the usual metal kitchen surfaces. Be sure to remove any objects that might fall off from the rattling as you pound. Place a very thick wooden cutting board (such as the ones made by John Boos, which are widely available) on the surface to absorb the impact of the pounding. The best tool to use is a metal meat mallet/tenderizer, but they're not all created equal. The best for home use is a solid stainless-steel round disc because it's heavier and has a smaller center of weight than the more common square ones. It's a bit small to do the volume a restaurant requires, but it's perfect for home use—or for beginners. Use the flat side, not the scored one.

For each piece of chicken, tear off two equal size pieces of plastic wrap. Place one piece on the cutting board, lay the chicken on top, and drizzle 1 teaspoon of cold water over the chicken, which prevents it from sticking to the plastic. Lay the second piece of plastic on top. Now you're ready to pound, but do so strategically by starting from the center. Part of the art is using the right force; too much will rip holes in the meat or the plastic wrap. The time to exert a little extra pressure is not in the strike, but just as the mallet hits the meat. Rotate the piece (in the plastic) about 20 degrees clockwise after each strike, so you work your way around, and feel with your free hand to make sure it's evenly flat. From a 7-ounce chicken breast you should end up with a piece that's about the size of a 10-inch plate. About halfway through pounding, lift the top layer of plastic and drizzle the meat with a little olive oil so the plastic won't tear the meat as you remove it for cooking. When the piece is fully pounded, remove the top plastic again, and drizzle with a little more olive oil and with herbs, if desired. Cover with the plastic and store flat in the fridge until you're ready to cook it.

CHICKEN PAILLARDS

WITH TOMATO, ARUGULA, AND RED ONION SALAD

If any dish is tailor-made for my Upper East Side customers, it's a chicken paillard. It's lean protein, so it fits into whatever diet is in style at any moment. Combining salad with warm ingredients is a vestige of nouvelle cuisine, and I'm glad it's here to stay.

In this deceptively simple dish, the warmth of the just-cooked chicken releases the aroma of the dressing and enhances the slight bitterness of the arugula. The tomato and arugula add sweetness and sharpness, respectively. Like all simple dishes, making it perfect means all the elements have to be right. That starts with the best-quality chicken breasts from your local butcher. It's not that easy to pound a perfect paillard, one that's evenly thin all the way around, but not *too* thin in any one spot—especially when you're doing dozens per day.

In addition to being a fixture on the restaurant menu, the paillard is also one of the most popular items we serve for large catered dinners. Barneys' Public Relations and Special Events teams always create world-class events, so the challenge for us is making sure what we serve measures up, especially for events when we are feeding many people at the same time. We are Barneys, and can't serve anything less than delicious, so how *do* you cook something this thin and delicate for a large group? The answer, when you're cooking for a hundred or more: lots of staff! Six chefs cooking paillards, two people topping them with salad, and three food runners sprinting them quickly to our waiting, fashionable guests.

You probably won't be making them for quite as many people, but however many you make, you should pound the paillards ahead of time; in fact, you can prepare them up to 24 hours ahead of time and store them in the refrigerator.

Serves 2

EQUIPMENT

Heavy, thick, wooden cutting board

Metal meat mallet/tenderizer

Plastic wrap

Storage container with cover

12-inch nonstick skillet

Kitchen tongs

CHICKEN PAILLARDS

2 (7-ounce) boneless, skinless chicken breasts

2 tablespoon Freds Herb Mixture (page 12)

Drizzle of extra-virgin olive oil

SALAD

2 cups baby arugula

10 cherry tomatoes, halved
(or 2 plum tomatoes, quartered, seeds and center removed, then cut lengthwise into ¼-inch strips)

4 (¼-inch-thick) slices red onion

Kosher salt

Freshly ground black pepper

2 tablespoons Madison Avenue Dressing (page 44)

1 lemon, halved, for garnish

CONTINUES

Pound the paillards, in between sheets of plastic wrap, according to the instructions on page 102. Peel back the plastic, one side at a time, and sprinkle each paillard with a tablespoon of herb mixture and drizzle with olive oil. Keep refrigerated in the plastic wrap for up to 24 hours, until you're ready to cook.

Place the arugula, tomatoes, and onion in a mixing bowl. Place the dressing close at hand but do not add to the salad yet.

Unless you have two skillets, you'll need to cook the paillards one at a time. They cook quickly, so the first one will stay warm while you cook the second. Take one paillard out of the plastic wrap and sprinkle it on both sides with salt and pepper. Heat the skillet over medium heat until it's very hot. To check if it's ready, drizzle a drop of water into the pan. If it sizzles and balls up, the pan is ready. Briefly turn off the heat as you quickly remove the paillard from the plastic. Flip it into the hot pan, making sure it's flat in the pan, then turn the heat back to high. Cook

until the top side starts to look cooked, and then use tongs to turn it over. If the paillard is very thin, turn off the heat, but leave it in the pan to finish cooking. If it's a bit thicker and needs more time, keep the heat on until the piece is firm, but do not overcook. Use a large spatula to transfer the paillard to an oversize dinner plate. Repeat with the second paillard.

Quickly add the dressing to the salad, toss together, and then place in the center of each paillard. Garnish with half a lemon, and serve immediately.

———

UPPER EAST SIDE FILET OF SOLE
WITH SAUTÉED CARROTS AND SNOW PEAS

The Upper East Side of Manhattan has long been the home of New York society and the carriage trade, those who cater to that society. These are streets that have been graced by Jackie O. and Bill Cunningham, where Pierre Cardin opened an outpost of Maxim's from Paris, and Regine opened her famous disco, where Caviarteria opened its first shop, and where Le Pavillon brought classic French food to the United States in the first place. When it comes to food, there aren't many dishes from those grand days of high society that still feel modern the way filet of sole does. Back in the day, it would probably have been Dover sole flown in from England. Of course, you can still find Dover sole on the market, but it's prohibitively expensive, even for Madison Avenue. And eating fish flown in from England isn't exactly environmentally sustainable. Fortunately, the waters off Long Island are filled with flat fish that fill the same flavor profile as sole: They're flaky, pristinely white, mild, and "not too fishy-tasting," a request I get surprisingly often.

In the market there are a variety of fishes that are sold as sole; fluke, lemon sole, grey sole, and even flounder might be what you're getting. These are all fine, as long as the fish is impeccably fresh. You can gauge the freshness by searching for filets that are shiny and vibrant looking, not dull. Fresh fish feels firm to the touch and doesn't smell "fishy." Since those species vary in size, just make sure that all the pieces you purchase are more or less the same size and thickness so they cook evenly. This is a simple preparation, and yet (or possibly *because* of it) it's one of Freds' most popular and long-standing menu items. Snow peas are available year-round, but in the summer we like to use the delicious sugar snap peas that are around then.

Serves 2

VEGETABLES

18 baby carrots, halved lengthwise

1½ cups snow peas (or sugar snap peas)

2 tablespoons unsalted butter

1 teaspoon sugar

Pinch of salt

2 tablespoons mineral water

FISH

1 pound sole filets

Kosher salt

Freshly ground black pepper

1 cup all-purpose flour, for dredging

2 tablespoons clarified butter
(see page 14) or olive oil

1 cup white wine

2 lemon slices

1 tablespoon capers, rinsed of salt or brine

1½ tablespoons unsalted butter

1 tablespoon finely minced
fresh parsley

Make the vegetables: Blanch and shock the carrots and snow peas (see page 17). Set the snow peas aside. In a small skillet, melt the butter until it starts to brown. Add the carrots, sugar, and a sprinkling of salt, then sauté over medium heat for 2 minutes, just to warm them. Add the mineral water, mix together, and remove from the heat while you cook the fish.

Cook the fish: Sprinkle the fish filets with salt and pepper, then dredge in the flour. Heat the clarified butter or oil in a 14-inch nonstick skillet over medium heat. As you pick them up, gently shake the filets to remove excess flour, and then place carefully in the hot oil. Cook for about 1 minute, until they're lightly browned, then gently turn them over using a fish spatula, being careful to keep the filets intact. Add the wine, lemon slices, and capers, and simmer gently for 2 minutes. When the sauce starts to thicken, add the snow peas to the pan with the carrots. Turn the heat on under the vegetables so that they'll be warm when the fish is cooked. Add the unsalted butter to the pan with the fish, sprinkle in the parsley, and gently mix together to finish the sauce. Add more salt if needed. Place the carrots and snow peas on serving plates and lay the fish on top of them. Drizzle any remaining sauce over the fish and serve immediately.

Freds Gazpacho

CHAPTER 4
A YEAR IN SOUP

SPRING
English Pea Soup with Mint / 113
Spring Mushroom Soup / 114

SUMMER
Freds Gazpacho / 117
New Jersey Summer Heirloom Tomato Soup / 118
Summer Corn Soup / 120

FALL
Cauliflower Soup / 123
Lobster Bisque with Saffron Aioli / 124
White Bean Soup / 128

WINTER
Grain and Legume Soup with Kale / 130
Lentil and Vegetable Soup / 133

A good soup is like a well-tailored suit: It's a little old-school. There are other, flashier things you could wear. There are a lot of mediocre ones walking around, but when you see one that's well-made, you remember what's possible, how sharp that look can be. In soups, as in suits, classical under-pinning elevates the final product to something special. Quality work behind the scenes (or in the seams) makes the difference between so-so and spectacular.

Soup is the perfect light lunch for the fashionable, which is why we have a whole roster of them at Freds, rotating by the seasons. Along with salad, it's one of the chief weapons in a fashion-able person's fight against dietary excess: satisfying, satiating, and nutri-tious without weighing you down. In New York, there's a chill in the air at least nine months out of the year, so soup is never unwelcome.

You can tell a lot about a restaurant by eating its soup; it's a kind of litmus test of kitchen skills. One taste of a restau-rant's soup and I'll know whether or not I'm in good hands for the rest of the meal. A good chef will spend as much time planning and making soup as he or she does on their other, trendier dishes, because soup requires considerable care for it to be great. A great soup is layered with flavor, and the first element is starting with a good, richly flavored stock. Whether it's chicken, vegetable, or even, in some cases, veal, you want to choose a stock that will complement the soup you're making. Then, you want the other elements to be in harmony. If you're making a single-vegetable soup, such as asparagus or cauliflower, which tends to be light, you want to cram in as much flavor of the vegetable as possible, and you don't want to add any strong seasonings or ingredients that will overpower the delicate flavor. Texture is important—just ask Goldilocks. If a soup is too thick it will be unpleasantly porridge-like, perfect maybe for Goldilocks, but not for soup. So it's best to thin it, carefully, with a tiny bit more stock or even water. If it's too thin or watery it's not good either, in which case you should simmer it in an open pot awhile longer to allow some of the liquid to evaporate and for the flavor to concentrate. If there are chunky elements in your soup, like the vegetables in our Grain and Legume Soup with Kale, you want to make sure that they're all cut evenly and that each one is cooked through, so that they form a harmo-nious whole.

Then there's the question how to garnish. Croutons? A sprinkling of minced herbs? A drizzle of olive oil? What will give it a little extra kick of flavor and texture? For a seemingly simple dish, there's actually quite a lot to think about.

The production of our soups is one area where I have recently veered slightly from my classical training, not in method, but in ingredients. Traditionally, the stock of choice in a European kitchen is veal stock, although Americans tend to prefer chicken stock, which is what we used in the past at Freds. However, over the last few years I've received more and more requests from customers for vegan dishes, and so we've gradually transitioned to using vegetable stock for almost all our soups. Once you cut yourself loose from the flavor of meat, you begin to see how versatile vegetable stock can be. By varying the vegetables you use to make it, you vary the flavor of the stock. For example, use asparagus trimmings to make asparagus stock that will boost the delicate flavor of that vegetable in asparagus soup or risotto. Or maybe you prefer a rich mushroom stock as a soup base. The recipe on page 28 is a good generic vegetable stock, but I encourage you to experiment from there.

Even though a lot of Freds' soups use vegetable stock, feel free to substitute chicken stock if you prefer that flavor and nutritional profile.

There are a couple of exceptions to our vegan soup roster, our Lobster Bisque, for example, and then the biggest one of all: Estelle's Chicken Soup in Chapter 1 (page 27). Without a doubt, it's the crown jewel of Freds soups. There would be a riot among my customers if I ever took it off the menu. And why would I? It's like mother's milk to anyone who grew up in a New York Jewish household like I did—and that includes a lot of my customers. At Passover we add matzoh balls, for an added dose of nostalgia, although we also often offer an alternative that includes shaved baby artichokes and parsnips, to celebrate Passover in a lighter way.

Every single day at Freds finds huge stockpots simmering with some step of the Estelle process, but at home stock-making is bound to be an infrequent activity, even for people who like to make their own. There's no shame to using commercial stocks, but look for low-sodium versions. But, of course, in stocks as in most things, I always prefer home-made where possible. If you're thinking of making your own, freeze leftover bones and carcasses of roasted chickens until you have enough to make a large batch.

One small tip for flavoring soups, decidedly not vegan, is to add a small amount of cubed smoked pork when you're sautéing the aromatics (carrots, celery, onions, and garlic). It amps up the flavor immensely.

GARNISHES FOR SOUPS

We eat with our eyes, and so garnishes are an important visual element in a restaurant's presentation, but they're also a chance to add a "little something" with flavor or texture. We always garnish our soups, even if it's with a simple sprinkling of parsley. A drizzle of olive oil, a few homemade croutons (page 15), a bit of grated Parmesan, a dash of Freds Herb Mixture (page 12). It doesn't have to be elaborate, and usually isn't, but some form of garnish makes a simple bowl of soup into something a bit more special.

ENGLISH PEA SOUP WITH MINT

This gentle soup, which can be served warm or cold, is a sentimental favorite for me. It's one of the first foods I served to my children at the restaurant when they were infants. Both were winter babies, so by the time spring came around they were ready to eat some simple pureed foods. They're grown now and still love it, so I no longer need to make airplane noises to get them to spoon it up.

It appears every spring at Freds as part of our seasonal soup rotation, although the recipe has changed slightly over the years. It used to be made with a bit of cream, and a bit more butter. But it's always much loved by our customers—even more in its newest, lighter incarnation—because it's clean, delicious, and filling. For home cooks it also has the considerable advantage of being quick and easy to make.

If you reheat the soup, do so slowly and gently so that it retains the fresh pea quality that distinguishes it from split pea soup.

Serves 4 to 6

1 tablespoon unsalted butter

1 tablespoon extra-virgin olive oil

2 medium onions, diced

1¼ teaspoons kosher salt

¼ teaspoon white pepper

3 pounds fresh (or frozen) shelled peas

5 cups Vegetable Stock (page 28) or Chicken Stock (page 24)

½ cup white wine

12 fresh mint leaves; plus more for garnish (optional)

Homemade Croutons (page 15) for garnish (optional)

In a large soup pot, heat the butter and olive oil over medium heat. Add the onions, salt, and pepper and cook, stirring, until the onions are translucent, about 3 minutes. Add the peas and cook for about 2 minutes, stirring occasionally. Add the stock and wine, bring to a boil, reduce the heat to low, and simmer for 10 minutes. Add the mint leaves and simmer for another 10 minutes.

Using a food processor, blender, or immersion blender, puree the soup until smooth. Depending on the size of your machine, you may need to do this in several batches. Be especially careful as you do this because the soup is very hot. If the soup is thick, add additional stock. Adjust seasoning to taste, if desired. Serve the soup warm or cold.

Ladle into serving bowls and garnish each bowl with a mint leaf and a few croutons if desired.

SPRING MUSHROOM SOUP

Wild mushrooms enchant me, and the variety available boggles my mind, and inspires me as a chef. You'll find mushrooms, wild and cultivated, in many dishes at Freds—salads, pasta, risotto—and we actually have a mushroom soup for every season. In the fall and winter it's likely to be a hearty mixture fortified with barley, farro, or beans. But our version for spring doesn't require the mushrooms to share the limelight with grains and legumes. It's all mushroom, almost like a mushroom chowder, to celebrate the season when warmer weather and spring rains are coaxing them to pop up everywhere. Ramps, too, are a wild harbinger of spring, so they're a natural addition to this soup.

Of course, with wild mushrooms one has to be careful, which is why we buy ours from purveyors who specialize in them, who are experts in the field, and who fly them in from all over the world.

I like to include a generous amount of maitake mushrooms in the blend when I make this soup, but if you can't find them, a mixture of more common ones—button, oyster, cremini—will work just fine. You can use portobellos, too, although they're less desirable because they tend to turn the soup very dark. If you use them, be sure to trim away the black gills on the underside of the cap, so that you're left with only the meat of the cap. Except for a few dried porcini to amp up the flavor, I don't suggest using dried mushrooms, as they'll be too rubbery. Whatever type of mushrooms you use, it's important that they be sliced and chopped into more or less evenly sized pieces so that they cook evenly. Serve this soup with grated Parmigiano Reggiano and a crusty baguette (see photo, page 131).

Serves 8 to 10

1 cup hot water

½ cup dried porcini mushrooms

¼ cup extra-virgin olive oil

2 medium onions, diced

2 cloves garlic, minced

1 cup ramp bulbs, washed and sliced, with their leaves (can substitute 1 small leek, trimmed, well-washed, and thinly sliced)

2½ teaspoons kosher salt (if using low-sodium broth you may want to add 1 extra teaspoon)

1 teaspoon ground white pepper

1 large carrot, diced

1 stalk celery, diced

2 medium potatoes, peeled and diced

2 pounds assorted fresh mushrooms (such as maitake, cremini, oyster, or button), trimmed, wiped clean, and cut into ½-inch pieces

2 cups white wine (can substitute water)

1½ cups canned chopped Italian plum tomatoes

1½ quarts Vegetable Stock (page 28) or Chicken Stock (page 24)

3½ tablespoons chopped fresh rosemary leaves

8 leaves fresh sage, chopped

Piece of Parmigiano Reggiano cheese rind, roughly 3½ by 1¼ inches (optional)

Freshly grated Parmigiano Reggiano for garnish (optional)

In a small bowl, pour the hot water over the dried porcini, cover, and set aside to reconstitute while you prep the vegetables.

Heat the oil in a large stockpot over medium heat. Add the onions, garlic, ramp bulbs, salt, and white pepper and sauté until translucent, about 3 minutes. Add the carrot, celery, and potatoes and cook, stirring occasionally, for 2 more minutes. Add the fresh mushrooms in batches, stirring occasionally and waiting until the batch is wilted before adding another batch. Sauté about 5 minutes.

Squeeze the porcini and pour the reconstituting liquid into the pot. Roughly chop the porcini and add them as well. Pour in the wine, bring the mixture to a simmer, and cook for 1 minute. Add the tomatoes, stock, rosemary, sage, and Parmesan rind. Bring to a boil and reduce heat so that the soup is gently simmering. Cook, uncovered, for 1½ hours, until the mushrooms are tender and the soup has thickened.

Remove the Parmesan rind and check to see if you need to add more salt. Ladle into bowls and top with grated Parmigiano Reggiano if desired.

———

FREDS GAZPACHO

This traditional, no-cook Spanish chilled soup—light years ahead of the juicing trend—has been on the menu at Freds every summer since we opened. We also serve it as a specialty when Barneys hosts events or luncheons for Spanish designers. There's a reason this dish is a classic. It's perfectly refreshing, whether you're enjoying it with us on Madison Avenue or in your own backyard.

Traditionally, gazpacho was made with a mortar and pestle, but thank goodness we now have food processors to make it easy. Make sure this soup is very cold when you serve it.

Serves 6 to 8

4 cups local summer tomatoes (beefsteak, heirloom, or a mix of both), cut into 1-inch cubes

2 cups cucumber, peeled, seeded, and cut into 1-inch cubes

2 cups red bell peppers, cored, seeded, and cut into 1-inch cubes

1 cup chopped red onion

1 cup roughly chopped scallions, white part only

2 cloves garlic, peeled and halved

1 jalapeño, cored, seeded, and sliced, or more to taste (optional)

2 cups Vegetable Stock (page 28)

6 slices New England or brioche pullman bread, crusts removed

¼ cup sherry vinegar, or more to taste

¼ cup extra-virgin olive oil

¼ cup ketchup

¼ cup good commercial mayonnaise

Kosher salt

Freshly ground black pepper

Extra-virgin olive oil, for garnish

¼ cup *each* finely minced cucumber, tomato, and red bell pepper, for garnish

Homemade Croutons (page 15) for garnish

Combine all the vegetables and the stock in a large bowl, cover with plastic wrap, and refrigerate to marinate for 24 hours.

Puree the mixture in a blender or food processor: Working in batches, add the vegetables and liquid to the food processor and run the machine for 1 to 2 minutes to make sure the vegetables are very smooth. Pass the mixture through a mesh strainer into a large bowl and discard any solids.

Crumble the bread into the food processor or blender. Add the vinegar, oil, ketchup, and mayonnaise. Puree until it becomes a smooth paste. Add to the vegetable puree and mix everything together well. Season to taste with salt and pepper. Cover the soup and place in the fridge until thoroughly chilled, at least 2 hours.

To serve, stir the soup, as some of the liquid may have separated. Adjust seasonings, if needed. Ladle into bowls, drizzle with olive oil, sprinkle with finely minced vegetables and croutons, and serve immediately.

NEW JERSEY SUMMER
HEIRLOOM TOMATO SOUP

Toward the end of summer, when the local tomatoes have been baking in the sun and the juices are bursting their skins, *that's* the time to make this soup. The tiny amount of bacon adds a depth of flavor that's addictive, but if you're not a bacon fan, don't worry. The soup won't disappoint if you leave it out.

Serves 6 to 8

¼ cup extra-virgin olive oil

2 slices smoked bacon, finely minced (optional)

2 medium red onions, finely minced

2 scallions, finely minced

2 cloves garlic, thinly sliced

1 teaspoon kosher salt

2 medium carrots, finely minced

2 stalks celery, finely minced

2 tablespoons all-purpose flour

¼ cup tomato puree

4 cups Vegetable Stock (page 28) or water

6 pounds very ripe local summer tomatoes, quartered, with their juices

½ cup fresh basil leaves, julienned, plus additional whole leaves for garnish

1 bay leaf

Freshly ground black pepper

Heat the olive oil in a large, heavy stockpot over medium heat. Add the bacon (if using), onions, scallions, garlic, and salt and cook, stirring, until the onions are translucent, about 3 minutes. Add the carrots and celery and continue cooking until the vegetables are wilted but not brown, about 2 minutes. Add the flour, mix well, and continue cooking and stirring for about 3 minutes. Add the tomato puree and stir quickly together for about 1 minute to form a paste. Add the stock, a little at a time at first so that it thins the paste. Then add tomatoes and their juices, the basil, and bay leaf and bring to a boil. Reduce the heat to low so the soup is simmering lightly, and cook until the soup thickens and turns a deep red color, 20 to 30 minutes.

Let the soup cool slightly. Remove and discard the bay leaf. Run the soup, a little at a time, through a food mill to remove the tomato skins and seeds, or pulse in a food processor and then pass through a mesh strainer. Adjust seasoning to taste. Reheat to serve warm, or chill well to serve cold. Garnish each bowl with fresh whole basil leaves.

SUMMER CORN SOUP

This creamy soup is a recent and very popular addition to the Freds menu. It can easily be adapted to be vegan without losing the creaminess that makes it so satisfying. Chef's tip: Freeze some of the water when you cook corn and use it in the stock for this soup.

Serves 4

2 quarts Vegetable Stock (page 28) or Chicken Stock (page 24)

5 tablespoons unsalted butter (can substitute olive oil)

¼ teaspoon kosher salt

6 ears fresh summer corn, husked and cut in half

2 small potatoes, peeled and diced

2 yellow onions, diced

2 stalks celery, diced

1 large leek, white part only, trimmed, well-washed, and diced

½ cup heavy cream or 1 cup whole milk (can substitute 1 cup almond milk)

Freshly ground black pepper

Place the stock, butter, and salt in a large stockpot and bring to a boil. Add the corn and cook until tender, about 5 minutes. Remove the corn from the stock, set aside to cool, then use a sharp knife to shave the kernels off the cobs. Set the kernels aside, but do not discard the cobs.

Return the pot with the broth to medium-high heat. Add the corn cobs, potatoes, onions, celery, leek, and cream. Bring to a boil, reduce the heat to low, and simmer gently until the potatoes are soft, 35 to 45 minutes. Fish out the cobs and discard.

Add the corn kernels to the soup. Using a food processor, blender, or immersion blender, puree the soup until smooth. (Depending on the size of your machine, you may need to do this in several batches.) Be especially careful as you do this because the soup is very hot. If the soup is too thick, add additional stock and heat thoroughly. Adjust seasoning and serve.

CAULIFLOWER SOUP

It doesn't get more classic than this deceptively simple vegetable velouté soup. Like velvet, *velouté* (which means "velvet" in French) never really goes out of style. Escoffier classified velouté as one of the five mother sauces that forms the basis for many other dishes.

For Escoffier, velouté in the 19th century started with a roux of butter and flour thinned out with veal stock. That's a little heavy for people these days, and more and more of my customers request healthier dishes. So this is my updated velouté, thickened with a little potato. I use a small amount of butter, but you can substitute olive oil, and it's up to you whether you use chicken or vegetable stock.

The art is to wring every bit of flavor out of the cauliflower and to make the soup as velvety as possible by puréeing and straining it, so that all you're left with is pure, smooth taste. There's a smooth elegance to it that lives up to the comparisons to velvet. As we do at Freds, use this recipe as a template and substitute other vegetables for the cauliflower; the variations we make include carrot, zucchini, butternut squash, and potato. Just make sure that the vegetables and potatoes are cut to roughly the same size so that they cook evenly.

Serves 6 to 8

2 tablespoons extra-virgin olive oil

1 tablespoon unsalted butter
(can substitute olive oil)

2 medium white onions, cut
into large dice

1 clove garlic, chopped

2 teaspoons kosher salt

2 medium heads cauliflower,
cut into florets, stems cut into large dice

2 medium russet potatoes, peeled
and cut into large dice

1 cup white wine

2 quarts Vegetable Stock (page 28)
or Chicken Stock (page 24)

Drizzle of truffle oil for garnish
(optional)

Finely chopped fresh chives for
garnish (optional)

In an 8- to 10-quart stockpot, heat the oil and butter over medium heat. Add the onions, garlic, and salt and sauté for 2 minutes, until the onions are wilted but not browned. Add the cauliflower and potatoes, stir together, and then add the wine. Bring to a simmer and then add the stock. Bring just to a boil, then reduce the heat so that it's barely simmering. Cook uncovered for 1½ hours. The liquid should be reduced in volume by a third. Turn off the heat and let the pot sit for about 20 minutes to cool slightly.

Using a food processor, blender, or immersion blender, puree the soup until smooth. Pass through a mesh sieve to remove any remaining particles of fiber. Adjust the seasonings, if desired. If the soup is too thick for your liking, add a little stock to thin it. Conversely, if it's too thin, reduce it by simmering until it's reduced. Serve hot with a drizzle of truffle oil and a sprinkling of fresh chives, if desired.

LOBSTER BISQUE
WITH SAFFRON AIOLI

We steam and shell many, *many* lobsters every day at Freds because the Palace Warm Lobster Salad (page 48) and the Lobster Club Sandwich (page 96) are two very popular lunch items. With the mountain of lobster shells left over, it would be a shame if we didn't use them. So we make lobster stock, which we use for seafood stew, seafood risotto, and as a base for this incredibly flavorful lobster bisque. It's one of the most traditional, classical items on the menu, and it's especially popular with our European customers, who are surprised to find an authentic taste of home.

The process of making lobster stock is, *in theory*, similar to making chicken stock: You're wringing the flavor from the part of the animal you can't chew. In actuality, though, it's a bit more work and a whole lot messier, with an aroma that lingers around a lot longer. But there's nothing like it. I like to make it on the weekends when visiting friends at the beach to use in a traditional South of France–style bouillabaisse. I find the process relaxing and, besides, there's really no commercial product that will match the flavor of homemade (or *housemade*, as we say in restaurants) lobster stock. Making it at least once should be on the bucket list of every serious home chef.

The traditional garnish for lobster bisque is a large crouton, topped with some garlicky saffron aioli.

Serves 8 to 10

EQUIPMENT

Sharp butcher's knife or kitchen shears

Large, heavy cutting board
(too light and small and you risk it slipping)

Butcher's mallet

Kitchen towels

Oven mitts

Mesh or China cap strainer

Ladle

2 large mixing bowls

10- to 12-quart stockpot

Long-handled wooden spoon

LOBSTER STOCK

Makes 2 quarts

4 (1- to 1½-pound) lobsters (or culls)

¼ cup extra-virgin olive oil

2 carrots, cut into 1-inch dice

½ head of celery, cut into 1-inch slices

2 red onions, cut into 1-inch dice

1 leek, trimmed, well-washed, and cut into 1-inch slices

3 cloves garlic, smashed

1 cup cognac

1 cup white wine

1 cup canned crushed Italian tomatoes

7 quarts cold water

CONTINUES

BISQUE

Reserved tomalley and coral
from the lobsters

All-purpose flour*

1 tablespoon olive oil

4 large shallots, chopped into
½-inch pieces

1 clove garlic, peeled and smashed

1¼ teaspoons kosher salt

.25 gram saffron**

6 tablespoons cognac

2 quarts Lobster Stock

½ cup heavy cream

Freshly ground black pepper

Reserved lobster meat (roughly
1½ pounds), cut into chunks

8 to 10 diagonal ½-inch-thick
baguette slices, toasted
(see Homemade Croutons, page 15)

8 to 10 tablespoons Saffron Aioli
(opposite)

¼ cup minced fresh chives for garnish

*The amount of flour you need varies, because
no two lobsters contain the same amount of
tomalley and coral, but the ratio is equal
amounts tomalley/coral mixture and flour.

**Most saffron comes from Europe and is
sold in containers measured by the gram.

Make the stock: Cook the lobsters and extract the tail, body, and claw meat according to the instructions on page 48 (Palace Warm Lobster Salad). Use a spoon to remove the green tomalley and the reddish-black coral from the body by picking through the tail meat and pulling back the top shell of the lobster, including the head and antennae. Reserve the lobster meat separately from the tomalley and coral. Refrigerate until ready to use, up to 1 day.

Using a sharp butcher's knife or kitchen shears, cut the shells into 1- to 2-inch pieces. Place the pieces, a few at a time, on the cutting board and pound them with a butcher's mallet. (This can get messy, so keep kitchen towels close at hand. Also, I recommend wearing oven mitts when doing this, as some of the shells can be quite sharp when they're cut.)

Heat the olive oil in a large, heavy stockpot over medium heat. Add the lobster shell pieces and cook, stirring occasionally, until they begin to brown, 8 to 10 minutes. Add the carrots, celery, onions, leek, and garlic and reduce the heat to low. Cook, stirring occasionally to prevent burning or sticking, for 20 to 30 minutes, making sure to really soften the vegetables and cook the shells, which give the bisque its unique flavor. As the mixture is cooking, occasionally use the mallet to push down on the lobster shells in the pot. This will continue to pulverize them, which extracts the protein that will thicken the bisque. The longer you cook the shells the better, just make sure the flame is low so that the shells are roasting but not scorching.

Stand back and add the cognac, as it will flame. When the flame subsides, add the wine, tomatoes, and water. Turn up the heat to bring it just to a boil, then reduce the heat to low. Simmer for 3 hours, checking regularly to stir and press down on the lobster shells. The more you reduce the stock, the more the flavor will intensify. The stock is ready when the liquid is reduced to about half of the original amount. Turn off the heat and let it cool for 30 minutes.

Place the strainer over a large bowl. Use a ladle to move the soup, a ladleful at a time, to the strainer. Push down on the shells with the back of the ladle to make sure you press every bit of liquid out of them, then discard them. You should end up with roughly 2 quarts of lobster stock.

Make the bisque: To make the roux, place the reserved tomalley and coral in a mixing bowl and sprinkle with flour, a little at a time, mixing it all together until it forms a paste with the consistency of pancake batter.

Heat the olive oil in a large, heavy stockpot over medium heat. Add the shallots, garlic, and salt and cook, stirring, until the shallots are translucent, about 3 minutes. Add the saffron and stir with the wooden spoon to release the flavor and color.

Reduce the heat to low, add the roux, and continue to stir for 2 to 3 minutes. Stand back and add the cognac, as it will flame. Add the lobster stock, a little at a time so that the roux thins without lumps. Simmer slowly until the soup thickens to the consistency of heavy cream, then strain the soup through the strainer, pushing down a bit to make sure all the liquid makes it through.

Place the soup back into the pot and bring just to a boil. Reduce the heat to a gentle simmer and slowly add the cream. Simmer for 5 minutes, then adjust seasoning with salt and pepper, if necessary.

To serve, divide the lobster meat evenly among the serving bowls. For each bowl, spread a crouton with 1 tablespoon aioli. Ladle in the hot soup and place the crouton to float in the bowl. Garnish with minced chives and serve immediately.

SAFFRON AIOLI

Purists may object to the fact that I use commercial mayonnaise in this recipe, rather than making it from scratch. But there's such good commercial mayo on the market that I prefer to use it, rather than run the risk of using raw eggs. If you can, make this a day before you serve it, and store it in the fridge so that the flavors meld and the golden color of the saffron permeates. It's most convenient to make this in a food processor, but since it's such a small amount, if you don't have a small processor, you can make it the traditional way, by hand: Use a large knife to mash the garlic and salt together until it forms a paste, then whisk in the rest of the ingredients, in the order stated, and mix together well.

Makes 1 cup

2 small cloves garlic, peeled

1 teaspoon kosher salt

.25 gram saffron

2 tablespoons fresh lemon juice

1 cup good commercial mayonnaise

Pinch of cayenne pepper

Place the garlic and salt in a small food processor and blend together until they form a smooth paste. Add the saffron and lemon juice and pulse to mix. Add the mayonnaise and cayenne pepper and mix well. Cover and store in the fridge for up to 2 to 3 days.

WHITE BEAN SOUP

Even though it's made from the humble bean, this soup is as silky and soft as a cashmere sweater. The extra step of straining is what elevates it to something beautiful and elegant, even though it's made with everyday ingredients that you probably already have in your pantry. I've worked with both Frenchmen and Italians, and while they might not agree about much when it comes to food, the bean holds a place of honor in both culinary traditions as an ancient, nutritious, and sustaining food. Reconstituting dried beans doesn't take much effort—just a little planning ahead—and is well worth it, especially for a recipe like this where you want the flavor and creaminess of the beans to take center stage.

Serves 6 to 8

2 cups dried white beans (cannellini, navy, or Great Northern)

3 tablespoons extra-virgin olive oil

2 cloves garlic, minced

1 large onion, cut into small dice

1 carrot, cut into small dice

2 celery stalks, cut into small dice

2 teaspoons kosher salt

2 medium russet potatoes, peeled and cut into small dice

1 cup dry white wine

3 quarts Vegetable Stock (page 28) or Chicken Stock (page 24)

Leaves from 6 sprigs fresh marjoram, chopped

Minced fresh chives for garnish

Extra-virgin olive oil for garnish

Place the beans in a container large enough to hold twice the amount of water as the volume of beans. Cover the beans with water and soak for 24 to 48 hours. Drain.

In an 8- to 10-quart stockpot, heat the olive oil over medium heat. Add the garlic, onion, carrot, celery, and salt and cook, stirring regularly, until the onion is translucent, about 5 minutes. Add the drained beans and potatoes, stir everything together, and cook for 2 minutes. Add the wine, stock, and marjoram. Bring to a boil, then turn down the heat so that the soup is just simmering. Simmer gently, uncovered, for 1½ hours, stirring every 10 to 15 minutes to make sure it's not sticking on the bottom. Turn off the heat, cover the pot, and let the beans steep for about an hour.

Puree the soup using a blender, food processor, or immersion blender, then pass the soup through a mesh sieve or food mill to remove any pieces of fiber. Adjust the seasoning, if desired, and place the soup back in the pot and heat through. Serve hot, topped with minced chives and a drizzle of extra-virgin olive oil.

GRAIN AND LEGUME SOUP WITH KALE

This soup hits every trend button—kale, whole grains, turmeric, international flavors—but don't hold that against it. It's one of the newer recipes I created in answer to my customers' increasing interest in cutting out meat. The combination of legumes, grains, and vegetables in one dish means this soup can be considered a complete meal, and for many of our lunchtime regulars it often is.

The many observant Muslims who are part of my longtime staff at Freds inspired the combination of roasted spices in this dish. Every year during Ramadan, they bring foods from home, and then they—servers, bussers, food runners—all sit down at sundown for a quick meal to break the fast. Even though I'm Jewish, I look forward to the ritual myself, and I enjoy watching them savor the food. I love to eat it, too, when I'm offered. The slight hint of Bengali flavors in this dish is homage to them.

The white beans for this soup need to be soaked for at least 8 hours before cooking, but the yellow lentils and barley do not need to be soaked, although they need to be rinsed.

Serves 8 to 10

½ cup dried white beans (cannellini, navy, or Great Northern)

¼ cup extra-virgin olive oil

1 tablespoon ground turmeric

1½ teaspoons ground coriander

1 teaspoon ground cumin

1 teaspoon ground cardamom

2 cloves garlic, thinly sliced

1 onion, coarsely chopped

2 teaspoons kosher salt

1 teaspoon white pepper

2 bunches kale, washed, rough stems removed, leaves chopped

1 cup dry red wine

3 quarts Vegetable Stock (page 28) or Chicken Stock (page 24)

2 cups canned Italian crushed tomatoes

1 cup pearled barley, rinsed and drained

½ cup yellow lentils, rinsed and drained

¼ cup chopped fresh parsley

2 tablespoons chopped fresh sage

Parmigiano Reggiano cheese rind, about 2 by 2 inches (optional)

Extra-virgin olive oil for garnish

Minced scallions for garnish

Freshly grated Parmigiano Reggiano for garnish

Spring Mushroom
Soup (page 114)

Grain and Legume
Soup with Kale

Place the beans in a container large enough to hold twice the amount of water as the volume of beans. Cover the beans with water and soak for 24 to 48 hours. Drain.

In a large soup pot, heat the olive oil over medium heat. Add the spices and roast in the oil, stirring constantly, until they have darkened slightly, about 1 to 2 minutes. Take care not to burn them or they'll become very bitter. Add the garlic, onion, salt, and pepper and cook, stirring, for a few minutes, until the onion has wilted. Add the kale and wine and cook, stirring, until the kale wilts. Add the remaining ingredients (except the garnishes), stir together, and bring to a boil. Lower the heat until it's barely simmering and cook, uncovered, for about 1½ hours, until the beans are tender. Remove the cheese rind and adjust the seasoning, if necessary.

Serve garnished with a drizzle of olive oil, sprinkling of minced scallions, and grated Parmesan.

LENTIL AND VEGETABLE SOUP

This simple wintery soup is as warming and healthy as it gets. It's also light, with equal parts lentil, vegetable, and broth, so it's not thick and cloying. I think of it as chicken soup for vegetarians—something light yet sustaining that you can eat every day. It's easy to make, since it doesn't require anything to be done ahead of time: No 24-hour soaking here. In fact, lentils shouldn't be soaked. Soaking germinates beans and legumes, which is a good thing for beans, but actually makes lentils harder to digest.

At Freds, we use French green or black beluga lentils. Extremely important, though: Always pick through the lentils before you use them to make sure there are no small stones lurking in the mix, waiting to crack someone's tooth. This recipe makes quite a lot of soup, but that means you will probably be able to stash some in the freezer, which is never a bad thing.

Serves 8 to 10

2 sprigs fresh rosemary

6 leaves fresh sage

2 bay leaves

2 whole cloves

1 (3-inch) cinnamon stick

3 tablespoons extra-virgin olive oil; (plus more for optional garnish)

2 medium onions, minced

2 cloves garlic, thinly sliced

1 teaspoon kosher salt

½ teaspoon ground white pepper

2 russet potatoes, peeled and cut into ½-inch dice

2 carrots, cut into ½-inch dice

2 celery stalks, cut into ½-inch dice

2 large leeks, well-washed, and cut into ½-inch dice

1 turnip, peeled and cut into ½-inch dice

1 cup lentils, preferably French green or black beluga

2½ quarts Vegetable Stock (page 28) or Chicken Stock (page 24)

1 cup canned chopped Italian plum tomatoes

1 cup white wine

Make a bouquet garni by placing the herbs, cloves, and cinnamon stick in a square piece of cheesecloth. Tie the corners together (or tie with kitchen twine) so that it will stay closed during cooking.

Heat the oil in a large soup pot over medium heat. Add the onions, garlic, salt, and pepper and sauté until the onions are translucent, about 3 minutes. Add the potatoes, carrots, celery, leeks, and turnip and cook, stirring, until wilted, about 4 minutes. Next, add the lentils and cook, stirring, for 1 minute. Finally, add the bouquet garni, stock, tomatoes, and wine and bring to a boil. Reduce the heat to low and simmer, uncovered, for 1½ hours, until the lentils are soft, the vegetables are cooked through, and the soup has thickened. As the soup simmers, skim off any froth that comes to the surface. When the soup is cooked, remove and discard the bouquet garni. Season to taste with additional salt and pepper. Garnish with a drizzle of extra-virgin olive oil if desired and enjoy with some crusty artisan bread.

Double-Cut American Lamb Chops
alla Scottadito with Mint Port Wine
Sauce, Jewish-Style Artichokes, and
Lyonnaise Potatoes (page 165)

DINNER

CHAPTER 5

NEIGHBORHOOD STANDARDS AND ROOM SERVICE

Charred Octopus with Shishito Peppers
over Caponata / 141

Shrimp Oreganata with White Wine, Butter,
and Herbs, Served over Grain Salad / 144

Fried Zucchini / 147

Medley of Seasonal Vegetables / 148

Roasted Sea Bass with Avocado Salsa and
Family-Meal-Style Spanish Rice / 149

Whole Roasted Branzino Côte d'Azur with Pernod
and Saffron and Sautéed Spinach à la Française / 152

Sea Scallops, Scampi-Style, with Mashed Potatoes / 154

Tuna with Soy and Blood Orange Glaze
with Couscous / 156

Chicken Francese / 159

Balsamic Chicken / 162

Double-Cut American Lamb Chops alla Scottadito
with Mint–Port Wine Sauce, Jewish-Style Artichokes,
and Lyonnaise Potatoes / 165

Freds Madison lives a double life, and that duality is one of the unique things about it. By day, it's power lunches, table-hopping, and air kisses. But at night, all that gives way to an intimate restaurant where the large windows invite the darkness in to be dispelled by candlelight. At lunch, people from all over the world come to Barneys and to Freds, for shopping and business lunches. But at night it's mostly couples and families from the neighborhood, stopping in for dinner on the way home from work, or quietly celebrating an anniversary or birthday. Even when it's busy at dinner, there's a special tranquility about the room.

I love the way Freds' dinner business connects us to the neighborhood, especially for the longtime customers I adore. But it wasn't always that way. Freds served dinner from the day we opened, but it didn't take on a life of its own right away. Our dinner business had to be explored, cultivated, thought out, and nurtured, and there were challenges along the way. For one thing, lunch business boomed so quickly from day one that it was like jumping on a moving train, clinging for dear life. On most days, by the time 5:30 rolled around we were just catching our breath. And then there was the obstacle that while people are accustomed to the idea of eating lunch in a luxury fashion store, they don't automatically think of it as an option for dinner. Plus, when Freds made the move from the basement to the ninth floor we lost our separate entrance on 61st Street. It took people a few years to get used to the idea of entering through a closed store at night.

I was clear from the beginning what I wanted the lunch menu to look like: a comprehensive menu offering something for everyone, one that followed in the steps of the Brown Derby or Mortimer's, with salads and club sandwiches, but that also featured European classic dishes, with a little bit of my Italian stuff thrown in. The vision was so clear that the lunch menu hasn't changed substantially—with the exception of tweaking for seasonal items and food trends—since we opened.

I didn't, however, have a vision for a separate dinner menu, and for a long time didn't realize one was necessary. Dinner was basically lunch, just at a later hour of the day. But gradually I began to see the creative and business potential of nurturing a more substantial dinner business. From an entrepreneurial point of view, dinner was an underutilized resource. Lunch was at peak capacity; there are only a certain number of tables you can fill at 1 p.m. But dinner had development potential.

Still, it took me awhile to "find the character" at dinner, to figure out how to integrate people's expectations based on lunch with the different atmosphere at dinner. The dinner menu has settled into a bit of a hybrid: Freds Classics, our lunch staples (because people always ask for them at dinner anyway), and Chef's Selections, slightly more formal dishes, comfort foods, and seasonal specialties. Honestly, for many of our regular customers, the dinner menu functions more as a guideline, anyway, because they know that we're happy to do special orders. Nine times out of ten it will be a request for something very light, like grilled fish with steamed vegetables. It's part of the ethos at Freds that we are happy to do so; every single one of our employees knows that. It's one of the great things about having a large and fully stocked kitchen, and something, I think, that makes Freds' service exceptional.

Freds Room Service

Long before there was Seamless, UberEATS, or Postmates, there was Freds Room Service, our home delivery service from the Madison location. We deliver within the boundaries of the Upper East Side, and it's one of the ways Freds extends the boutique customer service Barneys is known for. We initially started by offering standard menu items, like many restaurants in New York City, but it's gone way beyond that now. Neighborhood customers tell me, "We don't need to cook! We just get delivery from Freds!" Freds Room Service basically functions as a neighborhood canteen, delivering everything from quarts of chicken broth, pints of salad dressing, containers of hearts of palm, to a few plain grilled shrimp, and pretty much anything edible a person could want, as long as we have it in house. Sometimes I'm really surprised by what people ask for, but if we have it in the kitchen, we'll deliver it. Some dishes were actually added to the Freds regular menu because they were requested so many times as a special order through Room Service. I don't know of any other restaurant in the world that does this kind of thing—I certainly wish I had a place like Freds to deliver in *my* neighborhood—and it's a function of the size of our kitchen that we can handle it.

CHARRED OCTOPUS
WITH SHISHITO PEPPERS OVER CAPONATA

The catalyst for the Pressman family inviting me to run Freds was the reputation of my own successful restaurant, Campagna, located downtown in the Flatiron District of New York City. Campagna was known for hearty Italian peasant food, and even though I planned for the Freds menu to have a classical European bent, a few of Campagna's dishes snuck into my briefcase and made the trip up Madison Avenue with me. One of those dishes was caponata, the wonderful, savory/sweet eggplant condiment from Sicily. Beyond its *Godfather* associations, Sicily is one of Italy's most culturally rich areas. Because of its proximity to North Africa, and the fact that this small island was occupied at various points by Greeks, Romans, Arabs, and Spaniards, among others, Sicily has food traditions you don't find elsewhere in Italy. The delicious, pungent flavor of caponata—umami before that was even a thing—in which the local crops of eggplant, tomatoes, and peppers are stewed to a delicious mess with raisins and vinegar, contains a lingering resonance of Sicily's exotic past.

It was somewhat recently that I had the urge to pair the caponata with octopus. Octopus is a polarizing food: Like anchovies, people either hate it or love it passionately. There's no middle ground. But if you're looking for wild, sustainable, low-calorie seafood with a mild flavor, look no further than octopus, because it ticks all those boxes. Even those who love it may be hesitant to cook it at home, however, for fear of it being tough, but it's actually not that difficult to make tender octopus. It simply needs to be boiled long enough. Once it's cooked, it's actually a very forgiving food and can be baked, charred, sautéed, and even frozen to enjoy later.

We serve the caponata at room temperature and the rest of the dish blazing hot; the heady contrasts of flavors and temperatures have made this an instant Freds classic. If you can't find shishitos, substitute Padrón peppers. Although we usually serve this as an appetizer, you can serve it as a main course, which is especially nice with the addition of a side of Couscous (recipe on page 156).

Serves 4 as an appetizer

2 tablespoons extra-virgin olive oil

1 clove garlic, thinly sliced

8 shishito peppers

1 pound cooked octopus, or 1 (4-pound) raw/frozen octopus, cooked (see About Octopus, page 142)

3 tablespoons chopped fresh Italian parsley

½ lemon, cut into ½-inch wheels

3 sprigs fresh thyme

1 teaspoon crushed red pepper

Kosher salt

Caponata (page 143)

CONTINUES

Place the olive oil in a large frying pan. Add the garlic and sauté until it's lightly browned. Add the peppers and cook until they are slightly seared, about 2 minutes on each side. Add the octopus, parsley, lemon, thyme, red pepper, and a sprinkling of salt to taste and sauté, stirring only occasionally so they brown, for about 5 minutes, until the octopus and peppers are nicely charred.

Place a generous scoop of the caponata on a serving plate at the 12 o'clock position and cascade the octopus and peppers coming down toward the 6 o'clock position.

—

ABOUT OCTOPUS

On the East coast, many fishmongers sell tender aleady-cooked octopus. If you can find it, use it. Most of the octopus coming into this country is frozen, so you may also find frozen whole octopus. A 4-pound octopus is the most common size; it will shrink when cooking, and with trimming, to yield around 1 pound. It's actually easy to cook, and the good news is it's almost indestructible. You don't really need to thaw it before throwing it into boiling unsalted water. If you don't use it all after you cook it, it can be frozen to enjoy at a later date.

To cook octopus, bring a large pot of unsalted water to a boil. Add the octopus and boil for 45 minutes, or until tender when pierced with a knife. Carefully lift it out of the pot and drain it. While it's still hot, remove the eye and cut the tentacles and body into the size pieces you desire.

CAPONATA

Makes 4 cups, serving 4 to 6

2 medium eggplants, unpeeled,
cut into ½-inch dice

Kosher salt

1 cup all-purpose flour for dredging

4 cups vegetable or peanut oil for frying

¼ cup extra-virgin olive oil

1 medium onion, cut into ¼-inch dice

1 clove garlic, thinly sliced

4 celery stalks, cut into ¼-inch-thick slices

1 red bell pepper, cored, seeded,
and cut into 1-inch pieces

1 yellow bell pepper, cored, seeded,
and cut into 1-inch pieces

1 (16-ounce) can crushed Italian plum
tomatoes, or 6 fresh ripe plum tomatoes, diced

¼ cup red wine vinegar

½ cup golden raisins

½ cup pitted green olives, chopped

1 tablespoon capers, rinsed of
vinegar or salt

2 teaspoons sugar

Freshly ground black pepper

Place the eggplant cubes in a colander and sprinkle with 2 teaspoons salt. Place the colander in a larger bowl or on a tray to catch the juices, cover with a towel, and refrigerate for 2 to 24 hours. After the eggplant cubes have drained, do not rinse them, but pat dry with paper towels.

Place the flour in a shallow bowl. Line a baking sheet with paper towels.

In a deep, heavy skillet, heat the vegetable oil over medium-high heat until hot but not smoking. Working in batches to avoid crowding the pan, roll the eggplant pieces in flour, shake off any excess, and add to the hot oil. Fry, turning once, until golden brown. Transfer with a slotted spoon to drain on the paper towels.

Preheat the oven to 325°F.

In a large Dutch oven with a lid, heat the olive oil over medium heat. Add the onion, garlic, celery, and bell peppers and cook, stirring, until the onion is translucent, about 5 minutes. Add the tomatoes, reduce the heat to a simmer, and cook, uncovered, for 15 minutes. Stir in the cooked eggplant, vinegar, raisins, olives, capers, sugar, and salt and black pepper to taste, and mix well. Cover, transfer to the oven, and bake for 10 minutes. Taste for sugar, vinegar, salt, and pepper, and adjust those as desired. Cool and serve at room temperature.

SHRIMP OREGANATA

WITH WHITE WINE, BUTTER, AND HERBS, SERVED OVER GRAIN SALAD

If you're Italian American, you call this delicious coating of breadcrumbs *oreganata*. If you're in Italy, you'll call it *spiedino*. That's all semantics, because it's equally delicious whether you're eating it in New York City's Little Italy, or Italy's Ancona on the Adriatic, which is where I first enjoyed the Italian version. Or at Freds, for that matter, where we've been dishing it up since we first opened. Sometimes we substitute calamari for the shrimp, which is equally delicious.

Serves 2 as a main course, 4 as an appetizer

2 lemons: 1 juiced, 1 sliced into ¼-inch-thick wheels

½ cup breadcrumbs

2 tablespoons chopped fresh Italian parsley

1 tablespoon dried oregano, preferably Sicilian

2 cloves garlic, minced

2 tablespoons extra-virgin olive oil, plus more for drizzling

1¼ tablespoons kosher salt

½ cup white wine

12 jumbo shrimp (ask your fishmonger for Mexican or Ecuadorian white shrimp, U-12 size)

2 tablespoons unsalted butter

1 teaspoon chopped fresh chives

¼ teaspoon white pepper

Grain Salad (opposite)

Preheat the oven to 425°F. Grease a small flame-proof Dutch oven or casserole dish.

In a large mixing bowl, combine the lemon juice, breadcrumbs, parsley, oregano, garlic, olive oil, and 1 tablespoon salt. Mix together until the breadcrumbs are well moistened. Place the wine in a small bowl, and dip the shrimp into the wine to moisten them before placing them in the breadcrumb mixture. Press the shrimp into the breadcrumbs so they are well coated on all sides. Set the wine aside to use in the sauce.

Lay the lemon wheels on the bottom of the greased Dutch oven. Place the breaded shrimp on top of the lemon slices. Bake until the shrimp are cooked through and the breading is golden brown. Transfer the Dutch oven to a stovetop burner to make the sauce. Carefully pour the wine into the bottom of the pan, being careful not to pour it directly over the shrimp so they stay crisp on top. Add the butter, chives, remaining ¼ teaspoon salt, and pepper, and simmer over medium heat until the sauce is reduced and slightly thickened.

To serve, place a mound of the grain salad on each serving plate. Arrange the shrimp over the grains, and drizzle sauce from the pan over them. Finish with a drizzle of good olive oil.

GRAIN SALAD

The grains and lentils should be cooked and cooled before assembling the salad.

Serves 4–6

DRESSING

3 tablespoons extra-virgin olive oil

1 tablespoon red wine vinegar

Kosher salt

Freshly ground black pepper

1 teaspoon hot red pepper flakes (optional, or to taste)

SALAD

1 cup cooked pearl barley, cooled

1 cup cooked wheat berries, cooled (can substitute 1 additional cup cooked pearl barley)

1 cup cooked couscous, cooled

1 cup cooked lentils, cooled

1 cup diced tomato

½ red bell pepper, cored, seeded, and diced

½ yellow bell pepper, cored, seeded, and diced

¼ cup chopped fresh Italian parsley

1 scallion, thinly sliced

Make the dressing by whisking together ingredients in a small bowl and set aside.

Combine all the salad ingredients in a large mixing bowl and mix together well. Add the dressing and mix again. Adjust seasoning as needed.

FRIED ZUCCHINI

This dish is near and dear to my heart because it's the one that got my youngest son, Dan, to finally eat vegetables. He won't mind me telling the story now, because he's grown up to be a vegetarian, but when he was a kid, despite the fact that he had a whole "son of a chef" comedy routine, Dan ate about five foods: chicken fingers, French fries, pizza, pasta, and ketchup (he completely agreed with Ronald Reagan that it was a vegetable). It was cute for a little while, then it was annoying, but at a certain point it became concerning.

I was testing this recipe for Fried Zucchini one day when he was at the restaurant and I asked him to try it. I mean, it's fried, how bad can it be? He shook his head no and started going into his "son of a chef" schtick. I stopped him, and said, "Well, you might be the *son* of a chef, but I *am* the chef. No French fries until you try this," and handed him a piece of fried zucchini. Of course he loved it, but tried to blunt my satisfaction by pointing out that it was fried. I countered that it was green, and we agreed to a truce. But from that day on he was less afraid of vegetables. Whether it's the starter for a lifetime of eating veg, or a starter for dinner, this lightly coated zucchini is a very enjoyable little indulgence. If you make it, it's very important to shake off any excess flour before putting the zucchini into the oil, to keep the oil clean of particles that will burn and affect the flavor.

Serves 4 as an appetizer

1 cup whole milk

Kosher salt

2 medium zucchini

6 cups peanut oil for frying

1 cup all-purpose flour for dredging

Pour the milk into a large mixing bowl, add a sprinkling of salt, and mix together. Use a Japanese slicer or a mandoline to carefully slice the zucchini into very thin, but not transparent, discs. Place the discs in the milk to soak.

Pour the peanut oil into a large stockpot to fill the pot no more than halfway (so make sure to choose a pot that's big enough). This is important because you don't want oil to spill over when the zucchini is added. Heat the oil over medium heat until hot. (If you have a candy thermometer to place in the oil, the optimum temperature for frying is 350°F.) While the oil is heating, place several layers of paper towels on a baking sheet or flat surface, and set it aside by the stove.

Use a slotted spoon to remove the zucchini from the milk and let excess liquid drain off before you place the zucchini in the flour. (If the slices are too wet they'll turn the flour to batter instead of being thinly dusted with it.) In batches of 8 to 10 pieces, shake off any excess flour and fry the zucchini until golden brown on each side. Use a spider skimmer to move them around as they fry and then to transfer to the paper towels to drain. Sprinkle with salt and serve immediately.

MEDLEY OF SEASONAL VEGETABLES

This flavorful mix of perfectly cooked vegetables, a very popular order for Room Service and in the restaurant, could be the poster child for the beauty and elegance of simplicity in cooking—and of the importance of getting every element just right. If there's one dish that epitomizes the reason many of my regular customers come here several times a week, rather than saving Freds for special occasions, this would be it. You really could eat this every day and be satisfied and healthy. Its simplicity makes it seem more like home cooking than restaurant food, which is generally more caloric than what you'd make at home, and it's not going to win any awards for culinary originality. But my customers have shown me that there's more to hospitality than dazzling your guests with your creativity. There's a place in hospitality for well-done simplicity, too. We use pretty much the same mix of vegetables year-round, except in the summer when we add sugar snap and English peas. I like to serve this with simply cooked fish or with Chicken Francese (page 159) or Chicken Parmesan (page 174).

Key to this dish is blanching the vegetables that need a bit longer to cook, and then sautéing them with the ones that cook more quickly. For appearance and uniformity of cooking time, try to cut all the vegetables to roughly the same size. The tablespoon of butter at the end is a restaurant finishing touch that can easily be omitted if you prefer.

Serves 4 to 6 as a side dish

¼ medium head cauliflower, cut into florets

1 small head broccoli, trimmed and cut into florets

1 medium carrot, trimmed, peeled, and cut into ½-inch-thick discs

¼ pound string beans, ends snipped, cut into 1-inch pieces

2 tablespoons extra-virgin olive oil or clarified butter

1 clove garlic, peeled and smashed

1 red bell pepper, cored, seeded, and cut into 1-inch pieces

1 yellow bell pepper, cored, seeded, and cut into 1-inch pieces

1 small zucchini, trimmed, cut in half lengthwise, and cut into ½-inch-thick half-moons

1 small summer squash, trimmed, cut in half lengthwise, and cut into ½-inch-thick half-moons

2 tablespoons white wine or water

Kosher salt

1 tablespoon unsalted butter (optional)

Blanch the cauliflower, broccoli, carrot, and string beans according to the instructions on page 17, and set aside.

Heat the olive oil and garlic in a nonstick skillet over medium heat until the garlic starts to brown. Add the bell peppers, zucchini, and summer squash and cook, stirring occasionally, for 2 minutes, lowering the heat if necessary so they don't burn. Add the blanched vegetables, wine, and salt, and cook, stirring regularly, for about 5 minutes, until the raw vegetables are wilted. Add the tablespoon of butter if desired, mix well, and serve immediately.

ROASTED SEA BASS
WITH AVOCADO SALSA AND
FAMILY-MEAL-STYLE SPANISH RICE

In New York City, we're in close proximity to the waters off Long Island, which yield some wonderful fish and seafood. The sea bass—either wild striped bass or black sea bass—from this region truly is the king fish of the Northeast. When it's available it's almost always our Fish of the Day, in some kind of seasonal preparation. Most popular of all the preparations is this one, though, because people just can't get enough of the avocado salsa. In fact, avocado is by far my most requested ingredient these days.

It helps that my guys in the kitchen have such a deft way of handling them. Many of my cooks are of Latin backgrounds, and their cooking has become a delicious new influence in recent years, as I have started incorporating some of the dishes they make for family meal for the staff onto the Freds menu.

The Spanish Rice recipe, however, has actually never been on the menu. It's a little kitchen secret, the only recipe in this book that's not on our menu. Its inclusion is homage to my hardworking cooks, and to the ritual of family meal that's served twice a day, every single day we're open. We have three different Latin communities in the kitchen, and they each have their own preferred rice preparation. Of the three, this is my favorite, but only the cooks will know whose it is.

Serves 2

SPANISH RICE

2 tablespoons olive oil or butter, plus more for the ramekins

½ onion, minced

2 cloves garlic, mashed

.25 gram saffron

1 cup long-grain white rice

1 cup cooked black beans (optional but preferred)

1 cup canned crushed tomatoes

1 cup cooked green peas

2 tablespoons minced red bell pepper

1 bay leaf

½ teaspoon kosher salt

Pinch cayenne pepper

2 cups water

AVOCADO SALSA

1 ripe Mexican avocado

Juice of 1 lime

½ tablespoon olive oil

1 ripe plum tomato, cored, seeded, and cut into small dice

2 tablespoons chopped scallions

8 fresh basil leaves, finely shredded

CONTINUES

1 teaspoon finely chopped jalapeño (optional)

½ teaspoon sea salt

FISH

2 (6- to 8-ounce) trimmed skin-on sea bass filets

½ teaspoon sea salt

Freshly ground black pepper

2 tablespoons extra-virgin olive oil

½ lemon, sliced

2 sprigs fresh rosemary

Preheat the oven to 350°F.

Make the rice: Heat the olive oil in a heavy, flameproof casserole dish over medium-high heat. Add the onion and garlic and sauté until the onion is translucent. Add the saffron and mix it through. Add the rice, stir well, then add the remaining rice ingredients and mix again. Transfer to the oven and bake for about 16 minutes, until the rice is tender. Remove and discard the bay leaf before serving. Make the avocado salsa and prep the fish ingredients while the rice is cooking.

Make the salsa: Cut the avocado in half, remove the pit, and cut into very small dice. Place in a medium bowl, sprinkle with the lime juice, and add the remaining salsa ingredients. Gently mix everything together, then set aside in the fridge while you cook the fish.

Cook the fish: After the rice is cooked, switch the oven to high/broiler setting. Place the fish in a roasting pan, season the tops with salt and pepper, and drizzle with the olive oil. Top each filet with a slice of lemon, then place a rosemary sprig on top. Place on the oven's middle rack and cook until the fish is browned, cooked through, but flaky in the center, about 6 to 8 minutes.

Rub oil on the inside of two 4-ounce ramekins and stuff each with as much hot rice as possible, pressing down with a spoon to make sure it's really full. For each serving, turn a ramekin over at the 11 o'clock on the serving plate. Place the fish at the 6 o'clock position, spoon avocado salsa over the top of the fish, and serve.

—

WHOLE ROASTED BRANZINO CÔTE D'AZUR

WITH PERNOD AND SAFFRON AND SAUTÉED SPINACH À LA FRANÇAISE

If the South of France had an official taste, it might be the combination of saffron and Pernod mingling with butter in a silky sauce. A whiff of that instantly transports me to the Côte d'Azur, which is a beautiful place to be transported to, whether in real life or in the imagination, and I think my customers agree.

Using sustainable fish is a top priority for Freds. Chefs today need to be stewards of the land and the sea—as do home cooks. I recommend following the Monterey Bay Aquarium Seafood Watch, an organization that constantly tracks the sustainability of fish and seafood. Besides the website (seafoodwatch.org), they have an app, so you can actually check their information while standing right at the fish counter. When in doubt, ask your fishmonger about the origin of any fish you purchase. Our grandchildren will thank us for it—or if they don't exactly thank us, at least there might still be fish for them to eat.

Branzino, also known as *loup de mer*, is one of the fishes that is generally given a green light from Seafood Watch. If you can't find branzino, feel free to substitute another fish, such as salmon or sea bass.

Whole roasted fish fileted tableside is a European coastal tradition, and this presentation approximates that. If you want to cook whole fish at home, you can ask your fishmonger to remove the head and bones for you.

Serves 2

BRANZINO

2 (1- to 1½-pound) whole branzino, tails on, heads removed, deboned, and butterflied

Kosher salt

Freshly ground black pepper

2 tablespoons olive oil

SAUCE

2 tablespoons unsalted butter

1 clove garlic, minced

.25 gram saffron

½ cup minced fennel bulb

2 tablespoons minced shallots

¼ cup Pernod or Ricard

Juice of ½ orange

SPINACH

2 tablespoons clarified butter (see page 14) or unsalted butter

1 large shallot, minced

1 pound triple-washed curly spinach (*not baby spinach*)*

Kosher salt

*Do not use baby spinach for this recipe because it will become slimy.

Preheat the oven to 450°F.

Cook the branzino: Sprinkle the fish generously with salt and pepper. Place the olive oil in an ovenproof 14-inch frying pan and heat over medium-high heat until it just starts to smoke. Lay the fish in the pan skin side down. Adjust the heat, if necessary, so that the fish is sizzling but not burning. When browned lightly, about 2 minutes, use a spatula to turn the fish over. Place the pan in the oven and bake for about 5 to 7 minutes, until the fish is cooked through.

While the fish is in the oven, make the spinach.

Make the spinach: In a 5- to 8-quart round double-handled casserole pot, melt the butter and add the shallot. Using a wooden spoon, mix for 30 seconds, then add the spinach, sprinkle with salt, and cover. Cook for 1 to 2 minutes, until the spinach is wilted.

Make the sauce: Use a spatula to remove the cooked fish from the pan, and set them aside while you make the sauce. Use paper towels to carefully wipe the oil from the pan then place it over medium heat. Add the butter, garlic, and saffron and stir together until the butter melts. Add the remaining sauce ingredients and simmer gently for about 2 minutes, while the alcohol cooks out of the Pernod. Gently lay the fish in the pan and simmer together for 2 minutes longer, ladling sauce over the fish as it simmers. Transfer the fish to serving plates, and drizzle with remaining sauce.

To serve, place a mound of spinach at the 12 o'clock position on each plate. Lay the fish diagonally on the plate with the head at 6 o'clock and the tail resting on the hill of spinach.

———

SEA SCALLOPS, SCAMPI-STYLE,
WITH MASHED POTATOES

Working day to day in the business corridors of New York, it's easy to forget that it's a coastal city and port. But where I grew up in Queens, awareness of water was more constant, especially in summer when we spent a lot of time at the beach, always looking forward to a seafood dinner at the end of the long, hot day. Back then, it was de rigueur for a good seafood restaurant to have a cheesy nautical theme. My mother liked to splurge on lobster, and shrimp scampi was my standing order; my Dad, though, loved scallops. The cheesy nautical décor might be a thing of the past, but some of the great recipes are still with us, and scampi is one of them. When I worked in the Hamptons, on the East End of Long Island, I was inspired to cook the excellent local scallops scampi-style, and then added my own comfort food twist by serving them with mashed potatoes so all that delicious sauce didn't go to waste.

Prepare the mashed potatoes and keep them warm before starting the scallops. If you cover the potatoes they should stay warm for 20 to 30 minutes, much longer than it will take to cook the scallops. If needed, reheat them over low heat while you're cooking the scallops.

Serves 2

16 large sea scallops

Kosher salt

Freshly ground black pepper

½ cup all-purpose flour for dredging

1 whole clove garlic, peeled and smashed

2 tablespoons clarified butter (see page 14)

2 tablespoons unsalted butter

2 cloves garlic, minced

1 cup dry white wine

2 tablespoons chopped fresh parsley

2 tablespoons chopped fresh chives

Mashed Potatoes (opposite)

Sprinkle the scallops with salt and pepper. Place the flour in a shallow bowl and, working in batches, dredge the scallops, shaking off any excess flour. Add more flour if needed to dredge them all.

In a large skillet over medium-high heat, heat the smashed garlic clove and clarified butter. When the butter is hot, add about half the dredged scallops and sauté them, turning once, until golden brown on both sides, about 4 to 6 minutes total. As they cook, remove and set aside on a plate, and add more scallops until they're all cooked. Turn off the burner and use paper towels to wipe any remaining butter and garlic cloves from the pan.

To the same pan, add the unsalted butter and minced garlic and sauté over medium-high heat for 1 minute. Briefly remove the pan from the burner, and tilt it away from you as you pour in the wine. Place the pan back on the heat and simmer for 1 to 2 minutes. Return the scallops to the pan, add the parsley and chives, and mix together until the scallops are covered in sauce. Make sure the mashed potatoes are warm before plating the scallops.

Place a dollop of mashed potatoes in the center of each serving plate. Divide the scallops between the two plates, and place them in a ring around the potatoes. Drizzle with remaining sauce and serve.

MASHED POTATOES

Serves 4

2 pounds Yukon Gold potatoes

1 teaspoon kosher salt
(or more as needed)

1 cup milk

2 tablespoons unsalted butter

½ cup freshly grated Parmigiano
Reggiano cheese

Fill a large stainless-steel mixing bowl with ice water and set it by your cutting board. Peel and quarter the potatoes and place them in the ice water as you work so they don't discolor.

Fill a large pot with water and add the salt. Remove the potatoes from their ice bath, drain, and place them in the pot. Boil until they are soft, then drain off the cooking water, leaving the potatoes in the pot. While they're still very hot, use a potato masher to mash them well, so there are no lumps.

In a small saucepan, heat the milk and butter until the butter is melted. Add to the warm potatoes, warm and mix together, then add the Parmesan. Stir together over low heat until the cheese melts. Taste and add more salt as needed.

——

TUNA WITH SOY
AND BLOOD ORANGE GLAZE
WITH COUSCOUS

Tuna is probably the most popular species of wild fish on restaurant menus today. It's the prize catch for deep-sea fishermen and a high-yield fish in both price and ratio of meat to bone. Tuna's popularity has landed some varieties on the endangered list as compiled by Monterey Bay Aquarium Seafood Watch. Our tuna purveyor checks this list (at seafoodwatch .org) every day before deciding what variety and from which waters to purchase.

I prefer my tuna seared on the outside and rare—raw,* really—on the inside, but obviously you should cook it to your preference. This preparation is one of Freds' oldest dinner recipes, and even when it's not on the menu people ask if we can make it for them. As long as we have the ingredients on hand the answer is always yes.

Couscous varies, and these instructions are for the standard kind you would buy in bulk. If you purchase a boxed brand, please follow their instructions for cooking it. Make sure to follow the exact measurements for the liquid and couscous so it will come out fluffy, not clumpy.

If desired, serve this with Sautéed Spinach (page 87).

Serves 2

COUSCOUS

1 cup couscous

1½ cups water, Vegetable Stock (page 28), or Chicken Stock (page 24)

2 tablespoons finely minced red bell pepper

2 tablespoons finely minced yellow bell pepper

1 tablespoon finely minced fresh chives

½ tablespoon finely chopped fresh parsley

Kosher salt

Knob of butter (for reheating)

TUNA AND GLAZE

1 tablespoon olive oil or clarified butter

2 (6- to 8-ounce) sushi-grade tuna steaks**

Kosher salt

Freshly ground black pepper

1 teaspoon sesame oil

1 tablespoon minced scallion

½ teaspoon minced fresh ginger

¼ cup fresh blood orange juice

2 tablespoons white wine

1 teaspoon soy sauce

Eating undercooked fish may be hazardous to your health. Please refer to your local health department for guidelines.

**If you like tuna cooked rare, order thick slices that cook more slowly.*

CONTINUES

Make the couscous: Spread the couscous evenly on the bottom of a baking dish with a lid. Place the water or stock in a saucepan and bring it to a rapid boil. Once it's boiling, pour it evenly over the couscous. Cover the baking dish and let the couscous steep for 10 minutes. Remove the cover and use a fork to fluff up the grains. Add the bell peppers, chives, parsley, and salt and mix through. Set the couscous aside while you cook the tuna.

Cook the tuna: Heat the olive oil in a large skillet until it starts to smoke. Season the tuna with salt and pepper and carefully place the filets in the hot pan. Place them in the pan away from you, not toward, in case the oil splatters. Sear the tuna for 2 minutes, then turn over and sear for 2 minutes on the other side. The amount of time you sear it will depend on the thickness of the tuna, and the degree to which you like it cooked. If you want to check, use a paring knife to cut the meat a little so you can see internal color of the meat. If it's too raw for you, continue sautéing, turning it regularly so it doesn't burn. When the tuna is done to your liking, remove it from the pan and set aside while you make the glaze.

While you make the glaze, heat the couscous with the knob of butter in a nonstick pan over low heat so that it will be warm when the fish is done.

Make the glaze: Use a paper towel to wipe out the oil residue from the tuna pan, and place the pan back on the burner over medium-high heat. Add the sesame oil, scallion, and ginger and stir together. As they start to sizzle, add the orange juice, wine, and soy sauce. Simmer on low heat for several minutes, until the sauce has reduced by half. Place the tuna back in the pan and turn it so that it's all covered in the glaze.

Spoon a bed of warm couscous onto each plate, place a filet on top, and serve immediately.

———

CHICKEN FRANCESE

One of my favorite sayings, the one my kids and my staff know so well they usually cut me off mid-sentence, is "A classic is a classic, and if you don't like it you just never had a good one." A genuine classic transcends food trends, even if it was once a trend, and stands the test of time from one generation to the next. It can be a simple dish, and often is, and doesn't need to utilize gourmet ingredients like caviar or truffles to make it special. By any measure, Chicken Francese, egg-battered chicken in a tart, buttery, lemony sauce, is a classic. Like Veal Marsala, it's graced many an Italian-American menu, but finding a really great rendition isn't that easy.

The chicken reheats well, and even tastes good cold, or in a sandwich. It's tasty, nostalgic, and delicious no matter how it's served. We serve it with Sautéed Spinach (page 87), or our Medley of Seasonal Vegetables (page 148) and Mashed Potatoes (155) to soak up all the rich sauce.

Serves 4

CHICKEN

4 skinless, boneless chicken breasts (about 1½ pounds)

Kosher salt

Freshly ground black pepper

½ cup white wine

Juice of 2 lemons

1 cup all-purpose flour

4 large eggs, whisked

1 cup freshly grated Parmigiano Reggiano cheese

2 tablespoons finely chopped fresh parsley

1 cup peanut oil (or clarified butter or other frying oil)

SAUCE

½ cup white wine

2 tablespoons fresh lemon juice, or more to taste

½ cup Chicken Stock (page 24)

2 tablespoons unsalted butter

1 tablespoon freshly grated Parmigiano Reggiano cheese

1 tablespoon finely chopped fresh parsley

CONTINUES

Preheat the oven to 350°F.

Prep the chicken: Butterfly the breasts by slicing through the middle horizontally, but not all the way through, and splaying the two sides open so it resembles two wings of a butterfly. Sprinkle each piece generously with salt and pepper.

In a large bowl, combine the wine and lemon juice. Add the chicken breasts and turn to coat them with the marinade. Set aside while you prepare the dredge.

On a plate or other shallow vessel, combine the flour, ½ teaspoon salt, and ½ teaspoon pepper. In a mixing bowl, mix together the eggs, Parmesan, parsley, ½ teaspoon salt, and ½ teaspoon pepper. Set aside an additional plate on which to place the chicken once it's dredged, as well as a baking sheet to bake the chicken once it's browned.

Cook the chicken: One at a time, dredge the breasts in the seasoned flour, shaking off any excess.

In a skillet large enough to hold the breasts without crowding (or cook in batches if needed), heat the peanut oil over high heat until shimmering and very hot. Dip the dredged breasts in the egg mixture so that they're evenly coated. Carefully place them in the hot oil and cook until golden brown on one side, 2 to 3 minutes. Turn over and brown the other side, 2 to 3 minutes. Transfer the chicken to the baking sheet, blotting off any oil as it drips off. Transfer to the oven and bake until cooked through, 8 to 10 minutes.

Prepare the sauce: While the chicken is in the oven, pour out any remaining cooking oil and wipe the skillet clean with a paper towel. Place it over medium heat, add the wine and lemon juice, and simmer until the liquid is reduced by half. Add the stock and cook, swirling the pan, until it's once again reduced by half. Swirl in the butter until melted, taste, and add more lemon juice or salt if desired. Add the cooked chicken breasts, sprinkle them with the Parmesan cheese and parsley, and baste them with the sauce, making sure the cheese and parsley are mixed through. Serve with mashed potatoes and your choice of vegetables.

— — —

BALSAMIC CHICKEN

One of the most rewarding parts of my job is the relationships I have with my customers. My regulars are not shy about voicing their tastes and preferences, which I happen to enjoy. When I started telling people that I was writing a Freds cookbook, the suggestions started flying in for recipes they thought should be included. This particular recipe was suggested by many customers, and by lots of the staff, too.

Balsamic Chicken came out of a hunch I had one day at my restaurant Campagna. In Switzerland, I had learned the two-day method for making coq au vin. One night it occurred to me that the same basic theory could be used for braising chicken with balsamic vinegar instead of red wine. The result is a dark, almost black dish that has the deep, rich flavor of the grape "must." When you slice into it, the white flesh of the chicken makes a startling contrast to the dark exterior.

Because it uses balsamic vinegar, not wine, it shouldn't marinate as long as coq au vin. Marinate for 2 to 4 hours only, and certainly not overnight; much longer than 4 hours and the vinegar will start to destroy the meat and the vinegary flavor will be too strong.

This dish needs to be baked at a low heat, preferably 325°F. If the oven temperature rises above 350°F, the natural sugar in the balsamic will start to caramelize and eventually burn. It also requires a little bit of attention and intuition on your part. After 30 minutes of cooking, check and make sure the balsamic isn't completely evaporated or thickened too much. If it has, add some chicken stock or water to the bottom of the pan. Even though the total cooking time is about 1½ hours, you should check it every 15 minutes after the initial 30 minutes. Add stock or water as needed until the chicken is cooked through and tender. This is especially good served with Mashed Potatoes (page 155), and seasonal vegetables (such as sugar snap peas, pictured) and is a perfect recipe to double and freeze for a night when you want a hearty dinner but don't have the time to cook.

Serves 2 to 3

2 cups inexpensive balsamic vinegar, plus more if needed

¼ cup extra-virgin olive oil

1 clove garlic, thinly sliced

Kosher salt

Freshly ground black pepper

1 (3-pound) chicken, preferably all-natural or organic, cut into quarters

1 cup Chicken Stock (page 24) or water

Mix together the vinegar, olive oil, garlic, salt, and pepper. Place the chicken in a large bowl and pour in the mixture, working it through so all the chicken is completely covered with marinade. Cover and marinate in the refrigerator for 2 to 4 hours.

Preheat the oven to 325°F.

Place the chicken in a 10-quart covered casserole dish and pour any marinade left in the bowl over the chicken. Cover the pot and bake for 30 minutes, then check to make sure all the liquid hasn't evaporated. If it has, or is becoming quite thick, pour a little of the stock or water into the bottom of the pot. Do not add more balsamic vinegar. Continue cooking, but check every 15 minutes for the rest of the cooking time, adding stock or water as needed to keep the bottom of the pot moist. Total cooking time should be about 1½ hours, until the chicken is cooked through. Remove the chicken from the pan; the sauce in the pan should be very thick, almost molasses-like, but if it's a bit thin place the pan on the stovetop and simmer until it thickens.

DOUBLE-CUT AMERICAN LAMB CHOPS ALLA SCOTTADITO

WITH MINT-PORT WINE SAUCE, JEWISH-STYLE ARTICHOKES, AND LYONNAISE POTATOES

I borrowed a page out of Glenn Bernbaum's society restaurant Mortimer's when I put double-cut lamb chops on the menu at Freds. He knew that cutting and chewing something unwieldy in public is one of the most unflattering things a socially conscious person can do, so he made sure food portions were always manageable: small burgers (long before sliders) that you could eat delicately, for example. And rather than serve rack of lamb, he served single lamb chops, and even Emily Post wouldn't object if you picked one up with your fingers.

I like lamb chops because they're kind of a retro, American fancy-dinner item. When you buy them, ask your butcher to *French* a rack of lamb for you (that's when the meat is scraped off the bones, which is how you'll pick them up to eat them), and cut it into double individual chops. Double chops are thicker than single chops, which means they'll cook more slowly and give you more of a margin for error so you don't overcook them.

Serves 2

2 tablespoons olive oil

½ rack of lamb split, chine removed, Frenched, cut into 4 double chops

1 tablespoon kosher salt

1 tablespoon coarsely ground black pepper

½ cup demi-glace (page 31 or store-bought)

2 tablespoons port wine

1 tablespoon chopped fresh mint

Jewish-Style Artichokes (page 166)

Lyonnaise Potatoes (page 167)

Note: Lamb chops cook quickly, so the artichokes and potatoes should be prepared just before you cook the lamb. To time the various elements in this dish so that they are ready to serve together, follow this sequence:

Bake the potatoes according to the recipe, and when they are cooked, remove from the oven and set aside to cool. Don't turn off the oven so it will remain hot to cook the lamb chops.

While the potatoes are cooling, make the Jewish-Style Artichokes according to the recipe. When the artichokes are cooked, set them aside in a warm place.

Sauté the potatoes and when they are a few minutes away from being done, place them in the oven while you cook the lamb. Keep an eye on them, though, so they don't get too brown; if they do, remove them from the oven and set aside in a warm place while you finish the lamb.

CONTINUES

Cook the lamb: Make sure the oven is preheated to 450°F. In an oven-proof heavy-duty 14-inch skillet, heat the oil over high heat just to the smoking point, then reduce to medium high. Season the chops on both sides with the salt and pepper. Sear the lamb chops in the skillet for 2 minutes on each side, creating a dark crust. Transfer the skillet to the oven and bake until desired doneness. (See my Tire Test on page 5 to check for doneness.) Most of my customers enjoy lamb chops English style, which is pink (or medium rare), which should take about 6 minutes in the oven.

In a small saucepan, heat the demi-glace, port, and mint until simmering. Cook for 2 minutes so the alcohol evaporates. Lay two lamb chops on each plate and drizzle with sauce (or serve the sauce on the side, if desired). Serve with the artichokes and potatoes.

JEWISH-STYLE ARTICHOKES

These fried baby artichokes are my homage to *Carciofi alla Giudia*, the Jewish artichokes served at Rome's famed restaurant Piperno. In America, the only artichokes suitable for this recipe are baby ones that have not developed a tough, hairy center. In the restaurant we fry them twice, the way we do French fries, which I must confess is not the traditional Italian way. At home or in a smaller setting I prefer to use the following method, which is how they're traditionally done in Italy (although they use larger artichokes). Adding a sprinkle of water at the end of the cooking time helps the leaves of the chokes to open.

I had never made them until one summer when I was in East Hampton giving a week-long cooking class. My late, great friend, the Italian cookbook author and teacher Anna Teresa Callen, was there, too, that week, and somehow we got to talking about *Carciofi alla Giudia*. She asked me to demonstrate making them in front of everyone, and under her guidance I was able to do it. To my surprise when I drizzled the water on them they opened like flower petals. To my relief, Anna approved.

I recommend using a candy thermometer to keep track of the oil temperature; you don't want it to exceed 350°F at any point or the leaves will burn. It goes without saying that you should be careful and stand back a bit as you add the sprinkle of water to the pan.

Serves 2

Juice of 1 lemon

6 baby artichokes, trimmed and cleaned

1 to 2 cups olive oil (just enough to submerge the chokes)

Splash of warm water

Kosher salt

Fill a mixing bowl with water and squeeze the lemon juice into it. Set it aside by your work area. Cut off the top third of one artichoke with a serrated knife. Peel off the leaves until only the light green leaves are left. Using a paring knife, carve away the dark green bottom until it is white and tender and all the hard exterior is removed. As you finish, place in the water to keep it from discoloring. Repeat with all the artichokes.

Remove the artichokes from the water and pat them dry. Use your finger to delicately spread open the top leaves of the chokes. Be gentle so as to loosen them slightly but not break the leaves. In a 10-inch-wide by 4-inch-high casserole dish, place the artichokes face down. Pour the olive oil onto the artichokes, just enough to cover them, and place a candy thermometer in the oil. Turn the heat to medium and cook the artichokes for 10 to 15 minutes, making sure the oil temperature doesn't exceed 350°F. The leaves of the chokes will begin to turn brown and crisp up. Once the whole artichokes have turned brown, remove the candy thermometer, and turn off the heat. Carefully drizzle a few drops of water around each artichoke. This will create a form of combustion—the oil will pop, so be careful—that helps the leaves of the artichoke expand. Once the popping has stopped, remove the artichokes from the oil and place them on a cutting board. While they're still hot, cover them with a kitchen towel, and press down firmly on each to flatten. Sprinkle with salt and serve hot.

LYONNAISE POTATOES

Lyonnaise potatoes are potato slices sautéed in butter with some type of onion, in this case shallots and scallion. They're insanely delicious, and making them is a two-step process. First, the whole potatoes are par-cooked and cooled. Then, they're sliced and sautéed.

Serves 2 to 3

Kosher salt (enough to spread on a baking pan)

3 large russet potatoes

2 tablespoons unsalted butter, clarified butter (see page 14), or extra-virgin olive oil

2 shallots, thinly sliced

1 scallion, minced

½ teaspoon chopped fresh marjoram

Freshly ground black pepper

Bake the potatoes: Preheat the oven to 450°F. Spread a layer of kosher salt on a baking pan with sides. Pierce each potato a time or two with a fork and lay them on the bed of salt. Bake until they are *almost* cooked through. The amount of baking time depends on the size of the potatoes, but you want them to be cooked slightly less than regular baked potatoes. Set them aside to cool.

Sauté the potatoes: Peel the cooled potatoes and cut them into ½-inch-thick slices. Heat the butter in a heavy-bottomed 12-inch skillet over medium heat until it's hot but not smoking. Carefully place the potatoes in a single layer in the pan and cook for about 2 minutes on each side, turning so that each side is golden brown, crispy, and completely soft in the center when pierced with a knife. Add the shallots, scallions, and marjoram to the pan and cook with the potatoes until the shallots are translucent. Lower the heat, if necessary, so the potatoes don't burn. Sprinkle generously with salt and pepper and serve.

Vegan Bolognese with
Whole Wheat Penne

CHAPTER 6

ITALIAN CLASSICS

Eggplant Parmesan / 171

Chicken Parmesan / 174

Freds Daily Focaccia / 177

Foolproof Pizza Dough / 178

Pizza Margherita / 180

Pizza Emilia-Romagna / 183

Focaccia Robiola with Truffle Oil / 185

Mark's Baby Clam Sauce with Spaghetti / 187

Vegan Bolognese with Whole Wheat Penne / 190

Fusilli al Basilico / 193

Fettuccine with Shrimp, Arugula, Garlic,
Cherry Tomatoes, and Basil / 194

Freds Spaghetti / 197

Wild Spring Ravioli / 199

Risotto alla Milanese / 201

Risotto with Fruits of the Sea / 202

Risotto alla Contadina / 203

Italian food occupies a singular place on the menu at Freds, as the restaurant itself is named after Fred Pressman, the man who first brought Giorgio Armani, Prada, and many other Italian fashion icons to America, before anyone else knew them, back when the store was still in its original 17th Street location. In many ways, the story of fashion begins with Italian design, so the Italian connection runs deep at Barneys.

Italian food is an integral part of my career as a chef as well, and so Italian food still has a substantial presence on the menu, and there are customers who come to Freds specifically to eat my lasagna, or spaghetti alla vongole, or meatballs.

All the time I spent in Italy early in my career—traveling, eating in restaurants and private homes, meeting people, taking notes, watching a Sicilian mama make pasta in her small Palermo kitchen, walking in vineyards and olive groves, visiting balsamico producers and Parmigiano makers, waking early to watch the fishermen bring in their catches on the coast—became a part of my professional DNA. And even though I'm not Italian, the Italian sensibility in food aligns perfectly with my own preferences: Use impeccable ingredients and prepare them simply.

We make three or four kinds of fresh pasta every morning—spaghetti and several kinds of seasonal ravioli and tortellini—and drape the thin sheets of pasta the way my Roman friend Maria taught me so many years ago. Risotto is always on the menu, and we vary that seasonally, too. In the spring, we pair tender, fresh raw fava beans with hunks of Pecorino cheese, just like you'd find in Tuscany, and winter will find us serving fennel with the oranges that come in season then.

This chapter includes my recipe for foolproof homemade pizza dough, adapted for cooking in a home oven. It's the recipe I use when I make it at home or on weekends with friends, and I hope you'll try it. Practice makes perfect with pizza dough, so be assured that your skill by the tenth attempt will be greater than the first time, as will your results.

There are a couple of Italian recipes and techniques I have purposefully not included. Fred's Spaghetti and Meatballs is a perennial favorite, but I included several different versions in my last book, *Two Meatballs in the Italian Kitchen*. I also have not included a recipe for making fresh pasta. It's a huge part of the prep that goes on every single day at Freds, but I don't think it's likely that many people will be interested in making it at home. Even *I* don't make it in my own home, because there's so much good commercial fresh pasta out there, especially at farmers' markets and gourmet stores. Two recipes in this chapter—Freds Spaghetti and Wild Spring Ravioli—are made at Freds with our house-made fresh pasta, but the sauces are good with commercially produced fresh, or even dried, pasta.

Of course, the two final words on the subject of Italian food must always be this: *Buon appetito!*

EGGPLANT PARMESAN

One thing I've heard over and over again from my friends in the music business is the importance of an artist playing the hits. The fans deserve it, and they'll be more open to new work if they get to hear the staples. The same theory applies in the restaurant business, to a certain degree. When I opened Freds, I was known for the rustic Italian food I served at my restaurant Campagna, and people would have been disappointed initially if there had been nothing like that on the menu at Freds. Anyway, Barneys is a huge supporter of Italian designers, so it made sense to include some Italian dishes. Eggplant Parmesan has always been a customer favorite, and people still clamor for it. I try to limit serving it to the fall and winter seasons, when local produce disappears and everyone craves comfort food.

I've lightened the dish substantially in recent years. We used to coat the eggplant heavily in flour before frying; now we use a little flour and dip it in an egg and cheese mixture that retains less oil than flour alone. Making this dish requires lots of counter space and time; I would make it a weekend project and enlist friends to help. Cooking is a social experience and recipes like this can fill a rainy afternoon with culinary entertainment—and eating pleasure. When frying a large amount of eggplant, it's a good idea to place a candy thermometer in the oil to make sure it stays at 350°F or just below. That will help you get maximum use of the oil and prevent it from burning. If the oil starts to get very dark brown it will make the eggplant bitter, so if that happens it's best to discard the burnt oil and start over with fresh (even if that means you use a smaller amount) for the remaining eggplant. A metal spider is the best tool to use to remove the eggplant from the hot oil.

Serves 4

EGGPLANT

2 medium eggplants (2 to 2½ pounds)

Kosher salt for sprinkling

6 large eggs

¼ cup freshly grated Parmigiano Reggiano cheese

3 tablespoons chopped fresh Italian parsley

2 cups all-purpose flour

4 cups vegetable or peanut oil for frying

TOMATO SAUCE

2 tablespoon extra-virgin olive oil

4 cloves garlic, thinly sliced

2 (28-ounce) cans crushed Italian tomatoes (preferably San Marzano)

2 teaspoons dried oregano, preferably Sicilian

1 teaspoon kosher salt, plus more to taste

1 tablespoon unsalted butter

8 fresh basil leaves

Freshly ground black pepper

½ cup freshly grated Parmigiano Reggiano cheese

CONTINUES

To make the eggplant: Cut off the tops of the eggplants, but do not peel them. Slice each eggplant lengthwise into ½-inch-thick slices. (If the eggplants are very long, first cut them in half crosswise and then slice the halves into ½-inch-thick lengthwise slices.) Lay the slices on a baking sheet with sides and sprinkle each slice generously with salt, then turn over and salt the other side (approximately ⅛ teaspoon per side). If you run out of space on the baking sheet, lay additional slices over the first layer, salting them the same way. Lay a second baking sheet on top and weight it down by placing some heavy objects on it (full tin cans work well for this, but anything heavy will do). Allow to sit for 2 to 4 hours.

While the eggplant is draining, make the tomato sauce.

To make the tomato sauce: Heat the olive oil in a heavy-bottomed saucepan over medium-low heat. Add the garlic and cook until it starts to brown and release a nutty aroma, about 5 minutes. Add the tomatoes, oregano, and salt and bring to a boil. Reduce the heat to low and cook, uncovered, stirring every 10 to 15 minutes to prevent the sauce from scorching, until the sauce is thick and dark red colored, 1 to 1½ hours. While it's still hot, stir in the butter and basil leaves, and season with pepper; remove from the heat and set aside.

To fry the eggplant: Remove the eggplant slices from the baking sheet and discard the bitter liquid. Rinse the slices under cold running water to remove excess salt. Drain and pat dry with kitchen or paper towels.

Whisk the eggs in a mixing bowl, add the ¼ cup Parmesan and parsley, and mix again. Place the flour on a separate plate by the egg mixture. Place several layers of paper towels on a baking sheet or serving platter for draining the cooked eggplant.

Place the oil in a deep fryer or 12- to 14-inch heavy-duty soup pot that's at least 4 inches deep. Heat the oil to 350°F; check with a candy thermometer. If you don't have a candy thermometer make sure the oil is very hot but not smoking.

Dredge the eggplant in the flour, being sure to cover both sides. Shake off any excess and immediately place into the egg mixture. Hold up to let excess egg drip off and then place in the hot oil. Cook the eggplant in batches, working with only a few pieces at a time, so as not to crowd the pot. Fry until golden brown on both sides. Remove from the oil and place on the paper towels to drain. Repeat until all the eggplant is cooked. If you run out of space on the paper towels, move the older slices to a cooling rack or baking dish instead of piling them on top of each other, otherwise they'll be greasy.

To assemble the dish: Preheat the oven to 350°F. Cover the bottom of a 9- by 13-inch baking dish with a generous ladle of tomato sauce and then arrange a layer of eggplant slices. Cover the eggplant with more sauce, spreading it with a pastry spatula so the vegetable is lightly covered. Sprinkle with some of the Parmesan and repeat until all the eggplant is layered in the baking dish. Spread a layer of tomato sauce over the top and Parmesan over that. Cover with aluminum foil and bake for 30 to 40 minutes, until heated through and browned on top. Remove from the oven and let it sit a few minutes before cutting. This can be served hot or cold, and reheats very well.

——

CHICKEN PARMESAN

This is another classic Italian dish that made the trip from my downtown restaurant Campagna. Every Sunday was southern Italian night at Campagna, and my uptown customers would trek down to get their fix of Italian-American dishes. The Chicken Parm was the most popular item on those nights, so it was a no-brainer to bring it uptown to Freds. Serve with Freds Seasonal Vegetable Medley (page 148). At Freds we use bone-in chicken breasts, but at home it's probably easiest to use boneless ones.

Serves 4

1 recipe Tomato Sauce (page 171)

4 skinless, boneless chicken breasts (about 1½ pounds)

Kosher salt

Freshly ground black pepper

2 cups all-purpose flour for dredging

4 large eggs

1¼ cups freshly grated Parmigiano Reggiano cheese

2 cups breadcrumbs

1 cup vegetable oil or pure olive oil

4 (1-ounce) slices fresh mozzarella cheese

Prepare the tomato sauce.

Prep the chicken: Butterfly the breasts by slicing through the middle horizontally, but not all the way through, and splaying the two sides open so it resembles two wings of a butterfly. Sprinkle each piece generously with salt and pepper. Spread the flour on a large plate. Whisk the eggs in a large shallow bowl, add 1 cup of the Parmesan, and mix well. Spread the breadcrumbs in a large baking dish. Working one at a time, first dredge each cutlet in the flour, then shake to remove any excess. Then place in the egg mixture and let sit for about 2 minutes. Remove and gently shake off dripping excess egg. Lay the cutlet in the breadcrumbs and use your hand to press the chicken into the breadcrumbs. Then turn it over and coat on the other side, pressing again, so that it's well coated. Place the coated cutlet on a plate. Repeat with the remaining chicken. Refrigerate the coated chicken for about 45 minutes for the coating to congeal so it will stay on the cutlets better when you cook them.

Preheat the oven to 350°F

Place several layers of paper towels on a plate or baking sheet and set aside near the stove. Heat the oil in a 14-inch skillet over medium heat until it starts to smoke. Carefully place two of the cutlets in the hot oil and brown on one side, about 2 minutes; reduce the heat to medium low if you see they are browning too quickly or starting to burn. When they're browned on one side, turn over and cook to brown the other side for 2 minutes more. Place on the paper towels to drain of oil, and repeat until all the meat is cooked.

Spoon a thin layer of tomato sauce in the bottom of a 10- by 12-inch baking dish. Lay the cutlets in the sauce and sprinkle with the remaining ¼ cup Parmesan. Spread each cutlet with about ½ cup of tomato sauce, then lay a slice of mozzarella on each one. Bake for 16 to 20 minutes, until the cheese is melted and the dish is sizzling. Test for doneness if needed by inserting a sharp paring knife into the center of a cutlet so you can see if it's cooked through. Serve immediately with remaining tomato sauce in a small bowl for those who like extra.

FREDS DAILY FOCACCIA

Focaccia has been part of the Freds daily bread since day one. We make sheet pans of it, every single day, without exception. I've tinkered with the recipe a lot over the years, and this version—perfected over a few summer weekends at my friend Robert's house at the beach—I think is the ultimate. At least until I tinker with it again.

Focaccia is best when eaten within 2 hours of being made. Artisan bakers consider eating hot bread an anathema, but most people I know, myself included, simply are not strong enough to resist.

Unlike the rest of the recipes in this book, I've given measurements in grams for this recipe and the pizza dough because it's more precise for baking.

Serves 6 to 8

EQUIPMENT

KitchenAid mixer with dough hook

Large bowl

Plastic wrap

2 baking sheets with 1-inch sides

INGREDIENTS

680 grams lukewarm water, 75°F to 78°F

1½ teaspoons Fleischmann's active dry yeast

1000 grams King Arthur Unbleached Bread Flour

20 grams kosher salt

1 cup extra-virgin olive oil

Sea salt for garnish

Small sprigs fresh rosemary for garnish

Place the water and yeast in the bowl of the KitchenAid with a dough hook and mix together on the lowest speed. Add the flour and kosher salt and mix on the lowest speed for 2 minutes, until everything is mixed together and looks like a thick paste. Increase the speed to medium and mix for 6 to 8 minutes, until the dough looks smooth and is starting to cling to the dough hook. Remove the dough from the machine, place in a large bowl, and cover the bowl with plastic wrap. Set aside in a warm place to rise for 45 minutes, or until it doubles in size.

Coat two baking sheets with some olive oil. Cut the dough in half and place each piece on an oil-coated baking sheet. Spread olive oil over the tops and let them sit for 10 minutes. Then use your fingers to gently spread each piece of dough until it covers the entire sheet pan. Let sit for 30 minutes.

After 30 minutes, the dough will probably have shrunk from the sides, but even if it hasn't, repeat the process of pushing and spreading the dough so it covers the whole baking sheet. Drizzle with a little more olive oil and let sit for 30 minutes longer. While the bread is resting, preheat the oven to 425°F.

Sprinkle the tops of the dough with olive oil and sea salt, and dot with the rosemary sprigs. Let rest for 10 minutes longer, then place in the preheated oven. Bake for 15 to 20 minutes, until golden brown. Rotate midway through the bake to ensure even baking. Ideally the focaccia should cool for at least 40 minutes before serving, but good luck waiting that long.

_____

FOOLPROOF PIZZA DOUGH

Making pizza at home is actually very easy, and it can be a fun activity for the whole family. Yes, you need the right equipment, but it's not that much: a metal bench scraper for cutting the dough, and possibly a digital scale to measure the ingredients, plus a pizza stone, wooden pizza peel, and metal pizza peel for the baking, and you're good to go. You don't need a special oven, just a bit of counter space for working with the dough. Like anything worth doing, practice makes perfect, and I guarantee that by the tenth pie you'll be handling that dough like a pro. In fact, I suggest you take a photo of the first pizza you make so you can compare it with later ones and see how far you've come. Or at least have a laugh. Even if it comes out a little rustic the first time, it's going to be delicious. And you'll look good, especially if you're entertaining, because homemade pizza cut into little squares is a really impressive cocktail snack.

I use a KitchenAid mixer with the dough hook to mix the dough, but you can make the dough by hand if you don't have one.

The digital scale comes in handy since I've given measurements in grams, which is more precise for baking. I even weigh the water, which is a trick artisan bakers use. The only ingredient that I measure with the imperial system is the yeast. I prefer instant yeast, particularly the readily available Fleischmann's active dry yeast, that you mix with warm water. The old wives' tale of keeping the salt and the yeast separate is actually a good idea. Why take the chance to kill the yeast with the salt? However the idea of adding sugar to the dough to activate the yeast is unnecessary Classic pizza dough is a pure product made with four things: flour, yeast, salt, and water. Period.

Since flour is the principal ingredient, it's important to use a good one. The only flour we use, and really the only one I recommend, is King Arthur Unbleached All-Purpose Flour—the one in a red bag that you can find at almost every supermarket in all fifty states. If you are not using King Arthur flour, make sure the flour you're using is not bleached or bromated. Both those processes allow for longer shelf life but make an inferior product, certainly not great for an artisan pie.

It's possible to make the dough the same day you bake the pie because it can be made in as little as 4 hours, but I prefer allowing 6 to 8 hours (stored in the fridge) so the dough has plenty of time to retard, ferment, and gain flavor. Fermenting it for the longer time will also make it easier to work with. Once made, pizza dough only keeps for about 48 hours, even when stored in the fridge. The dough is still useable after that, but it can taste a little yeasty or sour. It will start to die after 3 days and then it's not good for anything. The dough freezes well, though, and will keep in the freezer for 3 months, so if you know you won't use it within 2 days, freeze it in individual containers right after it's made. Just make sure you bring the dough fully to room temperature before rolling it out.

Makes 4 dough balls, or 4 individual 12-inch pies

KitchenAid mixer with dough hook

Plastic wrap

Metal bench scraper

4 (1-pint) containers

INGREDIENTS

300 grams lukewarm water, 75°F to 78°F

1 teaspoon Fleischmann's active dry yeast

500 grams King Arthur Unbleached All-Purpose Flour (in the red bag)

5 grams kosher salt

¼ teaspoon extra-virgin olive oil (to coat the finished ball of dough; this makes it easier to remove it from the storage container)

In the bowl of the KitchenAid with a dough hook, combine the water and yeast. Mix together for 2 minutes on the lowest speed. Add the flour and salt and mix on the lowest speed for 2 minutes, until everything is mixed together and looks like a thick paste. Increase the speed to medium and mix for 6 to 8 minutes, until the dough looks smooth and is starting to cling to the dough hook.

Remove the bowl from the machine, cover tightly with plastic wrap, and place in a cool spot in the kitchen to sit for 1 hour, or until doubled in size. With the dough still in the bowl, punch it so that it deflates, cover again with plastic wrap, and set aside for 1 hour longer, or until it doubles in size again.

Remove the dough from the bowl and place on a well-floured surface. Using a metal bench scraper, cut the dough into four equal pieces. Gently roll and shape each piece of dough into a round ball. Drizzle a little olive oil into each of the 1-pint containers and place a ball of the dough in each one. Move the dough around so it's all covered in a light covering of oil and cover each container. If you are using the dough on that day, let sit out in a cool spot until you're ready to use it, but don't let it sit out for more than 1 hour. Refrigerate or freeze at this point.

If you refrigerate or freeze the dough, bring it to room temp before using but use it within two hours.

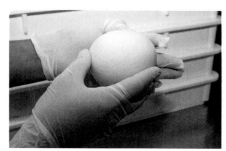

PIZZA MARGHERITA

Makes 1 (12-inch) pie

EQUIPMENT

Pizza stone

Rolling pin

Wooden pizza peel

Large serving ladle

Metal pizza peel

Pizza cutter

INGREDIENTS

1 ball Foolpoof Pizza Dough (page 178)

All-purpose flour for rolling out dough

Sprinkle of semolina or fine corn meal for coating wooden pizza peel

¼ cup Mutti brand Tomato Puree Passata (or similar brand, such as Pomi)

½ cup shredded mozzarella

Kosher salt

Sprinkle of dried oregano

1 tablespoon extra-virgin olive oil

2 teaspoons freshly grated Parmigiano Reggiano cheese

6 large leaves fresh basil

Place the pizza stone in the oven and preheat the oven to the oven's highest temperature for at least 2 hours to ensure that the stone is extremely hot.

If the dough has been refrigerated, let it sit out, covered so it stays moist, until it comes to room temperature, about 4 hours. Make sure you have plenty of room on the countertop and that the surface is smooth and completely dry. Dust the countertop with a sprinkling of flour, and place the dough on it. Push down to flatten the dough and, using a rolling pin and your hands, gently begin to roll and stretch it. Be careful not to stretch it so thinly that you put holes in it. Continue stretching and rolling until the dough is a 12-inch circle approximately ⅛ inch thick. Let it sit for 1 minute. Dust a wooden pizza peel with semolina or fine corn meal, so the pizza will not stick and will slide easily onto the stone. Slide the pizza dough onto the peel and then add the toppings: Ladle the tomato puree onto the center of the pizza and use the bottom of the ladle to carefully and quickly spread it evenly around the pie, leaving a ½-inch crust around the edges. Sprinkle the mozzarella evenly on the pie, sprinkle with salt and oregano, and drizzle with olive oil.

Slide the pie onto the pizza stone in the oven and bake until the crust is golden brown and the cheese is melted and bubbling. The crust may get a little charred at points, but don't be afraid of that; a little char adds flavor. Use the metal peel to remove the pizza from the oven and place it on a serving platter. While it's still sizzling hot, sprinkle with the Parmesan cheese and arrange the basil leaves on it. Let it sit for 1 or 2 minutes to let the cheese settle. Serve it uncut as an individual pie or use a pizza cutter to cut it into 6 to 8 small slices to share while you cook the next one!

PIZZA EMILIA-ROMAGNA

One of the highlights of the times I spent in Italy was a trip to Emilia-Romagna, the gastronomic center (and in many ways cultural center, although that statement could start an argument) of Italy. Emilia-Romagna's flatlands are known for farms, dairy production, Ferrari automobiles, and Europe's oldest university—the University of Bologna—not to mention prosciutto, Parmigiano, and balsamico, a unique must that is the basis for the universally loved balsamic vinegar.

Aceto balsamico tradizionale takes twelve to twenty-five years to produce. It's an artisanal product in the ultimate sense, and my visit to a traditional producer was one of the most charming and memorable experiences I've ever had in Italy—and that's saying a lot because Italy is full of the charming and memorable. The producer was housed in an ancient house in Modena, and we were guided through the whole process, starting on the ground floor of the house, with cooking the local white wine down and aging it in barrels. As time goes by, the liquid evaporates and is moved to smaller barrels, and those barrels are stored on higher floors of the house. The higher you go in the house, the smaller the barrels and the older the balsamico. A small, dark attic room on the top floor housed extremely old, prized, and expensive balsamico in small containers—fifty years old, seventy-five years old, one hundred years old. For a chef, seeing something like that is an almost religious experience.

It's important to understand that balsamic vinegar is *not* what you want for this pizza. This calls for *aceto balsamico tradizionale*, which, while it shares a similar astringency, is thickened from aging, and is quite sweet, with an almost molasses-like quality. Better supermarkets and gourmet stores usually carry a selection of different ones. The balsamico is not cooked with the pizza, but drizzled on it in concentric circles after the pizza is baked.

Makes 1 (12-inch) pie

EQUIPMENT

Pizza stone

Rolling pin

Wooden pizza peel

Metal pizza peel

Pizza cutter

INGREDIENTS

1 ball Foolproof Pizza Dough (page 178)

All-purpose flour for rolling out dough

Sprinkle of semolina or fine corn meal for coating wooden pizza peel

½ cup shredded mozzarella

½ cup freshly grated Parmigiano Reggiano cheese

¼ cup grated Pecorino Romano cheese

1 tablespoon 12- or 25-year-old *aceto balsamico tradizionale* (*not* balsamic vinegar!)

CONTINUES

Place the pizza stone in the oven and preheat the oven to its highest temperature for at least 2 hours to ensure that the stone is extremely hot.

If the dough has been refrigerated, let it sit out, covered so it stays moist, until it comes to room temperature, about 4 hours. Make sure you have plenty of room on the countertop and that the surface is smooth and completely dry. Dust the countertop with a sprinkling of flour, and place the dough on it. Push down to flatten the dough and, using the rolling pin and your hands, gently begin to roll and stretch it. Be careful not to stretch it so thinly that you put holes in it. Continue stretching and rolling until the dough is a 12-inch circle approximately ⅛ inch thick. Let it sit for 1 minute. Dust a wooden pizza peel with semolina or fine corn meal. This ensures that the pizza will not stick to the peel and will slide easily into the oven. Slide the pizza dough onto the peel and add the toppings: Sprinkle the

cheeses, one at a time, evenly on the pie. Slide the pie onto the pizza stone in the oven and bake until the crust is golden brown and the cheese is melted and bubbling. The crust may get a little charred at points, but don't be afraid of that; a little char adds flavor. Use the metal peel to remove the pizza from the oven and place it on a serving platter. Let it sit for 1 or 2 minutes to let the cheese settle. Drizzle the balsamico in concentric circles around the pie, use a pizza cutter to cut it into 6 to 8 slices, and serve.

———

FOCACCIA ROBIOLA WITH TRUFFLE OIL

New Yorkers have the Italian chef and pizzaiola extraordinaire Ciro Verde to thank for this completely addictive disc of indulgence. Or curse, because it *is* definitely addictive. No one can resist the scent of hot bread and truffle oil as one of these pies is carried through the dining room. Along with the Belgian Fries (page 9), it's one of Freds' iconic dishes that people order to share among the whole table. It's rich, so that's really the best way to have it.

Although authentic individual Italian pizza is everywhere now, that wasn't always the case, and Ciro was one of the first Italian chefs to serve them here, changing the landscape of pizza in America. This pie—which is technically a focaccia because it has two layers—has become a genuine New York classic, and for that we will always have Ciro and his craft to thank.

Robiola cheese is sold at most gourmet cheese counters. There are two types: fresh and aged. For this recipe the fresh is the one to use, as it is soft and spreadable. That's why cream cheese is an acceptable substitute if you can't find robiola. If you do use cream cheese, blend it with a sprinkle of lemon juice to approximate the slightly more sour flavor of robiola.

This is a two-step process. First, the shell is made and then it's filled with cheese and baked again until the cheese melts and the crust is a nice golden brown. The top layer of the focaccia is dotted with little holes, which let air escape as the dough bakes. We use a tool called a *docker*, but at home you could use a fork to make the holes. The pie is usually docked two or three times before the pizza is baked.

Makes 1 (12-inch) focaccia

EQUIPMENT

Pizza stone

Rolling pin

Rolling dough docker
(or a fork) to prick the dough

Wooden pizza peel

Metal pizza peel

Pizza cutter

INGREDIENTS

2 balls Foolproof Pizza Dough
(page 178)

All-purpose flour for rolling out dough

Sprinkle of semolina or fine corn
meal for coating wooden pizza peel

6 ounces fresh robiola cheese
(or Philadelphia cream cheese
or fromage blanc)

2 tablespoons good-quality truffle oil

CONTINUES

Preheat the oven and pizza stone to your oven's highest temperature for at least 2 hours to ensure that the stone is extremely hot.

If the dough has been refrigerated, let it sit out, covered so it stays moist, until it comes to room temperature, about 4 hours. Make sure you have plenty of room on the countertop and that the surface is smooth and completely dry. Dust the countertop with a sprinkling of flour, and place one ball of dough on it. Sprinkle a little flour on the dough and place the other dough ball on top of it. Push down to flatten the dough, and use your hands or a rolling pin to stretch out the circle. Don't push down too hard; you don't want the two dough layers to be completely mashed together. Stretch and roll out the dough until it's a 12-inch circle that is approximately ¼ inch thick. Use the docker to make indentations in the top all the way around.

Dust a wooden pizza peel with semolina or fine corn meal. This ensures that the dough will not stick to the peel and will slide easily into the oven. Slide the dough onto the peel and then slide it onto the hot pizza stone. Bake for 10 to 12 minutes. Check it periodically to see if bubbles are forming in the dough. If so, run the docker gently over the dough to flatten the air bubbles. Repeat as needed during the bake. After 5 minutes, flip the pie over and repeat on the other side. When it's light brown and cooked, use the metal peel to remove it from the oven.

Let it cool for about 5 minutes, then use a sharp knife to slice horizontally through the center. You should end up with a top and a bottom circle. Spread the robiola evenly on the bottom circle and then place the top over it. Place back in the oven and cook until the cheese is warm and melted, about 4 minutes. Remove from the oven and sprinkle with truffle oil. Use a pizza wheel to cut into 6 wedges and serve immediately.

———

MARK'S BABY CLAM SAUCE
WITH SPAGHETTI

My former wife, Susan, and I spent our honeymoon traveling in Italy. We were lucky because we had six weeks, and for a chef that adds up to a lot of good eating. One of the things I remember most about the food, though, is how often Susan would have pasta with clam sauce during the weeks we were by the coast. It got to be a joke between us, but watching someone eat that night after night after night made an impression. I had a hunch that I would have a dining room full of similar taste buds waiting for me at home, and since I've never been one to fight human nature, I put pasta with clam sauce on the menu as soon as we got back. It's never left and people still ask me how to make it. Of course the clams are not the same as the ones they have in Italy, but I find New Zealand cockles or Manila clams from the Pacific Northwest are just as delicious.

One little change I eventually made from the classic coastal Italian version is adding a tiny bit of tomato. So many people requested tomato with it that I just caved. I add enough tomato to change the hue of the sauce, but not enough to turn it into a full-fledged tomato sauce or change the flavor from the garlicky, briny taste of the Italian coast. I don't recall Susan ever complaining about the change, and she would know.

Serves 4 as a main course, 6 as an appetizer

¼ cup extra-virgin olive oil

4 cloves garlic, thinly sliced

48 very small clams in the shell, such as cockles or baby clams (not littlenecks)

1 cup dry white wine (trebbiano, Gavi, or sauvignon blanc)

½ cup clam juice

¼ cup canned crushed Italian plum tomatoes

1 teaspoon hot red pepper flakes

1 pound dried spaghetti

3 tablespoons chopped fresh Italian parsley

Kosher salt

Freshly ground black pepper

CONTINUES

Fill a 10-quart pasta pot with 7 quarts of salted water and bring to a boil over high heat.

Heat a long-handled 14-inch braising pan over medium heat. Add the olive oil with the garlic and cook, stirring, until golden. Add the clams and cook, stirring, for 1 minute. Add the wine, clam juice, tomatoes, and red pepper flakes and stir. Cover, reduce the heat to a simmer, and cook until the clams open and the liquid has reduced and thickened slightly, about 5 minutes.

Add the pasta to the boiling water, stir, and cover until it returns to a boil. Uncover and boil the pasta until tender but al dente. Drain, saving ¼ cup of the pasta water.

Add the pasta to the sauce and toss in the parsley, a pinch of salt (only a small amount since the clams are already naturally salty), and pepper. Toss together until all the pasta is evenly coated. If the sauce is too thick, thin by adding some of the reserved pasta water a little at a time. Cook over low heat 1 minute. Serve immediately.

VEGAN BOLOGNESE
WITH WHOLE WHEAT PENNE

When I noticed that Italians are making gluten-free pasta, I realized that we were in a new era of Italian cookery. So I figured it wouldn't be too heretical to update traditional, rich Bolognese sauce for people who, whether through preference or doctor's orders, want a lighter version of this satisfying comfort food. In recent years I've been committed to providing more menu choices for customers who have health issues or food sensitivities. Guests don't necessarily want to announce their food preferences to the world, especially if they're at, say, an important business lunch, so having a range of dishes guests can eat without having to place a special order is a new part of hospitality.

This Vegan Bolognese is chock-full of vegetables, minced finely to approximate the texture of the ground meat in the traditional version. It's a bit of work to mince all the veg (a food processor on the pulse setting does the trick), so consider doubling the recipe and freezing half in single-serving containers for quick mid-week meals. And don't skimp on the cooking time; the key to this sauce is letting it simmer over very low heat for a long time—at least 1½ hours.

Serves 4 as a main course, 6 as an appetizer

1 eggplant, trimmed and cut into 1-inch cubes

4 bell peppers (preferably a mix of red and yellow), cored, seeded, and roughly chopped

1 small head cauliflower, trimmed and broken into florets

2 carrots, peeled, trimmed, and roughly chopped

½ pound button mushrooms, wiped clean of dirt and sliced

1 large bulb fennel, trimmed and roughly chopped

1 medium zucchini, trimmed and roughly chopped

1 small hot red pepper, seeded and chopped (optional)

¼ cup extra-virgin olive oil

2 large red onions, diced

5 cloves garlic, minced

1½ cups red wine

2 (28-ounce) cans crushed Italian plum tomatoes (preferably San Marzano)

2 tablespoons chopped fresh rosemary leaves

1 tablespoon dried oregano

1 tablespoon herbes de Provence

2 teaspoons kosher salt

Freshly ground black pepper

1 pound dried whole wheat penne

Using a food processor with the pulse setting and working in batches, mince the eggplant, bell peppers, cauliflower, carrots, mushrooms, fennel, zucchini, and hot pepper (if using). Pulse each batch 3 or 4 times, but only hold the pulse button for 1 second at a time, pausing between pulses so that the vegetables don't become pureed. You want them chopped to a size that resembles chopped meat. Mix them all together in a large bowl and set aside.

Heat the olive oil in a large, heavy stockpot over medium heat. Add the onions and garlic and sauté until wilted, then add the vegetable mixture. Stir together for 2 to 3 minutes, until they are wilted. Add the wine and stir together for 1 minute, then add the tomatoes, rosemary, oregano, herbes de Provence, salt, and black pepper. Reduce the heat to low and simmer gently, uncovered, stirring every 8 to 10 minutes, for 1½ to 2 hours, until the sauce is rich and thick. If the sauce becomes too thick before the vegetables are very soft, add a little water and continue cooking. Taste and add more salt and pepper, if desired. You can use this sauce immediately, but it's even better if it sits overnight in the fridge to let the flavors meld.

Fill a 10-quart pasta pot with 7 quarts of salted water and bring to a boil over high heat. Add the pasta to the boiling water, stir, and cover until it returns to a boil. Uncover and cook until the pasta is al dente. Drain in a colander, but reserve 1 cup of the cooking water.

Make sure the sauce is hot, then add the drained pasta and toss together well. If the sauce is too thick, add some of the pasta water, a little bit at a time, to thin it slightly. Heat together for 1 or 2 minutes, and serve.

FUSILLI AL BASILICO

Tomato, basil, cream, and Parmesan cheese make simple magic when combined, and they turn this pasta into comfort food that follows in a line from the cream of tomato soup every American kid grew up eating. This pasta is in heavy rotation in the summer when fresh basil is abundant. It's everywhere, both on the menu in the dining room and in the kitchen, too, because the staff likes to make it for family meal. They make mountains of it at the end of the night for all the employees, two enormous pots. It doesn't matter how much they make; it always disappears.

Serves 4 as a main course, 6 as an appetizer

2 tablespoons extra-virgin olive oil

1 teaspoon minced garlic

2½ cups canned puréed Italian plum tomatoes (preferably San Marzano, or substitute 1 pound fresh summer plum or heirloom tomatoes, chopped or crushed)

¾ cup heavy cream

3 tablespoons Freds Pesto (page 13)

1 teaspoon kosher salt

½ cup freshly grated Parmigiano Reggiano cheese

1 (16-ounce) box dried fusilli pasta

12 fresh basil leaves, ripped by hand

Fill a large stockpot with salted water and bring to a boil.

While waiting for the water to boil, prepare the sauce. Heat the olive oil in a 12-inch skillet over medium heat. Add the garlic and brown slightly, then add the tomatoes, cream, pesto, salt, and ¼ cup of the Parmesan. Reduce the heat to low and simmer gently for about 7 minutes, until the sauce thickens and darkens slightly.

When the water is boiling, add the pasta, stir, and cover until it returns to a boil. Uncover and cook until the pasta is al dente.

Reserve ¼ cup of the pasta cooking water, and drain the pasta. Add the pasta to the pan with the sauce and mix together over low heat. If the sauce is too thick or dry, add some of the pasta water, 1 tablespoon at a time, tossing together until it's all hot and mixed well. Add the fresh basil, mix again, and serve immediately with the remaining Parmesan cheese.

FETTUCCINE WITH SHRIMP, ARUGULA, GARLIC, CHERRY TOMATOES, AND BASIL

We have a running joke in the kitchen: If you want a dish to be loved, just add shrimp. It's actually true—everyone loves shrimp. I was Principal of the Day at a school in Harlem and the fifth grade class and I were talking about our favorite foods. In an informal poll right then and there, shrimp ran a close second to lobster. My mother would have agreed with that ranking. Because it contains seafood, we do not serve this pasta with Parmesan cheese unless a guest requests it.

Serves 4 as a main course, 6 as an appetizer

3 tablespoons extra-virgin olive oil, plus more for drizzling

3 cloves garlic, sliced ¼ inch thick

16 jumbo shrimp (ask your fishmonger for Mexican or Ecuadorian white shrimp, U-12 size), peeled and deveined

1 pound cherry tomatoes, whole or sliced in half, depending on size*

Crushed red pepper flakes (optional)

12 ounces fresh fettuccine

2 cups baby arugula

1 cup fresh basil leaves

Kosher salt

If the tomatoes are the size of marbles, then leave them whole. Larger tomatoes should be cut in half or quartered, so all pieces are the size of marbles.

Fill a 10-quart pot with 7 quarts of salted water and bring to a boil over high heat. While waiting for the water to boil, make the sauce.

Heat 1½ tablespoons of the oil in a large 14-inch skillet over medium heat and add half the garlic. As the garlic starts to brown, add the shrimp, turn the heat up, and cook until the shrimp are about halfway done. Flip and cook so they get a nice color and crust on both sides. Remove the shrimp from the pan and set aside.

Use a paper towel to wipe the oil out of the pan. Add the remaining 1½ tablespoons oil and remaining garlic and cook until the garlic starts to brown. Turn off the heat and carefully add the tomatoes. I say carefully because some of the oil will spatter from the moisture from the tomatoes. Turn the heat back to medium high and cook the tomatoes for 2 minutes, stirring occasionally. Add the shrimp and crushed red pepper (if using), and simmer until the shrimp are cooked through. Turn off the heat and cover to keep the shrimp moist while you cook the pasta.

When the water is boiling, add the pasta, stir, and cover until it returns to a boil. Uncover and cook until the pasta is al dente. Drain and reserve ½ cup of the cooking water. Turn the medium heat back under the skillet and add the arugula and basil to the shrimp and sauce, and then the pasta. Using tongs or a wooden spoon, gently mix the pasta with the other ingredients. If the pasta becomes dry, add water a tablespoon at a time. Drizzle with extra-virgin olive oil and taste to adjust the salt.

——

FREDS SPAGHETTI

This dish is a take-off on traditional pasta pesto alla Genovese, which is made with cubed potatoes, green beans, and pesto. Double carbs are a deal-breaker for most, so I've lightened the dish by using vegetables—asparagus, shiitake mushrooms, and sun-dried tomatoes—instead of potatoes. We make it with our house-made fresh spaghetti, and it's a delicate dish, perfect for summer when there's an abundance of fresh basil. It's served warm, not hot, since once you cook the mushrooms and mix everything together you don't want to split the pesto by heating it too much. You simply want to lightly warm it.

Serves 2 as a main course, 4 as an appetizer

2 bunches asparagus, trimmed and cut into 1-inch pieces

2 tablespoons extra-virgin olive oil

2 cloves garlic, minced

¾ pound shiitake mushrooms, stems removed and discarded, caps julienned

8 oil-preserved sundried tomatoes, julienned

½ cup Freds Pesto (page 13)

6 ounces fresh spaghetti

½ cup freshly grated Parmigiano Reggiano cheese

6 fresh basil leaves for garnish

Fill a 10-quart stockpot with 7 quarts of salted water and bring to a boil over high heat. While waiting for the pasta water to boil, make the sauce.

Blanch and drain the asparagus (see page 17) and set aside in a large mixing bowl.

Place the olive oil and garlic in a 12-inch skillet over medium-high heat and sauté for about 30 seconds, until the garlic is golden brown. Add the mushrooms and sauté until they are soft and deep brown, about 5 minutes. Transfer to the bowl with the asparagus, add the sundried tomatoes and pesto, and mix together well.

When the water is boiling, add the pasta, stir, and cover until it returns to a boil. Uncover and cook until the pasta is al dente.

While the pasta is cooking, place the vegetable mixture in a Dutch oven and warm over very low heat.

Drain the pasta, reserving ¼ cup of the cooking water. Add the pasta to the Dutch oven and toss to combine. If the pasta looks dry, add the reserved pasta cooking water 1 tablespoon at a time, tossing to combine between additions. Garnish with the cheese and fresh basil leaves and serve immediately.

WILD SPRING RAVIOLI

We make fresh pasta every day at Freds and always have some kind of seasonal ravioli on the menu. This is my favorite preparation, made up of mostly foraged foods that signal spring. There are ramps here, the daffodils of foraged food, since they're the first ones to stick their heads out of the thawing, muddy ground. It also contains stinging nettles, which must be handled with gloves, but don't sting once they're cooked. Nettles are full of antioxidants and taste rather like spinach. Of course I don't gather these items myself, but rely, as I have for twenty years, on my friend Hans of Mushrooms & More, supplier of exotic mushrooms and foraged foods. If you can't find nettles, you can substitute ½ cup frozen spinach puree for the nettle puree. We throw a few less exotic vegetables into the mix—asparagus, English peas, spring onion—and toss them with our homemade cheese ravioli.

Serves 4 as a main course, 6 as an appetizer

1 bunch fresh thin asparagus, trimmed and cut into 1-inch pieces

Leaves from 1 pound stinging nettles (wear gloves when working with raw nettles)

Ice

¼ cup extra-virgin olive oil

1 small spring onion bulb, washed, trimmed, and minced

1 stalk green garlic, thinly sliced

1 bunch ramps (about 6), trimmed and minced

1 cup shelled fresh or frozen English peas

1 teaspoon kosher salt

½ teaspoon freshly ground black pepper

½ cup dry white wine

24 standard-size cheese ravioli

2 tablespoons unsalted butter

¼ cup freshly grated Parmigiano Reggiano cheese

Put a large stockpot full of salted water on to boil for cooking the ravioli.

In separate batches, blanch the asparagus and nettles for about 2 minutes, then shock in ice water (see page 17). Drain and pat dry. When the nettles are cool, puree them in a food processor. (One pound of nettles leaves should yield about ½ cup puree, but if you happen to get a leafier bunch that makes more, freeze the extra to use another time.) Set the asparagus and nettle puree aside.

Heat the olive oil in a 12-inch skillet and add the spring onion, green garlic, and ramps. Sauté for about 2 minutes. Add the nettle puree, asparagus, and peas and cook for about 1 minute. Season with salt and pepper. Add the wine, cover, and simmer over very low heat.

Cook the ravioli in the boiling water according to the package instructions. Reserve ¼ cup of the cooking liquid, then scoop the ravioli out of the pasta water using a slotted spoon. Add them to the vegetables, along with the butter. Add a little of the pasta water if the sauce is too dry, and sprinkle in half of the Parmesan. Mix together, gently so the ravioli don't break, until the cheese is melted with the sauce. Place the ravioli on a serving platter, and spoon the vegetables over them. Serve with the remaining Parmesan cheese.

Clockwise from top: Risotto alla Contadina (page 203); Risotto alla Milanese; Risotto with Fruits of the Sea (page 202)

RISOTTO ALLA MILANESE

Risotto alla Milanese is the little black dress of Italian cooking. Timeless, simple, goes with anything, on any occasion. It's the kind of elegant, simple dish that I absolutely love to serve. It's also one of the prettiest, thanks to the saffron giving it its beautiful yellow hue. Sometimes we vary the recipe slightly, depending on the season or our mood; in spring we might throw in a handful of English peas and a bit of minced prosciutto. In summer we might include some Prince Edward Island mussels. I never get tired of the original, though, and after it's made you might find me with the pot, scraping out the leftovers.

Serves 4 as a main course, 6 as an appetizer

4 tablespoons (½ stick) unsalted butter

1 medium red onion, minced

.50 gram saffron

2 cups arborio rice

1 teaspoon kosher salt

1 cup dry white wine

4 to 5 cups Chicken Stock (page 24)

¼ cup freshly grated Parmigiano Reggiano cheese

Freshly ground black pepper

1 tablespoon chopped fresh parsley

Melt 2 tablespoons of the butter in a heavy-bottomed 6-quart pot over medium heat. Add the onion, mix well with a long-handled wooden spoon, and sauté until the onion is softened, about 3 minutes. Add the saffron and let it melt into the onions, then immediately add the rice and salt. Stir until all the grains are coated with butter and are turning a deep yellow, about 2 minutes.

Add the wine and cook, stirring constantly, until the rice absorbs most of the wine. Add ½ cup of the stock and simmer, stirring, until it has been absorbed. Continue adding stock, ½ cup at a time and stirring until it is absorbed, until the rice is al dente, about 18 minutes total. Stir in the remaining 2 tablespoons butter and the Parmesan, and a grinding of black pepper. Mix and then taste, adjusting the seasoning if needed. Stir in the parsley and serve immediately.

RISOTTO WITH FRUITS OF THE SEA

If you love seafood, this dish contains a little bit of everything—shrimp, scallops, mussels, clams, octopus, and calamari. It's a combination that I like to use many different ways— tossed with pasta, made into a seafood salad, or served in a broth. But this warm, comforting risotto just might be my favorite way.

Because each seafood item cooks at a slightly different pace, and you don't want to overcook any of it, each ingredient needs to be added at a different point in the cooking process. For this dish, you might consider setting a timer to help you. The rice takes 18 to 20 minutes of cooking and stirring, so the scallops should be added at about halfway through.

Serves 4 as a main course, 6 as an appetizer

4 tablespoons (½ stick) unsalted butter

1 large onion, minced

1 clove garlic, minced

2 cups arborio rice

1 cup raw calamari, cut into ½-inch rings

½ cup cooked octopus (buy from your fishmonger or see About Octopus, page 142, to cook your own)

8 littleneck clams in the shell, rinsed

8 mussels in the shell, rinsed

1 cup dry white wine

½ cup canned crushed Italian tomatoes

4 cups Vegetable Stock (page 28), or 3 cups Vegetable Stock plus 1 cup Lobster Stock (page 124)

6 sea scallops, cut in half

6 jumbo shrimp (ask your fishmonger for Mexican or Ecuadorian white shrimp, U-12 size), peeled, deveined, and cut in half

2 tablespoons chopped fresh parsley

2 tablespoons chopped fresh basil

Freshly ground black pepper

Kosher salt*

Because seafood is saline, I don't recommend adding salt until the end of the cooking process, since none may be needed.

Heat a heavy-bottomed 6-quart pot over medium heat and add 2 tablespoons of the butter. When the butter melts, add the onion and garlic, mix well with a wooden spoon, and sauté until the onion is softened, about 3 minutes. Add the rice and stir together so the rice is coated with butter, then add the calamari and octopus and stir for 1 minute. Add the clams and mussels. Stir together, then add the wine and simmer until most of the wine has evaporated. Add the tomatoes and cook, constantly stirring, until the sauce thickens, about 3 minutes.

Start adding the stock, ½ cup at a time, and simmer, stirring, until it has been absorbed. If you are using lobster stock, start with that, and keep stirring and adding stock as it evaporates. At about the 10-minute mark, add the scallops and keep stirring. About 5 minutes from the end, add the shrimp. When the rice is al dente, add the remaining 2 tablespoons butter, the parsley, basil, and black pepper, and mix together well. Taste to see if you need to add salt, adjust accordingly, and serve immediately.

RISOTTO ALLA CONTADINA

This is a play on a massively popular pasta dish—Rigatoni alla Buttera—containing sausage, tomato, peas, and cream, that is the love of every business mogul who's ever eaten in my restaurants. We rarely have it on the menu these days, but people ask for it, and we're always happy to make it. Of course, you must eat it with heaps of Parmesan cheese.

Serves 4 as a main course, 6 as an appetizer

1 tablespoon extra-virgin olive oil

2 hot Italian sausages, removed from casings and crumbled

2 sweet Italian sausages, removed from casings and crumbled

2 tablespoons unsalted butter

1 red onion, finely chopped

2 cups arborio rice

1 teaspoon kosher salt

1 cup dry white wine

1 cup pureed Italian plum tomatoes (preferably San Marzano)

½ cup fresh or frozen peas

4 to 5 cups Chicken Stock (page 24)

½ cup freshly grated Parmigiano Reggiano cheese, plus more for garnish

2 tablespoons chopped fresh Italian parsley

Freshly ground black pepper

Heat a 12-inch skillet over medium heat. Add the olive oil and crumbled sausage meat and cook until it has browned and released most of its fat. Using a slotted spoon, remove the sausage and set aside to drain on a paper towel–lined plate.

Heat a 6-quart heavy-bottomed stockpot over medium heat and melt the butter. Add the onion, stir well with a long-handled wooden spoon, and sauté until the onion is soft and golden, 2 to 3 minutes. Add the rice and salt and stir thoroughly until all the grains are coated with butter, about 2 minutes. Add the wine and keep stirring. When the rice has absorbed the wine, add the tomatoes, constantly stirring. Once the rice starts absorbing that, add the sausage and peas and mix well.

Start adding the stock, ½ cup at a time, and simmer, stirring, until it has been absorbed. Continue adding stock, cooking and stirring, until the rice is al dente, about 18 minutes total. Add the Parmesan, parsley, and black pepper. Stir together well and serve immediately.

FREDS

CHAPTER 7
BRUNCH

Drinks, Juices, and Weekend Frolicking / 209

Perfect Egg Techniques / 215

    Scrambled Eggs / 216

    Poached Eggs / 216

    Hard-Boiled Eggs / 217

Cheese Fondue Scrambled Eggs with Local
Artisanal Cheeses, Ramps, and Green Garlic
with Pommes Anna / 219

Alfredo's Huevos Rancheros with Puebla-Style
Black Beans, Crispy Sunny-Side-Up Eggs, Warm Corn
Tortillas, Guacamole, and Tomatillo Salsa / 221

Freds Classic Eggs Benedict / 226

Asparagus, Prosciutto, and Parmesan Omelet / 229

Eggs alla Campagna / 231

Steak and Eggs with Rösti / 234

Vegan Frittata / 237

Banana French Toast with Maple Syrup / 240

Freds Downtown Grilled Local Artisanal Cheese
Sandwiches with Onion Jam and Bacon / 242

Drinks, Juices, and Weekend Frolicking

Weekday lunches at Freds might be geared for the power lunch, but Saturday and Sunday brunch is purely, blissfully social. People are more relaxed and the tone and volume of the conversations floating around the room are more exuberant. The restaurant is packed with groups of friends taking a break from shopping in Barneys, and our large, round tables are full of families dining together. I often see three generations at one table, and the hottest seats in the house are the kiddie high chairs. It's sweet when I see one of my high-powered customers, who entertained clients at Freds earlier in the week, trying to nab one of those high chairs for a grandchild.

It's kind of a restaurant industry secret, but ask anyone who's worked it: Brunch is a form of madness. Of course, to be happy in the restaurant business you have to thrive on madness, so we're fine with that. At brunch the normal dining routine is hijacked by the addition of a completely different menu, different drinks (endless coffee and juice), and different breads (our homemade scones, muffins, bagels, and bialys replace the regular bread basket). Only the quick survive in the kitchen, where brunch even has its own equipment—stacks of omelet pans that we hide away during the week so they're not used for anything else—to handle the quick turnaround of egg orders.

Drinks, spiked or not, are a brunch tradition, and twenty years ago when we opened Freds, a drink at brunch meant a mimosa or a Bloody Mary, or maybe a Bellini, if you were really adventurous. The cocktail game has changed a lot since then, along with the rising popularity of juicing. Genes Café was the first of our restaurants to offer a menu of juices pressed in house, and when we opened Freds Beverly Hills the proximity to all the great California citrus was exciting. Now all Freds restaurants offer fresh juices pressed or squeezed on a daily basis.

The juices started out virtuous, but inevitably they crept onto the cocktail menu. Inventing drinks is somehow more fun than inventing dishes. It brings out the mad scientist in me, or maybe it's just more fun to consume the experiments! The recipes here give measurements for one drink, but obviously when you're juicing you'll want to make sure you make enough to serve all your guests. Whether you have them virgin or spiked, to celebrate the weekend at brunch or to relax after work, these are some of Freds' favorite drinks.

HASSAN'S BLOODY MARY

It wouldn't be brunch in New York without a Bloody Mary, and this is Freds' bartender Hassan's recipe, beloved by many a brunch devotee. Hassan has been a fixture behind the bar at Freds for fifteen years, and he is also part of one of my fondest memories at Freds. My son's grade school class came on a tour of Freds because they'd been studying immigration and a commercial kitchen is a great place to see what a truly wonderful melting pot New York City really is. We figured out that there were people from nineteen different national backgrounds working at Freds and we had a representative from each country to talk to the kids. There were lots of questions, but one in particular choked up every adult in the room. One kid asked Hassan, who had come from Senegal when he was nineteen, if he had been scared to leave his Mommy and Daddy. He answered, "I was so scared that I didn't even realize I was scared." None of us had considered this, and it was a moving lesson in empathy for all of us, a lesson that's more timely than ever.

Serves 1

4 ounces tomato juice

½ ounce freshly squeezed lemon juice

1 teaspoon horseradish

1 teaspoon Old Bay seasoning

1 teaspoon Worcestershire sauce

Pinch salt

Pinch freshly ground black pepper

2 ounces vodka

TO GARNISH

1 stalk celery

1 stuffed green olive

1 wedge lemon

1 wedge lime

In a bowl or cocktail shaker, mix together the tomato juice, lemon juice, horseradish, Old Bay, Worcestershire, salt, and pepper.

Fill a highball or stem glass with ice. Pour half the vodka over the ice, then add the tomato juice mixture. Place the celery stalk in the glass and drizzle in the remaining vodka. Decorate with the other garnishes and serve.

FRED AND GINGER

This champagne cocktail was named for a different Fred, but its light elegance partners well with the Barneys bar scene. Besides, it contains two "super foods," ginger and pomegranate. Doesn't that make it a health food?

Serves 1

1 ounce Canton ginger liqueur

6 ounces champagne
(or dry sparkling wine, such as prosecco)

Splash of pomegranate juice
(such as from Pom)

Small slice of crystallized ginger, cut
to fit on the glass rim, to garnish (optional)

Pour the ginger liqueur into a chilled champagne flute. Slowly add the champagne and the splash of pomegranate juice. Garnish with the crystallized ginger. Serve immediately, with a toast to your health.

FASHION WEEK FIZZ

Genes Café opened at about the same time that the Aperol spritz was at its zenith of popularity. I have a weakness for Aperol, and we were pressing fresh juices at Genes, so the two things were bound to collide. Orange and carrot juice is a magical combination, and sweet/bitter Aperol gives it a nice kick. To juice the ginger, peel a large knob and run it through the juicer. This drink is made in a cocktail shaker, and can be served straight up or on the rocks.

Serves 1

1 ounce Aperol

2 ounces vodka

2 ounces freshly squeezed orange juice

2 ounces freshly pressed carrot juice

¼ ounce freshly pressed ginger juice

Splash of prosecco
(or other dry sparkling wine, or club soda)

1 orange slice, split to fit on glass rim,
to garnish (optional)

Place ice cubes in a cocktail shaker. Add the Aperol, vodka, and juices and shake well. Strain into a highball glass or pour over ice. Pour in prosecco to the rim and garnish with a slice of orange.

LAUREL CANYON SUNRISE

The perfect spot to enjoy this drink is the place that inspired it: Freds Beverly Hills' outdoor terrace, with its view of the Hollywood Hills. It's a little bit of heaven to sit up there, especially for this New York boy who grew up loving '70s West Coast rock and roll. I can see Laurel Canyon in the distance, and "Hotel California" is playing in my head.

Serves 1

8 strawberries, pureed

2 ounces freshly pressed pineapple juice

2 ounces freshly squeezed orange juice

2 ounces freshly squeezed white grapefruit juice

To spike: 2 ounces tequila or vodka (optional)

Dash of club soda

In a highball glass, place half the strawberry puree. Add ice and then add the juices. If you're spiking the drink, add the alcohol now, too. Top with a dash of club soda and then float the rest of the strawberry puree on top. Serve immediately.

Brunch = Eggs (well, mostly)

Brunch is, naturally, all about eggs, and the many different ways to consume that nutritious little miracle of a foodstuff. Of course we have other things on the menu; I've recently added a vegan frittata made entirely from vegetables (page 237), for example, and some of our locations offer our delicious rendition of Avocado Toast (page 75). Because of Barneys New York roots, bagels and lox—with or without eggs—will always have pride of place on the menu. On top of that, our regular lunch menu is also available. But the reality is, at brunch, most people are looking for the familiar comfort of a beautifully cooked plate of eggs.

At Freds, we use more than a hundred dozen eggs each week for the Madison dining room alone, so sourcing them is a fluid and ongoing part of our purchasing program. We make every effort to use eggs from local farms in all Freds locations, which in New York City includes farms in New Jersey and Vermont. Because of the volume we do, no one farm is ever going to provide us with all we need. The good news is that because demand for farm eggs is growing—from restaurants and home cooks alike—more farmers are producing them. So it's heartening to observe how demand absolutely affects supply on the food chain. Locally sourced farm eggs are superior in every way to the eggs produced on mass industrial chicken farms. The chickens have received better feed, the eggs are fresher, congeal better, and have a richer flavor, and the simpler the egg preparation, the more you appreciate the quality of the egg.

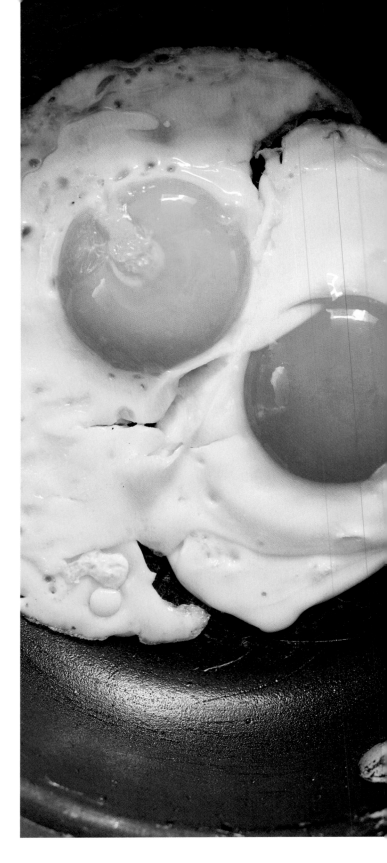

Perfect Egg Techniques

Everyone knows how to cook eggs. Who doesn't make them at home? But cooking them *perfectly*, every time, is an art form, because they're so simple and fragile. According to chef legend, the renowned André Soltner—head chef of Lutèce, one of the most important restaurants in American restaurant history—used eggs as the test of a chef's skill. He would hand job applicants two eggs and a frying pan. If the applicant couldn't cook the eggs perfectly he wouldn't consider hiring them. At Lutèce, bastion of French cuisine, that would probably have meant eggs over easy with immaculate, pristine whites and lovely runny yolks. I'm not sure the legend is actually true, but it's the kind of story that could be. With eggs there's no margin for error, no place to hide a mistake. They cook quickly, so if you want the presentation to be perfect and beautiful, you need to be deft. In a restaurant, if you break the yolk of a poached or sunny-side-up egg, or brown an omelet (in the French tradition, omelets should be as pristine as Lutèce's egg whites, with no trace of brown from sautéing), you need to start all over again. Happily, some preparations are more forgiving, such as Italian frittatas, or the crispy Spanish-style sunny-side-up eggs we serve with our Huevos Rancheros, where browning is actually desired and adds a dimension of texture.

In this chapter, I'll show you how to make a beautifully folded omelet, how to make perfect poached eggs, and much more, alongside recipes for Freds' classic brunch dishes.

> ### EGGS
>
> It must be stated that even though many of us like our eggs lightly cooked with the yolks still runny, the USDA advises against the consumption of raw eggs, especially by the young, old, or individuals with compromised immune systems.

SCRAMBLED EGGS

Everyone knows how to make scrambled eggs, but making *perfect* scrambled eggs, while simple, is an art. By perfect, I mean eggs that are fluffy and golden, and completely free of brown specks from sticking to the pan. It's crucial to use the right pan; I recommend a heavy-duty nonstick one. If you cook eggs frequently, you may want to keep a designated pan to use only for cooking scrambled or fried eggs, to make sure it retains its nonstick quality and isn't burned from using it over high temperatures for other foods.

If you use a good nonstick pan, you will only need a heatproof rubber spatula as a cooking implement. Whisk the eggs until the yolk and white are completely mixed together and slightly creamy. Add any seasonings (even if it's only salt) or ingredients at this point. Place the pan over medium heat. Slow and steady is the way to work with eggs, so don't turn the heat above medium. Add butter or oil to the pan, and when it's hot give the eggs one more whisk before pouring them in. Let the eggs start to congeal for a minute or so, and then, using the spatula, gently push the eggs on the edges toward the center of the pan, letting the raw egg in the center run to fill the edges. Continue to do this until all the egg is cooked to your liking, either soft scrambled or firm. If at any point the egg starts to brown lift it off the heat to let the pan cool slightly and then reduce the heat before returning it to the burner. Once they're cooked to your liking take them off the heat so they don't overcook and become rubbery.

POACHED EGGS

The elegance of Eggs Benedict (page 226) depends largely on the magic of poached eggs, pristine white pouches with beautiful, runny yellow centers. But making poached eggs can be a nightmare, where things—usually the egg whites—can quickly spin out of control. Thankfully, a few simple steps can help avoid poaching disasters. The method is simple, with no room for improvisation. As with most things, practice makes perfect.

Fill a 5-quart saucepan halfway full of water. Bring to a boil and add 2 tablespoons white vinegar and some salt. The vinegar aids in the coagulation of the whites. Turn the heat down to a very gentle simmer. Make sure the eggs are very cold. Instead of cracking the eggs directly into the pan, crack each one into a small cup or container, and use that to transfer it to the water. This gives you more control of the egg's plunge into the water. As you add each egg, use a spoon to stir the water and create a slight vortex where you are placing the egg. Use the spoon also to gently move the eggs away from each other so they don't stick together.

When they have cooked to your liking (about 3 minutes if you like them very runny; 4 to 5 minutes if you prefer firmer), use a slotted spoon or spider skimmer to gently remove them from the water. Obviously you want to do so without damaging the whites and breaking the yolks. Dab the bottom of the spoon on a paper towel to drain off any excess poaching liquid before serving.

HARD-BOILED EGGS

Most of the hard-boiled eggs we make at Freds go into entrée salads, but clocking in at less than 100 calories, a hard-boiled egg is also the perfect snack. When you look online, you'll find a million ways to boil eggs. This is what works for us at Freds. The addition of vinegar to the water should help the peel come off easier.

Yields 12 eggs

EQUIPMENT

5-quart soup pot with lid

Stainless-steel bowl (for ice bath)

Large slotted spoon or spider skimmer

INGREDIENTS

12 eggs

1 tablespoon salt

2 tablespoons white vinegar

Ice

Place the eggs gently in the bottom of the soup pot. Add enough cold water to cover the eggs; fill the pot about three-fourths full. Add the salt and vinegar. Turn the burner on high and bring the water to a boil. As soon as it starts boiling, turn off the heat and cover the pot. Let sit covered for 15 minutes.

Meanwhile, prepare the ice water bath by putting ice in a large stainless-steel bowl and adding water. Remove the eggs with a slotted spoon or spider skimmer and place in the ice water bath. When they've cooled for about 10 minutes, they probably will be cool enough to pat dry and start peeling, although you may opt to wait until they've completely chilled in the fridge.

CHEESE FONDUE SCRAMBLED EGGS

WITH LOCAL ARTISANAL CHEESES, RAMPS, AND GREEN GARLIC WITH POMMES ANNA

The wealth of wonderful, locally produced cheeses inspired me to find ways to use them, and this is one. We vary this dish by the season, depending on which member of the lily (onion) family is in bloom. This is the early spring version, made with ramps (wild leeks) and green garlic, which is young garlic. Later in the spring, and throughout the summer, we'll use bulb onions. In the fall and winter, it's best made with leeks. Use the amount given, whichever lily you use.

The cheeses we use are local to New York City. Beecher's Flagship is a Cheddar-style cheese made here in the Flatiron district. (Beecher's originated in Seattle, where you'll find them at the Pike Place Market.) Arethusa Farm Dairy's Crybaby cheese is a Swiss/Emmental/Jarlsberg–style cheese. Happily, artisan cheeses are being made all over the country, so feel free to substitute good-quality ones from your area.

Serves 4

2 tablespoons extra-virgin olive oil

2 tablespoons finely chopped green garlic (can substitute scallions)

1 cup minced peeled ramps, including leaves

¼ teaspoon kosher salt

8 eggs

1 cup shredded Beecher's Flagship cheese

1 cup shredded Arethusa Farm Dairy Crybaby cheese

2 tablespoons clarified butter (see page 14) or olive oil

Pommes Anna (page 220)

In a small skillet, heat the olive oil over medium heat. Add the green garlic and sauté for 30 seconds, then add the ramps. Reduce the heat to low and sauté until the mixture is very soft, about 3 minutes. Add the salt, mix well, and set aside to cool.

Crack the eggs into a large stainless-steel bowl and whisk vigorously and well, until they're creamy. (You can use an immersion blender to do this, but don't use it when you add the cheese or the cheese will get stuck in the blade.) Add the cooled ramp mixture and the cheeses and mix together well.

Heat the butter in a 12-inch nonstick skillet over medium heat just until it sizzles. Whisk the eggs one more time, then pour them into the pan. Immediately lower the heat to medium low. Using a wooden spoon or spatula, gently stir the eggs, moving the cooked eggs at the edge to the center so the uncooked eggs spread out in their place. Do not let the eggs brown or stick to the pan. If they're cooking too quickly, reduce the heat. Continue gently moving the eggs around until they are cooked to your liking. Serve with Pommes Anna.

CONTINUES

POMMES ANNA

The traditional preparation of this dish calls for layering slices of potatoes in a round baking dish—with plenty of clarified butter. While a beautiful approach, it is a little too precious for the kind of volume we do at brunch. So we make our own twist by slicing individual potatoes and fanning them out to cook in butter. They're kind of a sideways version of Hasselback potatoes, which have become popular in recent years. Our Pommes Anna have the same seasoning and delicious flavor as the original, but they're a bit more practical. This recipe is best made with clarified butter because it won't burn. If you absolutely don't have the time to clarify it, use melted butter; just know that the potatoes may become quite brown in places.

Serves 4

½ cup (1 stick) unsalted butter, clarified (see page 14)

4 medium Yukon Gold potatoes

Kosher salt

1 teaspoon paprika

Preheat the oven to 375°F.

Place the clarified butter in a large mixing bowl and set aside.

Fill a large mixing bowl with cold water. Peel the potatoes and place them in the water. Working on the potatoes one at a time to prevent discoloration, trim the ends so that the potatoes are perfectly oval, then cut them in half lengthwise. Lay the flat side down on a cutting board between 2 chopsticks. Using a very sharp knife, slice a potato half into almost paper-thin slices, leaving ¼ inch at the bottom unsliced; the chopsticks will prevent you from slicing the potato all the way through. As each potato piece is finished, place it in the bowl of butter. When all the potatoes are cut, mix them gently in the butter so it gets in between the slices. Place the potatoes flat side down on a baking sheet, drizzle with the remaining butter, and sprinkle generously with salt and lightly with paprika.

Bake until they are tender inside and well browned, 35 to 45 minutes. Let cool on the sheet pan a few minutes until they've loosened from the pan, then press down on each one gently and fan it decoratively.

—

ALFREDO'S HUEVOS RANCHEROS

WITH PUEBLA-STYLE BLACK BEANS, CRISPY SUNNY-SIDE-UP EGGS, WARM CORN TORTILLAS, GUACAMOLE, AND TOMATILLO SALSA

This dish reflects the melting pot that is our country—and a typical New York restaurant kitchen. I think of this dish as a tribute to all of us whose families came to America for a better life—mine included—and to the classic foods they thankfully brought with them. Chef Alfredo at Madison suggested this dish when we opened, and it instantly became a Freds classic.

If you're going to serve this for brunch at home, it needs to be an all-in kind of morning because there are many components to prepare. On the other hand, several of them—the beans and tomatillo sauce—can be made up to a day ahead.

At Freds we don't make our guacamole tableside, but we do the next best thing. The restaurant opens for brunch at 11 a.m. and we start making the guac at about 10:45. The challenge with guacamole is to prevent it from oxidizing, and Chef Alfredo has a few tricks up his sleeve. First, he puts the avocado pits back in after the guacamole is mixed together (obviously we remove them before serving). He also puts the guacamole in a storage container that has a small opening, so less air gets in, so the guacamole doesn't discolor. You'll want to make your guacamole just before you assemble the dish, but if the top does discolor a little, simply scrape off that part and the rest will be fine.

Serves 4

GUACAMOLE

2 ripe avocados

Juice of 1 large lime, plus more to taste

½ cup finely minced red onion

1 large plum tomato, seeds and excess liquid removed, finely minced

1 jalapeño, seeds and membrane removed (depending on how spicy you like it), finely minced

¼ cup cilantro leaves, finely minced

2 teaspoons extra-virgin olive oil

½ teaspoon kosher salt

TO ASSEMBLE

2 cups Puebla-Style Black Beans (page 224)

8 soft corn tortillas

Extra-virgin olive oil

8 eggs

Kosher salt

½ cup shredded queso blanco

1 cup Tomatillo Salsa (page 225)

CONTINUES

Make the guacamole: Minutes before you're ready to cook and assemble the dish, halve the avocados and twist to open. Remove the pits but set them aside. Cut the avocados into large chunks—about 1-inch pieces—and place them in a large bowl. Sprinkle the lime juice all over the avocados. Add the onion, tomatoes, jalapeño, cilantro, olive oil, and salt. Mix together gently but well, so that most of the avocado is still in large pieces. Place the pits into the center of the guacamole, cover, and set aside while you cook the eggs.

Preheat the oven to 350°F.

Warm the beans in a small pot, and set in a warm place while you prepare everything else.

Warm the tortillas, either in a skillet on the stovetop, or by placing them on a baking sheet or pizza stone in the oven. While the tortillas are warming, cook the eggs.

If you use a 14-inch ovenproof sauté pan you can cook all 8 eggs in it at once. It doesn't matter if they all run together; just cut them up to serve them. Or you can split them between 2 pans. To cook them, place a small amount of olive oil in an ovenproof sauté pan over medium-high heat. Crack the eggs into the hot pan, sprinkle them with salt, but do not lower the heat so that the eggs get a little brown and crispy on the bottom. Cook on the stove for about 1 minute. If you want them over easy, turn them over at this point, otherwise leave them up. Sprinkle the queso blanco over the eggs. Transfer the pan to the oven and bake until the eggs are done to your liking: runny, approximately 4 minutes; medium, 6 minutes; or 8 minutes (well done).

To serve, lay a warm tortilla on each plate. Top with the eggs, beans, and guacamole and drizzle tomatillo sauce over the beans and eggs. Serve immediately, with any leftover guacamole on the side.

———

CONTINUES

PUEBLA-STYLE BLACK BEANS

If you're going to use home-cooked black beans instead of canned, this dish requires a little planning ahead. At Freds, black beans are the only beans we don't soak for 24 hours before cooking. We pre-cook them instead for an hour or two, and then cook them a second time with the seasonings. At the restaurant, we've engineered a way to pre-cook these very slowly: We place one stove grate on top of another so that the pot is lifted high over the low flame. That might not work for your stove, so if that's the case, make sure you simmer these beans in a heavy-gauge pot over the *lowest* of low heats so they don't burn.

Makes 5 cups

1 pound dried black beans

Water to cover

2 tablespoons extra-virgin olive oil

1 red onion, minced

4 cloves garlic, minced

1½ teaspoons kosher salt

1 teaspoon ground cumin

1 cup water

1 whole jalapeño

1 bay leaf

Lay the dried beans out on a tray or baking sheet and comb through them to remove any stones. Place the beans in a 10-quart stockpot and add water to cover. Bring to a boil, skimming any froth that rises to the top. Reduce the heat to low heat and simmer, covered, until the beans are soft but not mushy, about 1½ hours. If the beans start to dry out, add cold water as needed. When the beans are cooked through, drain off any water. Let cool for at least 1 hour.

Heat the olive oil in a 5-quart pot over medium heat. Add the onion, garlic, salt, and cumin and sauté until the onion is wilted, stirring frequently to make sure the cumin doesn't burn. Add the beans and 1 cup water and warm together. Add the whole jalapeño, bay leaf, and a sprinkling of salt. Simmer slowly over very low heat, stirring frequently to make sure the bottom isn't burning, until the beans are falling apart and the sauce is thickened, about 20 minutes. If it gets too thick before the beans are tender, add more water a little at a time. Add more salt if desired, and remove the bay leaf and jalapeño before serving, or serve the jalapeño to the family member who likes a bit of spice!

TOMATILLO SALSA

I love the tartness of green tomatillos, and fortunately they're becoming more widely available. This sauce brings Huevos Rancheros together, but it's also my favorite dip for corn chips. It's so easy to make and can be made ahead of time so you have one less thing to do at brunch.

Makes about 1½ cups

1 pound tomatillos, outer husks removed

1 whole jalapeño

1 red onion, minced

3 tablespoons chopped cilantro

1 clove garlic, peeled

2 tablespoons water

1 tablespoon olive oil

½ teaspoon kosher salt

Preheat the oven to 425°F. Place the tomatillos and jalapeño on a baking sheet and roast, turning if needed, until their skins are charred to a light brown color but are still soft, about 30 minutes. Remove them from the oven and let cool for 10 minutes, or until cool enough to handle. Wearing gloves, carefully remove the skins and discard the seeds.

Place the tomatillos and jalapeños in a blender or food processor and pulse to puree. Add the onion, cilantro, garlic, water, olive oil, and salt and blend until everything is pureed. Place in a sealed container to chill in the fridge for 1 hour.

FREDS CLASSIC EGGS BENEDICT

Eggs Benedict and brunch are a quintessentially American pairing, but there's no general consensus about where or when Eggs Benedict was invented. Having worked in Holland, land of dairy and eggs, I can clearly see how hollandaise, one of Escoffier's important mother sauces, would have been inspired, if not invented, there. The Benedict is a little less straightforward, with several New York City restaurants claiming credit. The prevailing opinion is that a hungover Englishman named Lemuel Benedict inspired its creation when he asked the Waldorf Hotel for similar breakfast items after a night on the town. Wherever it was created, it became a brunch megastar and virtually every American restaurant that's open during weekend lunchtime hours is likely to have a version of it. Its availability in restaurants, combined with the fear of making hollandaise, means people can be hesitant about making it at home. If you're a serious home cook, however, making hollandaise and perfectly poached eggs are skills you'll want to master.

Like most restaurants, Freds offers Classic Eggs Benedict, along with variations, using crab cakes (see Baltimore Crab Cakes on page 91), spinach, and smoked salmon.

Serves 2

2 English muffins, split

4 thin slices Canadian bacon

4 eggs, poached (see page 216)

Hollandaise Sauce (opposite)

Sprinkling of chive whispers for garnish (optional)

Heat water in a saucepan for poaching the eggs. Once it comes to a boil, add salt and white vinegar, and lower the heat until it's very gently simmering. While the water is heating, make the Hollandaise Sauce. When the sauce is finished, set it aside in a warm place. Toast the English muffins and place two halves on each serving plate. Brown the Canadian bacon in a nonstick frying pan and lay a slice on top of each English muffin. Poach the eggs (see page 216) and, when they are done to your liking, remove them from the water, drain, and place one on top of each slice of Canadian bacon. Give the warm Hollandaise a final whisk and ladle it generously over the eggs, making sure to leave a bit of the egg white showing, for color contrast. Sprinkle with the chives and serve immediately.

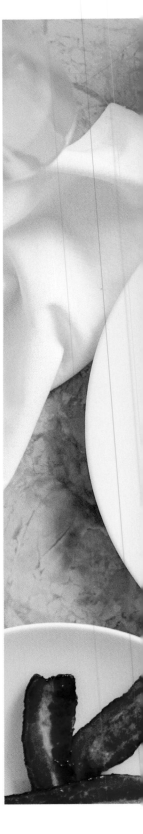

HOLLANDAISE SAUCE

Makes ¾ cup

4 egg yolks
1 tablespoon fresh lemon juice
½ cup warm clarified butter (see page 14)
¼ teaspoon kosher salt
Pinch of cayenne pepper

Vigorously whisk the egg yolks and lemon juice together in a stainless-steel bowl until thickened and doubled in volume. Place the bowl over a saucepan containing barely simmering water; the water should not touch the bottom of the bowl (or use a double boiler). Be careful not to let the eggs get too hot or they will scramble. Continue to whisk rapidly while slowly drizzling in the clarified butter; whisk until the sauce is thickened and doubled in volume. Remove from the heat and whisk in the salt and cayenne. Cover and place in a warm spot until ready to use. If the sauce gets too thick, whisk in a few drops of warm water before serving.

ASPARAGUS, PROSCIUTTO, AND PARMESAN OMELET

For many years, just around the corner from Freds Madison was Madame Romaine de Lyon, a restaurant famous for its beautiful omelets. A vestige of a different time, that restaurant is long gone, but we're carrying on the tradition because omelets never go out of style, especially if they're well made. We offer a different omelet every day, but we're happy to make special-request omelets, too, because our customers know we always have on hand many different cheeses, herbs, vegetables, mushrooms, and cured meats, and all they have to do is ask. If we have it, we'll make it. Our omelets are always served with a salad, never potatoes, because so many of our customers don't want to be tempted by carbs. Of course, many cave in to the Belgian fries, but that's only human.

We offer a different omelet every day (see some of the varieties on page 230), but this is one of the most popular.

Serves 1

3 eggs

1 tablespoon whole milk

Kosher salt

1 tablespoon clarified butter (see page 14)

4 asparagus stalks, and cut into ½-inch pieces and blanched (see page 17)

¼ cup plus 1 tablespoon shredded or grated Parmigiano Reggiano cheese

2 thin slices prosciutto di Parma (or similar ham)

Large handful Madison Salad Blend (see page 41) or other greens, tossed with 1 tablespoon simple vinaigrette, such as Madison Avenue Dressing (page 44)

Crack the eggs into a large mixing bowl and whip them until they are very well mixed, almost creamy. Add the milk and a sprinkling of salt and mix again.

Warm the clarified butter in an 8-inch nonstick pan over medium heat. Pour the egg mixture into the pan and turn off the heat to make sure the pan does not get too hot. Shake the pan slightly to distribute the eggs, and turn the heat back to medium. Let the eggs cook slightly, and then use the spatula to gently slide the cooked eggs and allow the uncooked eggs to flow into their place, shaking the pan gently to keep distributing them. When the eggs are about half cooked, place the asparagus, ¼ cup Parmesan, and prosciutto in a strip down the middle of the egg mixture. Whenever the pan gets too hot, and it seems like the eggs will brown, simply raise it off the burner for a few seconds. Keep gently moving any liquid eggs so that they flow to the bottom of the pan. When the eggs are cooked to your liking (I like my omelets a little runny, but you may prefer them well done), use

CONTINUES

the spatula to gently fold just one third of the omelet to the center. (You'll make the final fold as you transfer the omelet to the plate.) Remove the pan from the heat and tilt it a little so that the folded third is at the higher point. Use the spatula to help roll the eggs out of the pan onto the plate; as they slide out they will roll over the unfolded third, so that they end up resembling a burrito (although one with open ends). Sprinkle the remaining tablespoon of Parmesan cheese on top and serve with the mixed salad.

OMELETS OF THE DAY

Freds has served a daily omelet du jour for over twenty years. These are some of the most popular:

Porcini, Chanterelle, and Cheese

Spinach and Goat Cheese

Mozzarella, Tomato, and Basil

Ramps, Green Garlic, Spring Onions, and Local Artisanal Cheese

Four Cheese

White or Black Truffles with Parmesan Cheese

Zucchini, Onion, and Peppers

OMELETS

The ultimate poster child for simple-yet-difficult kitchen technique is without a doubt the omelet. Impeccably French: Simple, elegant, and flavorful, it's a point of pride for any aspiring chef to master. Anyone can make a plate of eggs, but only with care and practice will you end up with a perfect omelet. Here are my tips for doing so:

- A good-quality, heavy nonstick sauté pan is a must. A 10-inch sauté pan is the perfect size for the classic three-egg omelet. At Freds we don't use our egg pans for anything else so they stay pristine.

- Get your *mis en place* ready before you cook. Prepare the omelet filling and have it waiting next to the stove so you can quickly add it to the eggs.

- Vigorously whisk the eggs until they are very well mixed and creamy. We add a tablespoon of whole milk and salt and whisk it in, too. We do not, however, add black pepper; we let the customer add that at the table, if they like.

- Use clarified butter for cooking since it doesn't contain milk solids that could burn and discolor the eggs. If you don't have clarified butter, use olive oil.

- Use a heatproof rubber spatula to move the eggs in the pan, instead of a metal spatula which could cut the eggs and prevent you from making a perfect tri-fold.

- Cook the omelet over medium heat. This prevents it from browning, but also gives you time to control how the eggs are cooking.

- If you like your omelet well done, you might want to place it, still in the pan, in a 350°F oven for 2 or 3 minutes after you've folded it.

EGGS ALLA CAMPAGNA

One day in the kitchen of the Montreux Palace where I worked in Switzerland, one of the chefs—his name was Eric—persuaded the head chef to let him make something special for staff family meal. I was fascinated as I watched Eric make a quick, aromatic sauce of tomato, onion, garlic, and herbes de Provence in one of the hotel's big copper pots, crack some eggs into the sauce, and pop it in the oven. Since we were in Switzerland, he threw a little Swiss cheese on top. I had never seen eggs coddled that way—or that smelled so delicious. While it was cooking, Eric explained that he had grown up on a farm in Provence, and his family was quite poor, but they had a lot of hens. His grandmother often made this dish for supper, served with crusty bread to soak up the sauce and runny yolk. We all sat around to dig in together, and it was one of those magical food moments that has a lasting effect. I quickly learned how to make this incredible dish, which never fails to entice and is the perfect meal for any "family," whether that's at work or at home.

At Freds, we cook these in small individual pots, but at home I make it in a small Dutch oven, or any heavy ovenproof pot such as one from Le Creuset, a Staub ceramic pot (be careful of breakage with the Staub), or a 2-quart saucepan. At home I like to serve it rustically by putting the pot on the table straight from the oven and dishing it there, with two pieces of bruschetta per serving. However you serve it, remember that the handles of the pot will be extremely hot, so make sure you have enough kitchen towels for holding the handles, and make sure your guests don't touch it!

Serves 2

2 tablespoons extra-virgin olive oil

2 cloves garlic, sliced

1 large shallot, minced

¼ teaspoon herbs de Provence

Pinch of crushed red pepper

2 cups Italian canned crushed tomatoes

Kosher salt

6 leaves fresh basil, coarsely chopped

4 large eggs (6 if they're small)

2 tablespoons freshly grated Parmigiano Reggiano or Gruyère cheese

2 thick slices peasant-style bread

1 clove garlic, peeled

CONTINUES

Preheat the oven to 375°F.

In an ovenproof pot over medium heat, heat the olive oil and add the garlic. Cook until the garlic is lightly browned, then add the shallot. Stir together and cook until the shallot is translucent but not browned. Add the herbs de Provence and red pepper, stir together, and add the tomatoes and a pinch of salt. Simmer over medium-low heat for about 10 minutes, until the sauce is thickened and a deep red color. Turn off the heat, stir in the basil, and adjust salt if needed.

While the sauce is hot, crack the eggs one by one and place gently in the sauce, making sure they are in separate areas of the pan. I recommend cracking each egg into a small bowl and pouring them from the bowl. Sprinkle cheese over the top and transfer the uncovered pot to the oven. Bake until the eggs are done to your preference. If you like them runny, that should be about 5 minutes; longer if you like them more well done. Like the Frenchman Eric and most chefs, I think they're best when the whites are cooked but the yolks are still runny.

While the eggs are baking, toast the bread and while it's still hot, rub the edges with the garlic clove. Press firmly so that the oils of the garlic permeate the crust.

Just before serving, stick the toast decoratively into the edge of the pot, making sure not to disturb the coddled eggs. Serve immediately.

———

STEAK AND EGGS
WITH RÖSTI

Skier's breakfast

At Freds, we serve steak and eggs with sunny-side-up eggs, unless the customer prefers another preparation, such as scrambled. There's no judging—even if you ask for ketchup to go with it (everyone's got a guilty pleasure, and it's breakfast, after all). An 8-ounce steak, cooked here in the French style, in butter, is the perfect size for two people to share, especially since you have the added protein of the eggs. Be sure to season the steak generously with salt and pepper. While we typically serve it medium rare, obviously you'll be cooking the steak to your preferred degree of doneness. To help you determine that, refer to my Tire Test on page 5.

Combined with a rösti, or potato pancake, this breakfast is my ode to the European ski resorts I came to love. The game plan is to cook the rösti first. Then, leave the oven on after taking the rösti out, and use it to cook the steak and eggs, which cook fairly quickly.

Serves 2

1 tablespoon clarified butter (see page 14), or olive oil or unsalted butter

1 (8-ounce) shell steak

Kosher salt

Freshly ground black pepper

4 eggs

Rösti (page 236)

Watercress (optional)

Make the rösti according to the recipe on page 236. When it's cooked through, cook the steak and eggs.

Place the butter in a 12-inch cast-iron pan (or other heavy-duty ovenproof sauté pan) and heat over medium-high heat until very hot, almost starting to smoke. Season the steak generously with salt and pepper and place it carefully in the pan. Sear it for 2 to 3 minutes, then flip and sear for 2 to 3 minutes on the other side. If you like it rare, that's probably enough cooking time, but if you want it cooked more, continue cooking to your desired doneness.

There are several ways you can cook the eggs. My preferred method is to crack the eggs into the pan a minute or two before the steak is done and place everything in the already-hot oven for a few minutes, until the eggs are cooked (I like mine runny, so it doesn't take long). Alternately, you can set the steak aside to rest and cook the eggs (in the same pan or separately).

Cut the steak in half, divide the steak and rösti among 2 plates, and top with the eggs. If desired, garnish with watercress.

CONTINUES

RÖSTI

Potato pancakes are delicious in any language—whether you call them rösti, latkes, or hash browns. But unless it's Hanukkah (during which we fry up thousands of latkes), my favorite potato pancake is the German rösti. The Swiss make rösti, too, but they use shredded boiled potatoes, while the Germans make theirs with shredded raw potatoes. It takes a bit more care to cook a German rösti, but, if done correctly, it's crisper and more succulent. To cook rösti the German way, I think Yukon Gold potatoes are the best choice. If you were making the Swiss type (or regular hash browns) Idaho or russet potatoes would be better, as they're drier and less likely to stick to the pan.

Serves 2

2 medium Yukon Gold potatoes
(about ¾ pound), peeled

½ medium red onion, peeled

1 large egg

¼ cup shredded Gruyère cheese

¼ cup freshly grated Parmigiano
Reggiano cheese

¾ teaspoon kosher salt

Freshly ground black pepper

2 teaspoons clarified butter
(see page 14) or olive oil

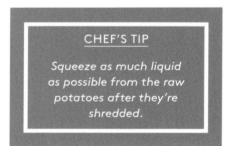

CHEF'S TIP

Squeeze as much liquid as possible from the raw potatoes after they're shredded.

Preheat the oven to 375°F.

Using a hand grater on the largest size shred, grate the potatoes into a large mixing bowl. Squeeze the potatoes well and drain off all the excess liquid, patting them with a towel to remove any excess. Grate the onion, being sure to retain the onion juices, and place in the bowl with the potatoes. Mix together well. Add the egg, the cheeses, salt, and pepper and mix again.

In a heavy 12-inch ovenproof skillet or cast-iron pan, heat the butter over medium-high heat. Add potato mixture, reduce the heat to medium, and, using the back of a spatula, spread and flatten it to form a large "cake." Cook, swirling the pan occasionally, until the underside is set and crispy, 3 to 5 minutes.

Transfer to the oven and bake until crispy and browned, 20 to 30 minutes. The potatoes are done when a skewer or knife blade piercing the middle of the rösti comes out clean. If the rösti needs to brown on top, place it under the broiler for an additional 3 to 4 minutes.

VEGAN FRITTATA

More and more of Freds customers are requesting vegan dishes, and I realized that brunch had a vegan-sized hole in it just waiting to be filled with something tantalizing and savory, something that hit the same comfort spot as, say, an omelet. Full disclosure: I'm a "home vegan," meaning that, while I'm an omnivore professionally, for the past several years I've chosen to be vegan in my day-to-day eating. People have strong feelings about dietary choices, so I won't wade into that debate here. But I will say that as a restaurateur a large part of hospitality is providing what my customers want, and increasingly they want vegan options.

When I'm creating a vegan dish, whether it's for myself or for the restaurant, I have two criteria. First, the dish has to taste good to the point that even a non-vegan would find it delicious. Secondly, I stick to whole foods, with no manufactured meat analogs made with soy or wheat gluten. That means I'm not generally a fan of vegan cheese, but I found one I like: Teese vegan mozzarella cheese is made from pea protein by a small company called Chicago Vegan Foods. It has a gentle taste and melting quality similar to mozzarella. Although I'm partial to this brand, if you can't find it, substitute any mozzarella-style vegan cheese.

In this dish, the sweet potatoes replace eggs as a binder for the other vegetables, some of which we change seasonally. Of course it's not nearly as firm as a dish made with eggs, so move it carefully when you transfer it from the pan. This frittata is delicious and savory, and both my palate and my cholesterol level thank me for eating it. I like to pair it with Grilled Hen of the Woods Mushrooms (page 84).

Makes one large frittata, serving 2 to 4

2 large sweet potatoes

5 tablespoons extra-virgin olive oil

½ cup diced onion

2 cloves garlic, minced

1 teaspoon ground turmeric

½ teaspoon ground cardamom

½ teaspoon ground cumin

1 teaspoon kosher salt

1 cup seasonal vegetables
(pick according to season)

1 cup shredded carrots

1 cup diced red and yellow
bell peppers

1 cup chopped mushrooms

1 cup diced zucchini

½ cup diced summer squash

¼ teaspoon ground white pepper

½ cup cubed Teese vegan
mozzarella cheese (or other
mozzarella-style vegan cheese)

> ## SEASONAL VEGETABLE SUGGESTIONS
>
> **Fall and winter:**
> *diced roasted butternut squash*
>
> **Spring:**
> *ramps, fiddlehead ferns, and green garlic*
>
> **Summer:**
> *cooked sweet corn kernels (from the cob)*

CONTINUES

Preheat the oven to 425°F. With a fork, poke several holes into each sweet potato, place them on a baking sheet, and roast until soft, 45 to 60 minutes. Let cool slightly. Reduce the oven temperature to 375°F.

While the potatoes are roasting, prepare the rest of the vegetables: Heat 2 tablespoons of the olive oil in a 12- to 14-inch ovenproof skillet over medium-high heat. Add the onion and garlic and sauté until the onion is translucent, about 3 minutes. Reduce the heat to medium and add the turmeric, cardamom, cumin, and ½ teaspoon of the salt. Cook, stirring, until aromatic, about a minute. Do not let it burn or it'll become bitter. Add the vegetables, one type at a time and starting with the seasonal vegetable, and sauté each for 1 minute before adding the next. Cook, stirring frequently, until the vegetables are tender. If the mixture gets too dry, add a little more olive oil, but not so much as to make the mixture oily or loose. Transfer the cooked vegetables to a mixing bowl and set aside. Wipe out the skillet with a paper towel and set aside.

Carefully remove the sweet potato flesh from the skin and place in a mixing bowl. Add the remaining ½ teaspoon salt and the white pepper and mash together well.

Add the sautéed vegetable mixture to the mashed sweet potatoes. Mix together gently, add the vegan cheese, and mix again. Taste and add more salt and pepper if needed.

Heat the remaining 3 tablespoons olive oil over medium-high heat in the reserved skillet. Place the sweet potato mixture in the pan and spread and flatten it to form a large "cake." Reduce the heat to medium and cook, swirling the pan occasionally, until the underside is set and crispy, 3 to 5 minutes. Transfer the skillet to the oven and bake until heated through, 15 to 20 minutes. If the top hasn't browned, place it under the broiler so the top gets brown and crisp.

———

BANANA FRENCH TOAST

WITH MAPLE SYRUP

I love it when Freds' chefs create something delicious, especially if it's something I wouldn't have come up with myself, and this stuffed French toast created by Chef Alfredo from Freds Madison is really special. It's one of those dishes that nobody can resist and, like the Belgian Fries (page 9), guests will order it for the table so everyone can indulge in a bite or two. It's beautiful and dramatic, yet surprisingly easy to make, so it's perfect for entertaining at home. Just make sure you buy the bread unsliced, so you can cut it yourself into extra-thick slices. A brioche or white pullman loaf, available at any good bakery, is best for the French toast, but of course you can use any bread you desire. Whatever you use, make sure it's day old, as old bread is sturdier for stuffing and soaking than fresh bread. And, of course, make sure to serve it with lots of warmed, real maple syrup!

Serves 2

3 eggs

½ cup milk

2 tablespoons sugar

1 teaspoon ground cinnamon

Pinch kosher salt

4 (1-inch-thick) slices brioche pullman bread

2 bananas, cut into ¼-inch-thick slices

1 tablespoon unsalted butter

4 strawberries, sliced

Confectioners' sugar for serving

Warm maple syrup for serving

Preheat the oven to 375°F.

Crack the eggs into a large mixing bowl and add the milk, sugar, cinnamon, and salt. Whisk together well and set aside.

Using a sharp knife, cut a pocket into one side of each bread slice, just through to the other sides, similar to a pita. Carefully stuff each slice with one-fourth of the banana slices. Carefully lay the stuffed slices in the egg mixture and turn once. Let the slices sit in the mixture for about 2 minutes to make sure all the bread is saturated with the egg.

Melt the butter in a 14-inch ovenproof skillet over medium heat. When the butter begins to sizzle, carefully transfer the stuffed slices to the pan, being careful not to let the bananas spill out. Brown the slices on both sides, then add the sliced strawberries to the pan. Transfer the pan to the oven and bake for 8 to 10 minutes. (Baking in the oven is an important step, since the centers will not cook enough on the stovetop.) The French toast is done when the centers of the slices have expanded.

Transfer the French toast to serving plates, dot with the baked strawberries from the pan, and sprinkle with confectioners' sugar. Serve immediately with warmed maple syrup on the side.

FREDS DOWNTOWN GRILLED LOCAL ARTISAN CHEESE SANDWICHES
WITH ONION JAM AND BACON

Fair warning: This sandwich is addictive. Just look at the ingredients; they cover the full range of the guilty pleasure spectrum, and yet when combined become a very sophisticated nosh. We'd been making grilled cheese sandwiches for children on request for years at Madison, but it wasn't until we opened Downtown that we got serious about them and put a grown-up one on the menu. Downtown's menu is geared for the slightly more casual crowd that you find there; they're a bit younger and love updates on classic comfort food, and I'm happy to oblige. I worked in Switzerland, home of melting cheese, after all, and the high-quality, locally produced artisanal cheeses available now inspired me to revisit some of the things I learned there. (If cheese is your thing, be sure to also try the Cheese Fondue Scrambled Eggs, page 219.)

It was from the head chef in Switzerland that I learned the little secret of adding just a bit of mustard to the butter in a cheese sandwich. The onion jam, too, is one of the condiments we made to go with the homemade pâté we made every day in Switzerland. The sharpness of the onion, the acidity of the wine, and the sweetness of the sugar in the jam temper the rich indulgence of the cheese and bacon.

Technically, this sandwich isn't grilled, but rather baked in the oven, which makes it perfect for entertaining, since you can make a lot of them all at once. Even better, the sandwiches can be assembled ahead of time and stored in the fridge until you're ready to bake them.

Makes 4 sandwiches

½ cup (1 stick) unsalted butter, softened

8 (½-inch-thick) slices brioche pullman bread (hand-cut, not machine sliced)

4 teaspoons Dijon mustard

4 tablespoons Onion Jam (opposite)

8 slices cooked Nueske's applewood-smoked bacon

2 cups mixed, shredded artisanal cheeses (we mix Beecher's Flagship Cheddar and Alpine-style Swiss)

Preheat the oven to 350°F.

Lightly butter both sides of each slice of bread. On one side of 4 of the slices, spread 1 teaspoon of mustard, followed by 1 tablespoon onion jam. Over that lay 2 slices of bacon and spread with one-fourth of the cheese per slice. Top each with one of the remaining buttered slices so you have 4 sandwiches. Place them in a full-size casserole dish or baking sheet with sides. (I do not recommend using a cookie sheet as the sandwiches might slide off when they're hot.) Bake the sandwiches, flipping them over halfway through, until they are lightly brown and the cheese is melted, 12 to 15 minutes.

Carefully (they're hot!) cut into quarters and serve with a mixed green salad.

ONION JAM

This condiment is so easy and delicious that you may find yourself making it regularly, and not just to use in the grilled cheese. It's nice to have on hand to accompany a cheese plate, or to serve with pâté or poultry (it pairs very well, for example, with Freds Sautéed Chicken Livers on Crostini, page 86). Make it a day before you want to serve it, so it can chill through and the flavors can meld. Stored in the fridge in a covered container, the jam will keep for up to one month.

Makes 1 cup

4 medium red onions

1 cup dry red wine

½ cup water

¼ cup sugar

1 teaspoon kosher salt

Sprinkling of freshly ground
black pepper

Peel the onions, cut in half vertically, and then slice paper thin. Place the onions and remaining ingredients in a 5-quart pot and bring to a boil over medium heat. As soon as it starts to simmer, reduce the heat to low and cook, uncovered, stirring frequently. Like any jam, you want it to be thick but not burn, so it needs to be watched carefully and stirred often. If the mixture starts to dry out before the onions are very soft, add water, a couple of tablespoons at a time, as needed. The jam is done when the onions are very soft, almost melted, the color is a dark purplish brown, and the mixture has reached a thick, jam-like consistency. Taste and adjust seasoning, if necessary, and store in the refrigerator.

DESSERTS

Profiteroles with Caramel Ice Cream
and Chocolate Sauce

CHAPTER 8

SWEET ENDINGS
Desserts and Fruits

Profiteroles with Caramel Ice Cream
and Chocolate Sauce / 250

Traditional Tiramisu / 252

Classic Crème Brûlée / 254

New York Cheesecake / 255

Chocolate Soufflé Cakes with Orange Compote / 257

Fashionista Churros / 259

Peach Melba / 261

Local Blueberry Crisp / 263

Summer Strawberry Shortcake / 264

Chocolate Biscotti / 267

Marilyn's Coconut Macaroons / 269

Freds and Fresh Fruit: How to Make a
Proper Fruit Plate / 270

It would be logical to assume that, with a clientele of fashion and society types, desserts are not a big thing at Freds. But that couldn't be further from the truth, because as it turns out, *everyone* has a sweet tooth, even the very fashionable. Desserts are very popular at Freds, and not just at the times of day (brunch, evenings, holidays) when families tend to dine here. Most of my customers like a bite of something sweet at the end of a meal just like everyone else, although desserts are often shared by the whole table, rather than ordered individually. For a restaurateur—and a home host, too—dessert is the last thing you serve your guest, so you want to leave them with a good impression. A great dessert can't make up for a botched meal (although every restaurateur known to mankind has apologized with free dessert at one point or other), but it can be the literal icing on the cake of a great one.

I'm the first to admit that I'm not a pastry chef. I actually have a bit of a fear of making pastry. Maybe it's the precise measuring that working with pastry requires, or the fact that I hate getting my hands sticky from sugar. Fortunately, that's where Freds' pastry chefs come in. Our pastry department makes everything from scratch (except for ice cream, because there's so much good-quality product out there). The Freds approach to desserts follows the style of the rest of the menu. I like simple, classic desserts done well. We're not necessarily looking to be innovative; we're probably not going to invent the next Cronut.

Of course, as I've said many times, the simpler the dish, the higher quality the ingredients need to be, and in that way the Freds pastry department is no different than any other part of the kitchen. We use only King Arthur flour in our baked desserts, because there really is no better flour available commercially in the United States. We use organic sugar exclusively, since most of the non-organic sugar comes from GMO beets. It's important to us that we use only farm eggs. We source the best local butter and heavy cream (often from Ronnybrook Farm Dairy in the Hudson Valley). Many of our desserts are fruit-based—in fact, a substantial fruit plate is one of our most popular desserts—and later in this chapter I detail a little bit about how carefully we select and tend the fruit we use so that it's served at its peak of deliciousness.

Dessert is often a celebratory part of the meal and at Freds we're ready at any time to help people celebrate a special occasion with candles, sprinkles, chocolate writing, and the like. We often use desserts as a way of saying thank you, sending out a complimentary plate of cookies or homemade chocolate truffles.

The classic desserts on the following pages are some of our favorites. Of course our pastry chefs make them in large quantities in the restaurant, but I've streamlined them, which hopefully will make it easy to provide sweet endings for the guests you entertain in your own home.

PROFITEROLES
WITH CARAMEL ICE CREAM AND CHOCOLATE SAUCE

These little choux puffs have been on the dessert menu since we opened. We just make a tiny twist on the classic: We fill them with caramel ice cream instead of vanilla pastry cream. You can make the profiteroles a few hours ahead, keep them at room temperature in an airtight container, and assemble the dish at the last minute. Just be sure to warm them slightly before filling with the ice cream.

Makes about 18 profiteroles, serving 6

EQUIPMENT

Saucepan

Long-handled wooden spoon

Stand mixer with paddle attachment

Pastry bag with large open star tip

Baking sheet

Parchment paper

Skewer (or sharp knife)

PROFITEROLES

1 cup water

½ cup (1 stick) unsalted butter

1 teaspoon granulated sugar

½ teaspoon kosher salt

1 cup all-purpose flour

4 large eggs (or 5 medium)

Chocolate Sauce (opposite)

1 pint caramel or dulce de leche ice cream

Make the profiteroles: Preheat the oven to 425°F. Combine the water, butter, sugar, and salt in a saucepan and slowly bring just to a boil over medium heat. Add the flour all at once and use a long-handled wooden spoon to stir everything, with the pan still on the heat, until the dough no longer sticks to the sides of the pan.

Transfer the dough to the mixing bowl of a stand mixer with the paddle attachment. Turn to medium speed and add the eggs one at a time, beating slowly until the mixture is smooth. (You can also do this by hand, but be prepared to use some serious elbow grease.)

Place the dough in a pastry bag with a large open star tip and set aside to sit for 5 minutes. Line a baking sheet with parchment paper. Pipe the dough onto the paper in 2-inch balls, making sure they're at least 3 inches apart. Rotate the tip as you pipe to make the balls a little decoratively shaped.

Bake for 8 minutes. Then reduce the heat to 350°F and bake for about 22 minutes longer, until the profiteroles are golden brown. Pierce each one with a skewer or knife to release the steam inside, which will help them remain dry and crisp. Set aside to cool for 10 to 15 minutes.

To serve: Cut each profiterole in half. Fill one half with a generous scoop of ice cream then put the halves back together. For each serving, place three profiteroles on a plate, drizzle generously with warm chocolate sauce (about a 4-ounce ladle per serving), and serve immediately.

CHOCOLATE SAUCE

Makes 2½ cups

EQUIPMENT

Heavy-duty stockpot

Mesh or China cap strainer

INGREDIENTS

1 cup whole milk

½ cup heavy cream

2 tablespoons unsalted butter

½ cup granulated sugar

1½ cups grated 70 percent cacao chocolate

Combine the milk, cream, butter, and sugar in a heavy-duty stockpot. Scald by bringing just to a boil, then lower the heat and add the chocolate. Stir with a wire whisk until the chocolate is melted. Strain through a fine-mesh or China cap strainer to remove any lumps. Serve warm.

TRADITIONAL TIRAMISU

There are a lot of different versions of tiramisu out there, but this is as close to the original Italian one as it gets. Tiramisu starts with making a good *zabaglione*, the fluffy, light Italian custard. Making the zabaglione is the only skill required here; the rest is an easy process of layering and waiting. And then, of course, eating.

Serves 10 to 12

1½ cups very strong coffee*

30 ladyfinger cookies

4 egg yolks

⅓ cup Marsala wine

6 tablespoons sugar

1 (17.6-ounce) container mascarpone cheese

1½ cups heavy cream

½ teaspoon vanilla extract

Cocoa powder for sprinkling

Make extra-strong coffee by mixing 4 tablespoons espresso powder with 12 ounces water, or brew using your favorite method with 4 tablespoons ground coffee and 12 ounces water.

Place the coffee in a wide mixing bowl. Dip half of the ladyfingers briefly in the coffee to moisten, but not so long as to soak them, then use them to line the bottom of a 10- to 12-inch baking dish.

To make the zabaglione, create a double boiler by filling a saucepan halfway with water and bringing it to a gentle boil, then place a large stainless-steel mixing bowl over the pan so it is not touching the water. Add the egg yolks, Marsala, and

4 tablespoons of the sugar to the bowl. Beat with a whisk or handheld electric mixer, whisking constantly so as not to scramble the eggs, until tripled in volume, 5 to 8 minutes. Remove the bowl from the pan and let cool. Stir the mascarpone until it is softened, then fold it into the cooled zabaglione until just combined.

Combine the remaining 2 tablespoons sugar with the cream and vanilla in a large mixing bowl and whip together until the cream forms stiff peaks. Gently fold the whipped cream into the mascarpone mixture until it's completely mixed in.

Spread half of the mixture evenly over the soaked ladyfingers. Dip the remaining cookies in the coffee and lay them on top of the cream mixture. Sprinkle the cookies with more coffee so they are dark and soaked, then spread the remaining cream mixture over them.

Use a fine mesh sifter to sprinkle cocoa powder on top. Refrigerate for at least 4 hours before serving.

CLASSIC CRÈME BRÛLÉE

It's not possible to improve upon perfection, so at Freds we make a simple, classic crème brûlée. To make this at home you'll need to invest in a kitchen blowtorch. They're not expensive, and sometimes come packaged with four small crème brûlée molds.

Makes 4 servings

EQUIPMENT

2-quart saucepan

Whisk

Fine mesh strainer

Mixing bowls

4 crème brûlée molds

Deep baking dish

Baking parchment or foil

Baking rack

Kitchen blowtorch

INGREDIENTS

2 cups heavy cream

1 vanilla bean, split lengthwise

4 large egg yolks

¼ cup plus 1 teaspoon granulated sugar

4 tablespoons demerara, light brown, or granulated sugar

Preheat the oven to 325°F.

Place the cream in a 2-quart saucepan. Using a paring knife, scrape the seeds out of the vanilla bean and add them and the whole vanilla pod to the cream. Bring the cream to a boil, remove from the heat, and let sit for 15 minutes to infuse the vanilla.

In a bowl, whisk together the egg yolks and granulated sugar. Whisk in the cream, a little at a time.

Place a fine-mesh strainer over a bowl and strain the mixture through it to remove the vanilla bean and any bits that might have coagulated. Place the molds in a baking dish and ladle or pour the custard into the molds, filling them almost to the top. Carefully pour hot water from the tap (not boiling) into the pan, being careful so it doesn't splash into the molds, to come halfway up the sides of the molds. Cover the pan with baking parchment or foil and carefully place it in the oven. Bake for around 30 minutes, until the custard is set but the centers are still slightly jiggly. Carefully remove the molds from the pan and cool on a rack. Refrigerate for 3 to 4 hours to cool completely.

Just before serving, brûlée the top of each mold individually: Spread an even layer of demerara sugar over the top, about 1 tablespoon per serving. Hold the blowtorch 2 to 3 inches from the top of the sugar and slowly move it back and forth over the surface until the sugar melts and turns a deep golden brown. Allow the sugar to cool and harden for a few minutes, and then serve immediately, before the sugar softens and gets sticky.

—

NEW YORK CHEESECAKE

It's become kind of a mission for me to save New York dishes that have been chased away by changing demographics and high rents. At one time, you couldn't walk four blocks in New York City without finding a diner or restaurant that served classic New York cheesecake. Along with bagels, bialys, and a few other delicious things, it's a taste of my childhood, as it is for many of my customers, and it still holds up. This cheesecake is relatively simple to make and is nice garnished with berries or other fresh seasonal fruits.

Serves 8 to 10

EQUIPMENT

1 (9-inch) nonstick springform pan

Aluminum foil

Food processor

Hand mixer

Large roasting pan with sides

Baking rack

INGREDIENTS

10 sheets graham crackers, crumbled

⅓ cup packed brown sugar

Pinch of salt

6 tablespoons melted unsalted butter, plus more to brush the pan

1 pound cream cheese, preferably Philadelphia brand, softened

1½ cups granulated sugar

1 teaspoon vanilla extract

4 eggs

1½ cups sour cream

Seasonal fruit for garnish

Preheat the oven to 350°F. Brush the bottom and sides of a 9-inch nonstick springform pan with melted butter or pan spray. Wrap two crossed layers of aluminum foil around the outside of the springform pan. Crimp the edges around the top to make a tight, waterproof outer covering. Set aside.

Process the graham crackers in a food processor until finely ground. You should have roughly 1½ cups. Combine the graham cracker crumbs, brown sugar, salt, and melted butter. Press the crumbs evenly onto the bottom of the pan and ½ inch up the sides, creating an even ¼-inch-thick layer. Set aside.

Using a mixer or by hand, beat the cream cheese, granulated sugar, and vanilla together until smooth and light, scraping down the sides of the bowl as needed, until combined. Add the eggs one at a time and mix well, then gently mix in the sour cream. Pour the mixture into the pan, over the crust.

Place the pan in a large roasting pan that has sides that are higher than the springform pan. Carefully pour hot water from the tap (not boiling water) into the baking pan, being careful so it doesn't splash into the filled crust, to come halfway up the sides of the springform pan. Bake for 1 hour, then reduce the heat to 325°F and bake for another 30 minutes, until the top is golden brown with no cracks, and the center of the cake jiggles just a little bit. Carefully lift the cheesecake from the water bath, remove the foil, and cool on a wire rack. When cool enough to handle, refrigerate for at least 4 hours, but ideally overnight. Serve with seasonal fruit.

CHOCOLATE SOUFFLÉ CAKES
WITH ORANGE COMPOTE

If you're lucky enough to have a restaurant that's been around for twenty years, you eventually come to realize that a lot of your menu items are written in stone. It's simply non-negotiable that they be available. No matter how much you might want to change them, people expect them to be there, and that must be respected. This soufflé cake falls into that category. We made it occasionally as a special dessert when Freds first opened, when molten chocolate cakes were all the rage. We added a little twist: Our molten chocolate is white, which makes for a pretty contrast. It was very popular, so eventually we put it on the permanent dessert menu. It now belongs in the league of immovable menu items, joining the Madison Avenue Salad (page 43) and Belgian Fries (page 9).

We bake these cakes to order in little 3-ounce disposable aluminum tins. The tins work really well for turning out the cakes, as long as you butter them generously before baking. Individual ramekins will work, too, although after trial and error we found that the disposable tins worked better. They're likely available in the baking section of your supermarket or can be ordered online.

The baking chocolate can really be any good-quality 70-percent bar; it doesn't have to be Valrhona or Callebaut. I find white chocolate discs in my supermarket, but you can also use grated white chocolate.

Makes 12 (3-ounce) cakes

ORANGE COMPOTE

3 Valencia oranges

½ cup granulated sugar

¼ cup water

2 tablespoons orange liqueur

CAKES

5 eggs, separated

5 tablespoons granulated sugar, plus more for the molds

Pinch of salt

6 ounces 70 percent cacao dark chocolate, grated or chopped

5 tablespoons unsalted butter, plus more softened butter for the molds

½ tablespoon King Arthur Unbleached All-Purpose Flour

24 to 36 small white chocolate discs (or ¾ cup shaved white chocolate, 1 tablespoon per cake)

2 pints vanilla ice cream

12 fresh mint sprigs for garnish (optional)

Sprinkling of confectioners' sugar for garnish (optional)

CONTINUES

Make the compote: Peel the oranges and then remove the segments and set aside. Combine the granulated sugar and water in a saucepan and simmer over medium-low heat until the sugar is melted. Add the liqueur and simmer for 2 minutes. Turn off the heat and add the orange segments. Stir together gently and set aside.

Make the cakes: Preheat the oven to 350°F. Create a double boiler by filling a saucepan halfway with water and bringing it to a gentle boil, then place a large stainless-steel mixing bowl over the pan so it is not touching the water.

Cream the egg yolks with the granulated sugar. Whip the egg whites and a pinch of salt until they reach stiff peak. Place the dark chocolate and butter in the large bowl over the boiling water. When the chocolate and butter are melted, remove the bowl from the heat and fold in the egg yolk and sugar mixture. Fold in the flour, and then gently fold in the egg whites until everything is mixed.

Generously butter the insides of twelve 3-inch disposable tins (or twelve 3-inch ramekins), then sprinkle the insides with granulated sugar, making sure it goes up the sides. (The sugar caramelizes during the cooking process and adds a lovely texture to the soufflés.) Fill each halfway with the chocolate batter, then place 2 or 3 white chocolate discs (or 1 tablespoon shaved white chocolate) in the center. Add more batter until the tins are full.

Place the tins on a baking sheet and bake for 6 minutes. Reduce the oven temperature to 325°F and bake for another 8 to 10 minutes. The soufflés should rise slightly above the tins and the tops should be firm and dry. Let cool for 2 minutes.

Place each cake upside down on a plate and remove the tin. The cake should be firm enough to stand. Spoon several tablespoons of compote onto one side of each soufflé and place a small scoop of ice cream on the other. Garnish with a sprig of mint and a sprinkle of confectioners' sugar, and serve.

FASHIONISTA CHURROS

Churros are the result of collaboration with the Latin American chefs in the Freds kitchen. They're basically choux pastry dough that's fried, so they're obviously extremely addictive. The ones we make are only about 4 inches long, and one or two from a shared plate is a perfect little indulgence. We serve them with small bowls of warm Chocolate Sauce (page 251), but they're delicious by themselves, too.

Serves 6 to 8

EQUIPMENT

Saucepan

Wooden spoon or heat-resistant spatula

Stand mixer fitted with a paddle

Pastry bag fitted with a ½- or ⅝-inch star tip

Deep fryer or 12- to 14-inch heavy-duty soup pot (at least 4 inches deep)

Candy thermometer (optional)

Large mixing bowl

Paper towels

Baking sheet

Kitchen scissors

Spider skimmer

INGREDIENTS

2 cups water

¼ cup packed light brown sugar

¼ cup (½ stick) unsalted butter

1 teaspoon vanilla extract

1 teaspoon kosher salt

2 cups all-purpose flour

4 eggs

6 cups peanut oil for frying

1 cup granulated sugar

3 tablespoons ground cinnamon (or more or less to taste)

Combine the water, brown sugar, butter, vanilla, and salt in a saucepan over medium heat. Bring to a boil and add the flour all at once. With the pot still on the heat, use the spoon to stir everything until the dough no longer sticks to the sides of the pot. Continue smearing the dough around the pot until the dough has a shiny appearance.

Transfer the dough to the mixing bowl of the stand mixer. Turn to medium speed and add the eggs, one at a time, beating slowly until the mixture is smooth. (You can also do this by hand, but be prepared to use some serious elbow grease.)

Place the dough in the pastry bag with the large tip, then set aside to sit for 5 minutes.

Heat the peanut oil in the deep fryer or soup pot to 350°F. (If you don't have a candy thermometer, make sure the oil is very hot but not smoking.) Keep an eye on the thermometer as you cook and adjust the heat as needed to keep the temperature at 350°F.

Mix the granulated sugar and cinnamon together and place in a large mixing bowl. Place several layers of paper towels onto a baking sheet or large platter.

Pipe the dough directly into the hot oil, squeezing about 4 inches of dough for each piece and snipping them off with scissors. Don't overcrowd them; fry in batches of 4 to 6 at a time,

CONTINUES

using a spider skimmer to turn and move them around as they cook. Fry until they start to brown on one side, and then turn them over. When browned all over, remove from the oil with the spider skimmer, pause for a moment to let any excess oil drip off, and place briefly on the paper towels to drain. If needed, break one open to make sure that it's cooked through and get a feel for the cooking time. While they're still hot, toss the churros in the cinnamon sugar mixture; serve immediately.

Churros can be held in a 200°F oven until all the dough has been fried, then tossed in the cinnamon sugar.

———

PEACH MELBA

We get fruits from different parts of the world all year long, but peaches are one of those fruits that are best bought locally at the height of their season in summer. That's when we make this light and flavorful classic dessert, using the sweetest, ripest summer peaches we can find. The color contrast of the chilled poached peaches with raspberry sauce is beautiful, and the dessert is perfect for entertaining as it's easy to make ahead and also a bit "fancy." To bring out the best flavor, let the raspberry sauce come to room temperature before serving.

Serves 6

POACHED PEACHES

3 large, ripe, local summer peaches

3 cups water

3 cups granulated sugar

½-inch piece vanilla bean, split in half

RASPBERRY SAUCE

4 half-pints fresh raspberries

1 cup granulated sugar

6 scoops vanilla ice cream

Poach the peaches: Score a 1-inch "X" into the skin at the bottom of each peach. Set aside.

In a heavy-duty 2-quart saucepan over high heat, combine the water and sugar. Scrape the seeds from the vanilla bean into the water and bring to a boil. Add the peaches, remove from the heat, and let them sit in the liquid for 10 minutes, or until the skins have loosened and they are cool enough to handle.

Remove the skin from each peach, cut in half, and remove the pit. Place the halves back in the poaching liquid and refrigerate to macerate for at least 2 hours.

Make the raspberry sauce: In a heavy-duty 2-quart saucepan over medium-low heat, combine the raspberries and sugar. Cook, stirring occasionally to release the raspberries' juices, until they just begin to send up thick bubbles and form a sauce. While still hot, puree the raspberries and sauce in a blender or with a hand mixer. Cool in the fridge for at least 2 hours, but bring to room temperature before serving for best flavor.

Assemble the dish: To serve, ladle a small pool of raspberry sauce onto each plate, then place a half peach on the sauce. Add a scoop of vanilla ice cream, drizzle with 2 tablespoons sauce from the peaches, and serve immediately.

LOCAL BLUEBERRY CRISP

One of my favorite desserts of all time is fruit crisp. It's the perfect seasonal dessert because it can be made with any kind of fruit; it's one of the original farm-to-table dishes. Our grandparents might be bemused by our love of kale and avocados, but they'd recognize a good fruit crisp when they saw one. Any type of fruit that makes a good jam will work for crisps: berries of any kind, individually or combined; stone fruits such as plums, apricots, or peaches (or all three combined); apples; or my personal favorite, quince. In summer, we use piles of sweet New Jersey blueberries. Top with a scoop of vanilla bean ice cream from Ronnybrook Farm Dairy in the Hudson Valley (or a local dairy near you) for a perfect summer treat.

We serve the crisp in individual ramekins at the restaurant because it's so busy that scooping it out of a large container gets messy. It's one of the few concessions I make to expedite service. At home, I recommend making it in a large baking dish the way I do for my friends and family.

Serves 6

1 tablespoon butter

FILLING

6 cups blueberries

1 cup granulated sugar

¼ cup all-purpose flour

2 tablespoons dry red wine

Pinch kosher salt

TOPPING

1 cup all-purpose flour

1 cup packed brown sugar

1 cup rolled oats or Swiss muesli

2 teaspoons ground cinnamon

1 teaspoon ground ginger

1 cup (2 sticks) unsalted butter, cut into small bits

Preheat the oven to 350°F. Use 1 tablespoon of butter to grease the inside of a 12-inch baking dish.

Make the filling: Combine all the filling ingredients in a large mixing bowl and toss together well. Transfer to the prepared baking dish and spread evenly.

Make the topping: In a separate bowl, mix together the flour, brown sugar, oats, cinnamon, and ginger. Rub the butter into the mixture until incorporated evenly and the mixture resembles little pebbles.

Spread the topping evenly over the filling. Cover with foil and bake for 45 minutes, until the filling is beginning to send up thick bubbles. Remove the foil and continue baking until the top is golden brown and crispy, about 15 minutes longer.

Serve hot or cold with vanilla ice cream, if desired.

SUMMER STRAWBERRY SHORTCAKE

Although we have strawberries available year-round at Freds, the only time we make strawberry shortcake is at the height of strawberry season, around the Fourth of July. Of course we use local berries in the summertime, but my all-time favorite strawberry is the little Starburst, the variety that is the artist's model for the iconic strawberry shape. They're not just good for their looks, however; they're incredibly sweet. At Freds we get them through Baldor Specialty Foods, which brings them to the East Coast. When we opened in Beverly Hills, I got to know the wonderful Harry's Berries in Oxnard, California; that's who supplies us with Starburst berries there.

Serves 6

BISCUITS

2 cups all-purpose flour, plus more for patting out and cutting

¼ cup sugar

2 tablespoons baking powder

½ teaspoon salt

1 stick unsalted butter, cut into small bits

2 eggs, beaten

1 cup heavy cream, plus more for brushing the biscuit tops

Crystallized sugar for the biscuit tops

Confectioners' sugar for plating (optional)

STRAWBERRY COMPOTE

6 cups fresh strawberries, hulled and halved

¾ cup sugar

WHIPPED CREAM

1 cup heavy cream

1 tablespoon confectioners' sugar, plus more for plating

1 teaspoon vanilla extract

Preheat the oven to 400°F.

Make the biscuits: Combine the flour, granulated sugar, baking powder, and salt in a medium bowl. Rub the butter into the dry mixture until incorporated evenly and the mixture resembles little pebbles. Combine the eggs and cream and add to the flour mixture. Mix slowly until the mixture just comes together, but do not overmix or the biscuits will be tough. Sprinkle a little flour onto a counter surface and turn the dough out onto it. Pat the dough into a uniform 1-inch thickness. Use a cookie cutter or glass to cut out six 2½-inch rounds. Gently reassemble remaining scraps of dough as you cut out the rounds if the first roll-out doesn't yield six. Place the biscuits at least 1 inch apart on a baking sheet, brush the tops with heavy cream, and sprinkle with crystalized sugar. Bake for 12 to 14 minutes, until lightly golden brown. Cool on a wire rack.

Make the compote: Place the strawberries and sugar in a heavy-duty saucepan, stirring to coat the berries. Bring to a boil, stirring occasionally so as not to scorch the sugar, then reduce the heat to low. Simmer until the sugar is melted and the berries are just barely soft, about 5 minutes. Set aside to cool to room temperature.

Strawberry Shortcake in
la-la-land at Freds Beverly Hills

We make the strawberries into a just-barely cooked compote that intensifies their flavor. This works well, too, if you want to enhance the flavor of strawberries when they're out of season. If you have succulent, fragile summer strawberries and don't want to cook them this way, slice them, toss them with the sugar, and then add 3 to 4 tablespoons of white wine (or 1 to 2 tablespoons lemon juice) and set them aside to macerate for 30 minutes.

In fact, a genius method I learned from the Italians is to use wine to gently wash delicate summer strawberries, rather than washing them with water.

Make the whipped cream: Combine all the ingredients in a large mixing bowl and whip using an electric mixer (or by hand using a large metal whisk) until the cream holds a peak—soft or stiff depending on your preference. Refrigerate until you are ready to assemble the shortcakes, but not more than 4 to 6 hours.

Assemble the shortcakes: Cut the biscuits in half. Place the bottom of a biscuit on each plate. Ladle on about ⅓ cup strawberry compote, then top with whipped cream. Place the top of the biscuit gently on top of that, and drizzle a generous spoonful of the compote on top. Top with a dollop of whipped cream, sprinkle with confectioners' sugar, and serve immediately.

CHOCOLATE BISCOTTI

We make a number of different types of cookies for our popular cookie assortment plate, and this signature biscotto is one of the most loved.

Makes 30 biscotti

1 cup (2 sticks) butter, softened

2 cups granulated sugar

4 eggs

1½ teaspoons vanilla extract

3½ cups all-purpose flour, plus more for shaping

1 cup cocoa powder

2 teaspoons instant espresso powder

1 teaspoon baking powder

½ teaspoon baking soda

¼ teaspoon kosher salt

1 cup shelled pistachios

Preheat the oven to 350°F. Line a baking sheet with parchment paper.

In an electric mixer fitted with a paddle (or in a large mixing bowl using a spoon), cream together the butter and sugar until light and fluffy. Add the eggs, one at a time, then the vanilla extract, and mix until smooth.

In a separate bowl, mix together the flour, cocoa powder, espresso powder, baking powder, baking soda, and salt, then stir into the butter mixture. Add the pistachios and mix into a stiff dough.

Place the dough on a lightly floured surface, and divide in half. Shape the dough into 2 logs about 3 inches wide and 12 inches long. Place them on the lined baking sheet and bake until slightly firm, about 25 minutes. Let the logs cool about 30 minutes.

Reduce the oven temperature to 325°F. Use a very sharp serrated bread knife to cut the logs into ¾-inch-thick slices. Use a slow back and forth sawing motion to cut them, rather than applying pressure from the top, since you don't want them to crumble, and you want to cut through the nuts. Place the biscotti, cut side down, on a freshly lined baking sheet. Bake until they're dry and crisp, 15 to 20 minutes. Cool to room temperature and store in an airtight container so they stay crisp.

———

MARILYN'S COCONUT MACAROONS

I started making these macaroons one Passover and they were so good that we revived them at Rosh Hashanah, then somehow they found their way to Hanukkah, and by that point it felt like we were about to round the corner to Passover again, so we just added a mini version to our regular cookie plate.

During the holidays we do a larger version—well, two versions: one plain and one dipped in chocolate. Each type has its devotees. The chocolate dipping is delicious but optional, and these are spectacular even without it. They are light and delicious, and a world away from the packaged macaroons of my childhood. It makes me happy to remember how much my mother, Marilyn, loved these macaroons—I kept her stocked so she always had a small stash in her freezer—so I've named them for her. This one's for you, Ma.

Makes about 3 dozen

MACAROONS

1 (14-ounce) bag sweetened coconut flakes

1 (14-ounce) can sweetened condensed milk

2 egg whites, beaten until frothy

2 teaspoons vanilla extract

CHOCOLATE DIP (OPTIONAL)

1 cup grated dark chocolate, preferably 70 percent cacao

6 tablespoons heavy cream

2 tablespoons unsalted butter

Preheat the oven to 350°F. Line 2 baking sheets with parchment paper.

In a large bowl, combine all the macaroon ingredients until the mixture is tight and sticky. Using a small scoop, shape small mounds and place them roughly 2 inches apart on the baking sheets. Bake for about 25 minutes, until the macaroons are golden brown. Allow them to cool completely before removing from the baking sheet.

To make them chocolate dipped: Create a double boiler by placing a stainless-steel bowl on top of a saucepan filled halfway with boiling water. Over medium heat, melt all the dip ingredients in the bowl, mixing together with a wooden spoon or spatula until the mixture is smooth and glossy.

Dip the macaroon tops in the chocolate, covering the cookie a little over halfway with chocolate. Place on a metal rack or in the refrigerator to set before serving.

Store in an airtight container for 4 to 5 days or in the freezer for 6 months.

FREDS AND FRESH FRUIT: HOW TO MAKE A PROPER FRUIT PLATE

One of the desserts Freds' customers can always count on being available is also one of our most popular: our fruit platter. On the face of it, it sounds simple, but actually it's a huge job to purchase, store, and perfectly ripen the best fruit platter we can assemble in any given season. It's not acceptable for us to offer wooden pieces of tasteless fruit; anyone can do that. Our fruit platter is what I would consider a traditional hotel fruit platter, and we work to deliver ripe, succulent, delicious mouthwatering pieces, slices, or chunks at the peak of perfection, every single day, even in the middle of winter. The fruit is managed by the purchasing agent and the head chef. Besides the fruit platter, fruit (which for kitchen purposes includes tomatoes and avocados) is used all over the kitchen—in other desserts, in salads, in salsas, guacamole, avocado toast, and other menu items.

Purchasing good fruit from good sources is the first step in our fruit program. If we used only local fruit we'd only be eating fruit for about three months out of the year, so we purchase from a wide variety of sources, depending on the day and the season.

Once the fruit arrives in house, it's our job to store it properly so that it ripens correctly and is served at the perfect moment. We carefully manage the inventory, constantly monitoring it, and using sight, smell, touch to serve each piece at its peak.

Then there's presentation. The five-star hotels where I worked in Europe are where I really learned how to handle fruit. Their extravagant weekly buffets called for spectacular presentations, and so I learned how to cut fruit with the precision of a surgeon, and how to fan slices like a Vegas card shark. I learned to carve apples into birds and swans, and turn a watermelon into a Viking ship full of melon balls. The fruit we served was completely manicured; every bit of seed, peel, or core was removed, even citrus slices were peeled of their membranes, all for several hundred guests on a weekly basis. No wonder I felt like a fruit surgeon.

Prepping fruit for a beautiful presentation begins with a very sharp paring knife. The fruit should be placed on a stable surface, so you have a good grip to make sure you're maintaining an even line all around the fruit as you peel. In the case of a fruit like pineapple, particularly since a pineapple is typically wider at the bottom than at the top, slice the bottom just enough so that it's flat, and then follow the natural line of the fruit down from the top as you peel the skin.

On a typical day our fruit plate consists of two types of melon, plus grapes, several types of berries, pineapple, kiwi, and whatever seasonal fruit is available, such as stone fruits or cherries in summer.

MELONS

Since we usually serve two types of melon, I like to make sure they're two different colors. In summer the staple is red and yellow watermelon, but we also mix in local musk or Crenshaw melons. The rest of the time it's cantaloupe and honeydew or casaba. Since those fruits are so common, it's especially important for us to pick tasty specimens. Fortunately, it's easy to identify a good-tasting melon (with the exception of watermelons, who don't like to reveal themselves). It's one of the first food lessons my mother taught me: Go by your sense of smell. Sniff the core where the fruit was attached to the stem to catch a good whiff of its fragrance. If you don't smell anything, let it continue to ripen.

To trim the skin of a melon evenly, first trim a 1-inch-thick slice off the top and the bottom, so it doesn't roll around. Stand it on one end and hold it steady while you peel off rind, working from top to bottom. When it's completely peeled, cut it in half and use a spoon to scoop out the seeds and any fibers. To cut into slices, place each half cut side down and slice it as evenly as possible. If you're careful and the slices are even, you should be able to fan the melon half out like a deck of cards.

BERRIES AND GRAPES

At Freds, we stick with the traditional berries: strawberries, blueberries, raspberries, and blackberries. To store berries, which are extremely fragile, we remove them from their containers, rinse them lightly, and then spread them in a single layer on a baking sheet. It's a little trick I learned in Europe that makes it easier to pick out any berries that are spoiling, and keeps them from contaminating the whole container. Storing them this way can easily extend their shelf life by a day or two.

Grapes are almost always from California and we buy both red and white Thompson Seedless. In season we buy black grapes from California and Muscat grapes from Italy. Grapes are best served in small clusters that are snipped with small grape scissors.

STONE FRUIT OR PITTED FRUIT

I never met a stone fruit I didn't like. These fruits only make it to the plate in summer when they're in season. Because their season is so short, we also take advantage by using them in pies, cakes, and crisps while they're available. On our catering menu in summer we have a popular dessert salad made only of mixed stone fruits with fresh mint. Our favorites: yellow and white peaches, nectarines, apricots, all types of plums, sugarplums, and cherries. When we serve stone fruits we cut them in half (except for cherries), remove the pit, and cut them into ½-inch-thick slices.

TROPICAL AND EXOTIC FRUIT

Pineapples and kiwis are standards on our fruit plate. When I can get good ones, I like to include prickly pears, star fruit, papayas, and mangoes. Exotic fruit can be hit or miss in New York City, and comes at such a premium that I hesitate to waste money on it if I'm not sure it's going to be good.

CITRUS

We sometimes include some type of orange on our fruit plate, but usually only in the winter when citrus is at its peak. We buy many different varieties; Valencia oranges are my favorite, but we also use blood oranges, tangerines, tangelos, and clementines, depending on the month. Most of our oranges come from Southern California or Florida, but occasionally we get some from further afield, such as Spain. Rather than slicing them, we often peel them the same way we do melons, then remove all the membranes and seeds so what's left is just the cleaned segments.

ACKNOWLEDGEMENTS

I'd like to thank the talented team at Barneys New York for their considerable help and support in putting together this book: Lisa and Richard Perry, Daniella Vitale, Mark Lee, Tony Mauro, Tomm Miller, Matthew Mazzucca, Grace Fu, Samantha Reilly, Karsten McVay, and Michael King.

For believing in this project, and for their encouragement, special thanks are due my agent, Jennifer Cohen, and the team at Grand Central Publishing, Gretchen Young and Katherine Stopa.

Freds at Barneys New York is a success because of the hard work, day after day, of Freds' dedicated staff. I'm proud of the teams at each Freds location, and must in particular thank the following:

Freds Madison: Executive Chef Alfredo Escobar, Loraine Ng, Tara Hollywood, Gianfranco Cherici, Nicola Gregg-Galarza, Elhadji Alassane Niang, Stephanie Richiardone, Angel Uzhca, Peter del Rosario, Luis Mendez, Luis Ramirez, Jose Rodriguez Mateo, Oscar García, Jaime Rosas, Jaime Rosete, Oscar Alvarez, Marina Kelman, Jose Cabrera, Jose Flores, John Calderon, Edwin Mata, Fernando Balcazar (special thanks for making the dressing perfectly every day), Freddy Alvarez, Luis Herrera, Juan Aniseto, Cesar Arias, Saul Reyes, Jesus Ocomatl, Angel Molina, and Juan Lima.

Freds Downtown: Executive Chef Jennifer Wasnesky, Mechel Thompson, Carlos Zhagui, Olimpia Flores, Gustavo Nunez, Hector Vazquez, Joseph Alejandrino, Amila Liyanage, Wahib Faouzi, Hubert Andre Williams.

Freds Beverly Hills: Executive Chef Emanuel Pradet and his staff.

Freds Chicago: Carlos Navarrete and his staff.

Special thanks to pastry chefs Jean Tippenhauer and Pearlita Stephens for help in adapting their dessert recipes for home use.

Freds is fortunate to use some of the finest food products in the world, and I'd like to specially thank the following individuals and purveyors: Marco Petrini from Monini; Baldor; Master Purveyors, Inc.; The Chefs' Warehouse; Local Bushel; Distinguished Seafood; D'Artagnan; and Wild Edibles, Inc.

Freds' beautiful tabletop items seen in the photos are thanks to these individuals and companies: Jeff Enda from M.Tucker; Bernardaud (china); Luigi Bormioli (stemware); and Sambonet (flatware).

The stunning photos in this book perfectly capture the Freds food and Barneys' aesthetic. They are the work of talented photographer Sidney Bensimon and her team, food stylist Olivia Mack Anderson and prop stylist Rebecca Bartoshesky. Thank you—and thanks for tolerating the early morning shoots.

Thanks to my friend Robert Hochberg, for giving me free rein in his kitchen. Those weekend cooking marathons helped me translate restaurant recipes to home recipes, and gave me the nerve to include some of the trickier ones—lobster bisque, focaccia and pizza dough—in this book.

And, finally, thanks to my co-author, Susan, for capturing my voice, helping me tell my stories, and putting up with my impossible restaurant hours and occasional nonsense.

Mark Strausman

August 2017
New York City

INDEX

A

aceto balsamico tradizionale, 183
  in Pizza Emilia-Romagna, 183
Ahrens, Thomas, xiv
Alfredo's Huevos Rancheros with
  Puebla-Style Black Beans, Crispy
  Sunny-Side-Up Eggs, Warm Corn
  Tortillas, Guacamole, and Tomatillo
  Salsa, 221
Amstel Hotel (Amsterdam), xv, 38, 39
artichokes (hearts)
  Baked Fresh Baby Artichoke Hearts, 56
  Jewish-Style Artichokes, 166
  in Palm Springs Shrimp Salad with
    Green Goddess Dressing, 55
Asian Chicken Salad, Beverly Hills, 68
Asian Dressing, 69
asparagus
  Asparagus, Prosciutto, and Parmesan
    Omelet, 229
  in Freds Spaghetti, 197
  in Mark's Madison Avenue Salad, 43
  in Palm Springs Shrimp Salad with
    Green Goddess Dressing, 55
  in Wild Spring Ravioli, 199
Asparagus, Prosciutto, and Parmesan
  Omelet, 229
Autumn Salad, 63
avocados
  Avocado Salsa, Roasted Sea Bass with
    Family-Meal-Style Spanish Rice and,
    149
  Avocado Toast, 75
  in Beverly Hills Club, 94
  in Freds Chopped Chicken Salad with
    Balsamic Dressing, 45
  in Palm Beach Shrimp Salad with
    Green Goddess Dressing, 53
  in Vegan Salad with Salsa Verde
    Vinaigrette, 65
Avocado Toast, 75

B

bacon
  in Beverly Hills Club, 94
  in The Club Salad, 61
  Freds Downtown Grilled Local
    Artisanal Cheese Sandwiches with
    Onion Jam and Bacon, 242
  in Lobster Club, 96
  in Madison Classic Club, 97
  Oven-Cooked Bacon, 18
Baked Fresh Baby Artichoke Hearts, 56
Balsamic Chicken, 162
Balsamic Dressing, 46
  Freds Chopped Chicken Salad with, 45
Baltimore Crab Cakes with Rémoulade
  and Classic Coleslaw, 91
Banana French Toast with Maple Syrup,
  240
barley
  Grain and Legume Soup with Kale, 130
  Grain Salad, 145
Barneys New York, ix–x, xii, 35, 170
basil
  Fettuccine with Shrimp, Arugula,
    Garlic, Cherry Tomatoes, and Basil,
    194
  in Freds Pesto, 13
beans. *See also* black beans; white beans
  cooking tips, 65
  Grain and Legume Soup with Kale, 130
  in Vegan Salad with Salsa Verde
    Vinaigrette, 65
beef
  checking for doneness, 5
  Steak and Eggs with Rösti, 234
beets, in Mark's Madison Avenue Salad, 43
Belgian Fries, 9
bell peppers
  in Freds Gazpacho, 117
  in Mark's Madison Avenue Salad, 43
  Medley of Seasonal Vegetables, 148

  in Vegan Bolognese with Whole Wheat
    Penne, 190
  in Vegan Frittata, 237
Bernbaum, Glenn, xv–xvi, 165
berries, about, 272
Beverly Hills Asian Chicken Salad, 68
Beverly Hills Club, 94
Biscotti, Chocolate, 267
black beans
  Puebla-Style Black Beans, 224
  in Roasted Sea Bass with Avocado
    Salsa and Family-Meal-Style Spanish
    Rice, 149
Blanched Vegetables, 17
bleu cheese, in The Club Salad, 61
Bloody Mary, Hassan's, 210
Blueberry Crisp, Local, 263
Bocuse, Paul, xv
Bolognese with Whole Wheat Penne,
  Vegan, 190
bouquet garni/sachet, 6
Branzino Côte d'Azur with Pernod and
  Saffron and Sautéed Spinach à la
  Française, Whole Roasted, 152
broccoli
  Blanched Vegetables, 17
  Medley of Seasonal Vegetables, 148
brunch
  about, 209, 214
  Alfredo's Huevos Rancheros with
    Puebla-Style Black Beans, Crispy
    Sunny-Side-Up Eggs, Warm Corn
    Tortillas, Guacamole, and Tomatillo
    Salsa, 221
  Asparagus, Prosciutto, and Parmesan
    Omelet, 229
  Banana French Toast with Maple
    Syrup, 240
  Cheese Fondue Scrambled Eggs with
    Local Artisanal Cheeses, Ramps,
    and Green Garlic with Pommes
    Anna, 219

brunch (*cont.*)
    Eggs alla Campagna, 231
    Freds Downtown Grilled Local
        Artisanal Cheese Sandwiches with
        Onion Jam and Bacon, 242
    Freds Classic Eggs Benedict, 226
    Perfect Egg Techniques, 215
    Steak and Eggs with Rösti, 234
    Vegan Frittata, 237
Brussels sprouts, in Autumn Salad, 63
Buatta, Mario, xv
butcher block, at Freds, 4
Butter, Clarified, 14
butternut squash, in Autumn Salad, 63

C

cabbage
    in Beverly Hills Asian Chicken Salad, 68
    Classic Coleslaw, 93
calamari, in Risotto with Fruits of the
    Sea, 202
Callen, Anna Teresa, 166
Calypso, Sauce, 10
Campagna, x, xvii, 141, 162, 171, 174
Caponata, 143
    Charred Octopus with Shishito
        Peppers over, 141
cashews, in Beverly Hills Asian Chicken
    Salad, 68
cauliflower
    Blanched Vegetables, 17
    Cauliflower Soup, 123
    Medley of Seasonal Vegetables, 148
    in Vegan Bolognese with Whole Wheat
        Penne, 190
Cauliflower Soup, 123
champagne, in Fred and Ginger, 212
Charred Octopus with Shishito Peppers
    over Caponata, 141
Cheesecake, New York, 255
Cheese Fondue Scrambled Eggs with
    Local Artisanal Cheeses, Ramps,
    and Green Garlic with Pommes
    Anna, 219
Cheese Sandwiches with Onion Jam and
    Bacon, Freds Downtown Grilled
    Local Artisanal, 242

Chicago Vegan Foods, 237
chicken. *See also* Chicken Soup Trilogy,
        Estelle's
    Balsamic Chicken, 162
    Beverly Hills Asian Chicken Salad, 68
    Chicken Francese, 159
    Chicken Paillards with Tomato,
        Arugula, and Red Onion Salad, 103
    Chicken Parmesan, 174
    Chicken Stock, 23
    Fortified Chicken Stock, 25
    Freds Chopped Chicken Salad with
        Balsamic Dressing, 45
    pounding a paillard, 102
    Sautéed Chicken Livers on Crostini
        with Shallots and Port Wine
        Sauce, 86
Chicken Francese, 159
Chicken Paillards with Tomato, Arugula,
    and Red Onion Salad, 103
Chicken Parmesan, 174
Chicken Soup Trilogy, Estelle's, 22, 27
    Chicken Stock, 24
    Fortified Chicken Stock, 25
Chicken Stock, 24
    Fortified, 25
Chocolate Biscotti, 267
Chocolate Sauce, 251
    Profiteroles with Caramel Ice Cream
        and, 250
Chocolate Soufflé Cakes with Orange
    Compote, 257
chopped salads
    Autumn Salad, 63
    Beverly Hills Asian Chicken Salad, 68
    The Club Salad, 61
    Freds Chopped Chicken Salad with
        Balsamic Dressing, 45
    Freds Niçoise Salad, 57
    Mark's Madison Avenue Salad, 43
    Palace Warm Lobster Salad with Freds
        Bistro Dressing, 48
    Palm Beach Shrimp Salad with Green
        Goddess Dressing, 53
    Palm Springs Shrimp Salad with
        Green Goddess Dressing, 55
    Vegan Salad with Salsa Verde
        Vinaigrette, 65

Churros, Fashionista, 259
citrus, about, 273
clams
    Mark's Baby Clam Sauce with
        Spaghetti, 187
    Risotto with Fruits of the Sea,
        202
Clarified Butter, 14
Classic Coleslaw, 93
    Baltimore Crab Cakes with Rémoulade
        and, 91
    in The Jewish Boy from Queens with
        Russian Dressing, 101
Classic Crème Brûlée, 254
classic cuts, 6
Club Dressing, 62
Club Salad, The, 61
Club Sandwiches, Freds
    Beverly Hills Club, 94
    Lobster Club, 96
    Madison Classic Club, 97
Coconut Macaroons, Marilyn's,
    269
Coco Pazzo, x, xvii, 39, 43
Coleslaw. *See* Classic Coleslaw
Corn Soup, Summer, 120
Court Bouillon, 32
couscous
    in Grain Salad, 145
    Tuna with Soy and Blood Orange
        Glaze with Couscous, 156
crab(meat)
    about, 91
    Baltimore Crab Cakes with Rémoulade
        and Classic Coleslaw, 91
    in Beverly Hills Club, 94
Crème Brûlée, Classic, 254
crostini
    Sautéed Chicken Livers on Crostini
        with Shallots and Port Wine
        Sauce, 86
    Tuna Tartare with Cucumber
        Carpaccio, Ginger, and Crostini, 79
Croutons, Homemade, 15
cucumbers
    in Freds Gazpacho, 117
    Tuna Tartare with Cucumber
        Carpaccio, Ginger, and Crostini, 79

D

daikon radishes, in Beverly Hills Asian Chicken Salad, 68
Danish cheese, in The Club Salad, 61
Demi-Glace, 31
desserts
about, 249
Chocolate Biscotti, 267
Chocolate Soufflé Cakes with Orange Compote, 257
Classic Crème Brûlée, 254
Fashionista Churros, 259
Fruit Plate, 270
Local Blueberry Crisp, 263
Marilyn's Coconut Macaroons, 269
New York Cheesecake, 255
Peach Melba, 261
Profiteroles with Caramel Ice Cream and Chocolate Sauce, 250
Summer Strawberry Shortcake, 264
Traditional Tiramisu, 252
dips
Garlic Mayonnaise, 10
Sauce Calypso, 10
doneness in meat, 5
Double-Cut American Lamb Chops alla Scottadito with Mint–Port Wine Sauce, Jewish-Style Artichokes, and Lyonnaise Potatoes, 165
dressings. See salad dressings
drinks
about, 209
Fashion Week Fizz, 212
Fred and Ginger, 212
Hassan's Bloody Mary, 210
Laurel Canyon Sunrise, 213

E

eggplants
Caponata, 143
Eggplant Parmesan, 171
in Vegan Bolognese with Whole Wheat Penne, 190
Eggplant Parmesan, 171
eggs
brunch, about, 214
perfect techniques, 215
Alfredo's Huevos Rancheros with Puebla-Style Black Beans, Crispy Sunny-Side-Up Eggs, Warm Corn Tortillas, Guacamole, and Tomatillo Salsa, 221
Asparagus, Prosciutto, and Parmesan Omelet, 229
Cheese Fondue Scrambled Eggs with Local Artisanal Cheeses, Ramps, and Green Garlic with Pommes Anna, 219
Eggs alla Campagna, 231
Freds Classic Eggs Benedict, 226
Hard-Boiled Eggs, 217
Hollandaise Sauce, 227
Poached Eggs, 216
Scrambled Eggs, 216
Steak and Eggs with Rösti, 234
Eggs alla Campagna, 231
Eggs Benedict, Freds Classic, 226
egg substitutes, for salad dressings, 40
Emilia-Romagna, Pizza, 183
emulsification, 40
endive
in Autumn Salad, 63
in The Club Salad, 61
in Freds Niçoise Salad, 57
in Palace Warm Lobster Salad with Freds Bistro Dressing, 48
English Pea Soup with Mint, 113
Escobar, Alfredo, xiv, 75, 221, 240
Escoffier fold, 6–7
Estelle's Chicken Soup Trilogy, 22, 27
Chicken Stock, 24
Fortified Chicken Stock, 25
exotic fruits, about, 273

F

Fairmont Le Montreux Palace, xv, 38, 48, 231
Fashionista Churros, 259
Fashion Week Fizz, 212
Fettuccine with Shrimp, Arugula, Garlic, Cherry Tomatoes, and Basil, 194
Filet of Sole with Sautéed Carrots and Snow Peas, Upper East Side, 106
Focaccia, Fred Daily, 177
Focaccia Robiola with Truffle Oil, 185
Foolproof Pizza Dough, 178
Fortified Chicken Stock, 25
Fred and Ginger, 212
Fred Daily Focaccia, 177
Freds Beverly Hills, 38, 55, 68, 75, 209, 213, 264
Freds Bistro Dressing, 50
Palace Warm Lobster Salad with, 48
Freds Chopped Chicken Salad with Balsamic Dressing, 45
Freds Classic Eggs Benedict, 226
Freds Club Sandwiches
Beverly Hills Club, 94
Lobster Club, 96
Madison Classic Club, 97
Freds Downtown, x, 242
Freds Downtown Grilled Local Artisanal Cheese Sandwiches with Onion Jam and Bacon, 242
Freds Gazpacho, 117
Freds Herb Mixture, 12
Freds Madison, x, xii–xiii, xvii–xviii
brunch at, 209, 214
day the in life of the kitchen, 2–7
dinner menu, 138–39
Italian food at, 170, 171
lunch, 35, 38–39, 74
purchasing office, 3
Room Service, 139
Freds Niçoise Salad, 57
Freds Pesto, 13
in Freds Spaghetti, 197
in Fusilli al Basilico, 193
Freds Potato Chips, 98
Freds Seasonal Vegetable Medley, 148
Freds Spaghetti, 197
French Toast with Maple Syrup, Banana, 240
Fried Zucchini, 147
Fries, Belgian, 9
Fruit Plate, 270
Fusilli al Basilico, 193

G

Garlic Mayonnaise, 10
Gazpacho, Freds, 117

Genes Café, x, 209, 212
goat cheese, in Autumn Salad, 63
Grain and Legume Soup with Kale, 130
Grain Salad, 145
    Shrimp Oreganata with White Wine,
        Butter, and Herbs, Served over, 144
Grandhotel Hessischer Hof (Frankfurt),
    xiv–xv, 16
grapes, about, 272
green beans
    in Freds Niçoise Salad, 57
    in Mark's Madison Avenue Salad, 43
Green Goddess Dressing, 54
    Palm Beach Shrimp Salad with, 53
    Palm Springs Shrimp Salad with, 55
green peas
    in Mark's Madison Avenue Salad, 43
    in Spanish Rice, Roasted Sea Bass with
        Avocado Salsa and Family-Meal-Style,
        149
Grilled Hen of the Woods Mushrooms in
    a Balsamic Glaze with Arugula and
    Shaved Parmesan, 84
Guacamole, Alfredo's Huevos Rancheros
    with Puebla-Style Black Beans, Crispy
    Sunny-Side-Up Eggs, Warm Corn
    Tortillas, Tomatillo Salsa, and, 221
Gutfreund, John, 38

H

Hard-Boiled Eggs, 217
Harry's Berries, 264
Hassan's Bloody Mary, 210
hearts of palm, in Palm Beach Shrimp
    Salad with Green Goddess
    Dressing, 53
herbs
    classic cuts, 6
    Freds Herb Mixture, 12
    Freds Pesto, 13
Hollandaise Sauce, 227
Homemade Croutons, 15
hotel buffets, 38–39, 270
Huevos Rancheros with Puebla-Style Black
    Beans, Crispy Sunny-Side-Up Eggs,
    Warm Corn Tortillas, Guacamole,
    and Tomatillo Salsa, Alfredo's, 221

I

Il Cantinori, xvi
InterContinental Amstel (Amsterdam), xv
Italian classics
    about, 170
    Chicken Parmesan, 174
    Eggplant Parmesan, 171
    Fettuccine with Shrimp, Arugula,
        Garlic, Cherry Tomatoes, and Basil,
        194
    Focaccia Robiola with Truffle Oil, 185
    Foolproof Pizza Dough, 178
    Fred Daily Focaccia, 177
    Freds Spaghetti, 197
    Fusilli al Basilico, 193
    Mark's Baby Clam Sauce with
        Spaghetti, 187
    Pizza Emilia-Romagna, 183
    Pizza Margherita, 180
    Risotto alla Contadina, 203
    Risotto alla Milanese, 201
    Risotto with Fruits of the Sea, 202
    Vegan Bolognese with Whole Wheat
        Penne, 190
    Wild Spring Ravioli, 199
Italian sausages, in Risotto alla
    Contadina, 203

J

Jacqueline's, xvi
Jewish Boy from Queens with Russian
    Dressing, 101
Jewish-Style Artichokes, 166
    Double-Cut American Lamb Chops
        alla Scottadito with Mint-Port Wine
        Sauce, Lyonnaise Potatoes, and,
        165
juices, about, 209

K

Kale, Grain and Legume Soup with,
    130
Kempinski Hotel (Frankfurt), xv
King Arthur Unbleached All-Purpose
    Flour, 178, 249
kitchen towels, 7

L

Lamb Chops alla Scottadito with Mint–
    Port Wine Sauce, Jewish-Style
    Artichokes, and Lyonnaise Potatoes,
    Double-Cut American, 165
Lane, Ronnie, 43
Laurel Canyon Sunrise, 213
Lee, Mark, 63
lentils
    in Grain and Legume Soup with Kale,
        130
    in Grain Salad, 145
    Lentil and Vegetable Soup, 133
    in Mark's Madison Avenue Salad, 43
Lentil and Vegetable Soup, 133
Littlefield, Susan, xvi, xviii, 187
lobster
    Lobster Bisque with Saffron Aioli,
        124
    Lobster Club, 96
    Palace Warm Lobster Salad with Freds
        Bistro Dressing, 48
Lobster Bisque with Saffron Aioli, 124
Lobster Club, 96
Local Blueberry Crisp, 263
lunch
    classics. See lunch classics
    at Freds, 35, 38–39, 74
    salads. See salads
    soups. See soups
lunch classics
    Baltimore Crab Cakes with Rémoulade
        and Classic Coleslaw, 91
    Beverly Hills Club, 94
    Chicken Paillards with Tomato,
        Arugula, and Red Onion Salad, 103
    Grilled Hen of the Woods Mushrooms
        in a Balsamic Glaze with Arugula
        and Shaved Parmesan, 84
    The Jewish Boy from Queens with
        Russian Dressing, 101
    Lobster Club, 96
    Madison Classic Club, 97
    Pan-Seared Salmon with Sautéed
        Spinach, Tomato and Scallion
        Salad, Salsa Verde Vinaigrette, and
        Roasted Fingerling Potatoes, 87

Roasted Shrimp with Lime and Ginger with Warm White Cannellini Beans, 81
Sautéed Chicken Livers on Crostini with Shallots and Port Wine Sauce, 86
Tuna Tartare with Cucumber Carpaccio, Ginger, and Crostini, 79
Upper East Side Filet of Sole with Sautéed Carrots and Snow Peas, 106
Luongo, Pino, xvi–xvii
Lutèce, 215
Lyonnaise Potatoes, 167
Double-Cut American Lamb Chops alla Scottadito with Mint-Port Wine Sauce, Jewish-Style Artichokes, and, 165

M

Macaroons, Marilyn's Coconut, 269
Madison Avenue Dressing, 44
Madison Avenue Salad, Mark's, 43
Madison Classic Club, 97
Madison Salad Blend, 41
Margherita, Pizza, 180
Marilyn's Coconut Macaroons, 269
Mark's Baby Clam Sauce with Spaghetti, 187
Mark's Madison Avenue Salad, 43
Mashed Potatoes, 155
Sea Scallops, Scampi-Style, with, 154
Mayonnaise, Garlic, 10
meats
checking for doneness, 5
pounding, 102
Medley of Seasonal Vegetables, 148
melons, about, 272
mis en place, 6
Monterey Bay Aquarium Seafood Watch, 152, 156
Mortimer's, xv–xvi, 165
mushrooms
in Freds Spaghetti, 197
Grilled Hen of the Woods Mushrooms in a Balsamic Glaze with Arugula and Shaved Parmesan, 84
Spring Mushroom Soup, 114
in Vegan Bolognese with Whole Wheat Penne, 190

in Vegan Frittata, 237
mussels, in Risotto with Fruits of the Sea, 202

N

New Jersey Summer Heirloom Tomato Soup, 118
New York Cheesecake, 255
Niçoise Dressing, 58
Niçoise Salad, Freds, 57
Noss, Jacqueline, xvi
nouvelle cuisine, xv

O

Obrycki's Crab House (Baltimore), 91
octopus
about, 142
Charred Octopus with Shishito Peppers over Caponata, 141
Risotto with Fruits of the Sea, 202
oils, for salad dressings, 40
olives
in Caponata, 143
in Freds Niçoise Salad, 57
omelets
about, 230
Asparagus, Prosciutto, and Parmesan Omelet, 229
Onion Jam, 243
Freds Downtown Grilled Local Artisanal Cheese Sandwiches with Bacon and, 242
Orange Compote, Chocolate Soufflé Cakes with, 257
Oven-Cooked Bacon, 18

P

paillard
Chicken Paillards with Tomato, Arugula, and Red Onion Salad, 103
pounding, 102
Palace Warm Lobster Salad with Freds Bistro Dressing, 48
Palm Beach Shrimp Salad with Green Goddess Dressing, 53

Palm Springs Shrimp Salad with Green Goddess Dressing, 55
Pan-Seared Salmon with Sautéed Spinach, Tomato and Scallion Salad, Salsa Verde Vinaigrette, and Roasted Fingerling Potatoes, 87
Parmigiano Reggiano
Asparagus, Prosciutto, and Parmesan Omelet, 229
in Chicken Francese, 159
Chicken Parmesan, 174
Eggplant Parmesan, 171
in Fusilli al Basilico, 193
Grilled Hen of the Woods Mushrooms in a Balsamic Glaze with Arugula and Shaved Parmesan, 84
pasta
about, 170
Fettuccine with Shrimp, Arugula, Garlic, Cherry Tomatoes, and Basil, 194
Freds Spaghetti, 197
Fusilli al Basilico, 193
Mark's Baby Clam Sauce with Spaghetti, 187
Vegan Bolognese with Whole Wheat Penne, 190
Wild Spring Ravioli, 199
pastry kitchen at Freds, 5, 249
Peach Melba, 261
pears, in Freds Chopped Chicken Salad with Balsamic Dressing, 45
Pea Soup with Mint, English, 113
Pesto, Freds, 13
in Freds Spaghetti, 197
in Fusilli al Basilico, 193
Pico de Gallo, 76
Piperno (Rome), 166
pitted fruits, about, 273
Pizza Dough, Foolproof, 178
Pizza Emilia-Romagna, 183
Pizza Margherita, 180
Poached Eggs, 216
Freds Classic Eggs Benedict, 226
Pommes Anna, 220
Cheese Fondue Scrambled Eggs with Local Artisanal Cheeses, Ramps, and Green Garlic with, 219

pork. *See also* bacon
   Italian sausages, in Risotto alla
      Contadina, 203
   Prosciutto, Asparagus, and Parmesan
      Omelet, 229
Potato Chips, Freds, 98
potatoes
   Belgian Fries, 9
   in Freds Niçoise Salad, 57
   Freds Potato Chips, 98
   Lyonnaise Potatoes, 167
   in Mark's Madison Avenue Salad, 43
   Mashed Potatoes, 155
   in Palace Warm Lobster Salad with
      Freds Bistro Dressing, 48
   Pommes Anna, 220
   Roasted Fingerling Potatoes, 88
   Rösti, 236
   Steamed Potatoes, 16
pounding a paillard, 102
Pradet, Emanuel, 68
prep kitchen at Freds, 3–4
Pressman, Barney, ix
Pressman, Bob, ix, x
Pressman, Fred, ix, *xi,* xii, 170
Pressman, Gene, ix, x
Profiteroles with Caramel Ice Cream and
   Chocolate Sauce, 250
Prosciutto, Asparagus, and Parmesan
   Omelet, 229
Puebla-Style Black Beans, 224
   Alfredo's Huevos Rancheros with
      Crispy Sunny-Side-Up Eggs,
      Warm Corn Tortillas, Guacamole,
      Tomatillo Salsa, and, 221

Q

quinoa
   cooking tips, 65
   in Vegan Salad with Salsa Verde
      Vinaigrette, 65

R

ramps
   Cheese Fondue Scrambled Eggs with
      Local Artisanal Cheeses, Ramps,
      and Green Garlic with Pommes
      Anna, 219

in Wild Spring Ravioli, 199
Raspberry Sauce, 261
Ravioli, Wild Spring, 199
Rémoulade, 92
   Baltimore Crab Cakes with Classic
      Coleslaw and, 91
Rice, Roasted Sea Bass with Avocado
   Salsa and Family-Meal-Style
   Spanish, 149
Risotto alla Contadina, 203
Risotto alla Milanese, 201
Risotto with Fruits of the Sea, 202
Roasted Fingerling Potatoes, 88
   Pan-Seared Salmon with Sautéed
      Spinach, Tomato and Scallion
      Salad, Salsa Verde Vinaigrette,
      and, 87
Roasted Sea Bass with Avocado Salsa and
   Family-Meal-Style Spanish Rice, 149
Roasted Shrimp with Lime and Ginger
   with Warm White Cannellini
   Beans, 81
Roasted Turkey Breast, 19
Robiola cheese, in Focaccia Robiola with
   Truffle Oil, 185
Rösti, 236
   Steak and Eggs with, 234
Russian Dressing, 102
   Jewish Boy from Queens with, 101

S

Saffron Aioli, 127
   Lobster Bisque with, 124
salads
   at Freds, 38–39
   Autumn Salad, 63
   Beverly Hills Asian Chicken Salad, 68
   Chicken Paillards with Tomato,
      Arugula, and Red Onion Salad, 103
   The Club Salad, 61
   Freds Chopped Chicken Salad with
      Balsamic Dressing, 45
   Freds Niçoise Salad, 57
   Grain Salad, 145
   Mark's Madison Avenue Salad, 43
   Palace Warm Lobster Salad with Freds
      Bistro Dressing, 48

Palm Beach Shrimp Salad with Green
   Goddess Dressing, 53
Palm Springs Shrimp Salad with
   Green Goddess Dressing, 55
Vegan Salad with Salsa Verde
   Vinaigrette, 65
salad blends, 41
salad dressings
   about, 39
   tips for making good, 40
   Asian Dressing, 69
   Balsamic Dressing, 46
   Club Dressing, 62
   Freds Bistro Dressing, 50
   Green Goddess Dressing, 54
   Madison Avenue Dressing, 44
   Niçoise Dressing, 58
   Salsa Verde Vinaigrette, 67
Salmon, Pan-Seared, with Sautéed
   Spinach, Tomato and Scallion
   Salad, Salsa Verde Vinaigrette, and
   Roasted Fingerling Potatoes, 87
Salsa Verde Vinaigrette, 67
   Pan-Seared Salmon with Sautéed
      Spinach, Tomato and Scallion
      Salad, Roasted Fingerling Potatoes,
      and, 87
   Vegan Salad with, 65
sandwiches. *See also* Freds Club
   Sandwiches
   Freds Downtown Grilled Local
      Artisanal Cheese Sandwiches with
      Onion Jam and Bacon, 242
   The Jewish Boy from Queens with
      Russian Dressing, 101
Sapore di Mare (East Hampton), ix, xvi, 43
Sarrazin, Marc, xvi
Sauce Calypso, 10
Sautéed Chicken Livers on Crostini with
   Shallots and Port Wine Sauce, 86
Scrambled Eggs, 216
   Cheese Fondue Scrambled Eggs with
      Local Artisanal Cheeses, Ramps,
      and Green Garlic with Pommes
      Anna, 219
Sea Bass, Roasted, with Avocado Salsa
   and Family-Meal-Style Spanish Rice,
   149

seafood. *See also* lobster; shrimp; tuna
    Court Bouillon, 32
    Mark's Baby Clam Sauce with
        Spaghetti, 187
    Pan-Seared Salmon with Sautéed
        Spinach, Tomato and Scallion
        Salad, Salsa Verde Vinaigrette, and
        Roasted Fingerling Potatoes, 87
    Risotto with Fruits of the Sea, 202
    Roasted Sea Bass with Avocado Salsa
        and Family-Meal-Style Spanish Rice,
        149
    Sea Scallops, Scampi-Style, with
        Mashed Potatoes, 154
    Whole Roasted Branzino Côte d'Azur
        with Pernod and Saffron and
        Sautéed Spinach à la Française,
        152
Sea Scallops, Scampi-Style, with Mashed
    Potatoes, 154
Seasonal Vegetable Medley, 148
Shishito Peppers over Caponata, Charred
    Octopus with, 141
shrimp
    in Court Bouillon, 32
    Fettuccine with Shrimp, Arugula,
        Garlic, Cherry Tomatoes, and Basil,
        194
    Palm Beach Shrimp Salad with Green
        Goddess Dressing, 53
    Palm Springs Shrimp Salad with
        Green Goddess Dressing, 55
    in Risotto with Fruits of the Sea, 202
    Roasted Shrimp with Lime and Ginger
        with Warm White Cannellini
        Beans, 81
    Shrimp Oreganata with White Wine,
        Butter, and Herbs, Served over Grain
        Salad, 144
Shrimp Oreganata with White Wine,
    Butter, and Herbs, Served over Grain
    Salad, 144
snow peas
    in Beverly Hills Asian Chicken
        Salad, 68
    Upper East Side Filet of Sole with
        Sautéed Carrots and Snow Peas,
        106

Soft Bed Salad Blend, 41
Sole with Sautéed Carrots and Snow
    Peas, Upper East Side Filet of, 106
Soltner, André, 215
soups. *See also* Estelle's Chicken Soup
    Trilogy
    about, 110–11
    Cauliflower Soup, 123
    English Pea Soup with Mint, 113
    Freds Gazpacho, 117
    garnishes for, 110, 111
    Grain and Legume Soup with Kale,
        130
    Lentil and Vegetable Soup, 133
    Lobster Bisque with Saffron Aioli,
        124
    New Jersey Summer Heirloom Tomato
        Soup, 118
    Spring Mushroom Soup, 114
    Summer Corn Soup, 120
    White Bean Soup, 128
Spaghetti, Freds, 197
Spaghetti, Mark's Baby Clam Sauce
    with, 187
Spanish Rice, Roasted Sea Bass with
    Avocado Salsa and Family-Meal-Style,
    149
spinach
    in Green Goddess Dressing, 54
    Pan-Seared Salmon with Sautéed
        Spinach, Tomato and Scallion
        Salad, Salsa Verde Vinaigrette, and
        Roasted Fingerling Potatoes, 87
    Whole Roasted Branzino Côte d'Azur
        with Pernod and Saffron and
        Sautéed Spinach à la Française,
        152
Spring Mushroom Soup, 114
Steak and Eggs with Rösti, 234
Steamed Potatoes, 16
stinging nettles, in Wild Spring Ravioli,
    199
stock
    basics of, 23
    best vegetables for making vegetable
        stock, 29
    Chicken Stock, 24
    Court Bouillon, 32

    Fortified Chicken Stock, 25
    for soups, 110–11
    Veal Stock, 30
    Vegetable Stock, 28
stone fruits, about, 273
storage, of salad dressings, 40
Strausman, Marilyn, ix, xiv, xv, 22, 48, 93,
    154, 194, 269
Strawberry Shortcake, Summer, 264
string beans
    in Freds Chopped Chicken Salad with
        Balsamic Dressing, 45
    Medley of Seasonal Vegetables, 148
    in Palace Warm Lobster Salad with
        Freds Bistro Dressing, 48
Summer Corn Soup, 120
summer squash, in Medley of Seasonal
    Vegetables, 148
Summer Strawberry Shortcake, 264
sweet potatoes, in Vegan Frittata,
    237

T

Tartare, Tuna, with Cucumber
    Carpaccio, Ginger, and Crostini, 79
Tiramisu, Traditional, 252
tire test, 5
Toast, Avocado, 75
Tomatillo Salsa, 225
    Alfredo's Huevos Rancheros with
        Puebla-Style Black Beans, Crispy
        Sunny-Side-Up Eggs, Warm Corn
        Tortillas, Guacamole, and, 221
tomatoes
    Chicken Paillards with Tomato,
        Arugula, and Red Onion Salad,
        103
    in Freds Gazpacho, 117
    New Jersey Summer Heirloom Tomato
        Soup, 118
    Pan-Seared Salmon with Sautéed
        Spinach, Tomato and Scallion
        Salad, Salsa Verde Vinaigrette, and
        Roasted Fingerling Potatoes, 87
    Pico de Gallo, 76
Traditional Tiramisu, 252
Tricolore Salad Blend, 41

tropical fruits, about, 273
Truffle Oil, Focaccia Robiola with, 185
tuna
    in Freds Niçoise Salad, 57
    in Mark's Madison Avenue Salad, 43
    Tuna Tartare with Cucumber
        Carpaccio, Ginger, and Crostini, 79
    Tuna with Soy and Blood Orange
        Glaze with Couscous, 156
Tuna Tartare with Cucumber Carpaccio,
    Ginger, and Crostini, 79
Tuna with Soy and Blood Orange Glaze
    with Couscous, 156
turkey
    in The Club Salad, 61
    in The Jewish Boy from Queens with
        Russian Dressing, 101
    in Madison Classic Club, 97
    Roasted Turkey Breast, 19

U

UN Plaza Hotel, xiv
Upper East Side Filet of Sole with
    Sautéed Carrots and Snow Peas,
    106

V

Van Noten, Dries, xii, xvii, 9
Veal Stock, 30
    Demi-Glace, 31
Vegan Bolognese with Whole Wheat
    Penne, 190
Vegan Frittata, 237
Vegan Salad with Salsa Verde
    Vinaigrette, 65
vegetables. *See also specific vegetables*
    best vegetables for making vegetable
        stock, 29
    Blanched Vegetables, 17
    classic cuts, 6
    Medley of Seasonal Vegetables, 148
Vegetable Stock, 28
velouté, 123
Verde, Ciro, 185
vinegars, for salad dressings, 40
Vitale, Daniella, 53

W

Warm White Cannellini Beans, 83
    Roasted Shrimp with Lime and Ginger
        with, 81

white beans
    Grain and Legume Soup with Kale,
        130
    Warm White Cannellini Beans, 83
    White Bean Soup, 128
White Bean Soup, 128
Whole Roasted Branzino Côte d'Azur
    with Pernod and Saffron and
    Sautéed Spinach à la Française,
    152
Wild Spring Ravioli, 199

Z

zucchini
    Fried Zucchini, 147
    in Mark's Madison Avenue Salad, 43
    Medley of Seasonal Vegetables, 148
    in Vegan Bolognese with Whole Wheat
        Penne, 190
    in Vegan Frittata, 237

ABOUT THE AUTHORS

Mark Strausman is a chef, restaurateur, and author based in New York City. In 1996, he created Freds at Barneys New York for the Madison Avenue flagship store. Subsequently he developed satellite Freds in Chicago and Los Angeles, and in Barneys' new Downtown New York City location, and remains Freds' managing director. In addition, he owned the groundbreaking Italian restaurant Campagna, in New York City, and Agriturismo in New York's Hudson Valley, and partnered to create and manage Coco Pazzo in New York City and Sapore di Mare in East Hampton, New York.

He is the author of the James Beard Award–nominated *Two Meatballs in the Italian Kitchen* and *The Campagna Table*. Online, he has written for the Huffington Post and Yahoo. He consults widely within the food and beverage industry. markstrausman.com

Susan Littlefield is a freelance writer and editor who lives in New York City. susanlittlefield.com